Knowledge in Context

This book develops a social psychological approach to knowledge, analysing the personal, interpersonal and sociocultural worlds in which it is produced. Sandra Jovchelovitch argues that representation is at the basis of all knowledge. Representation is viewed as the interrelations between self, other and object-world. Understanding its genesis, development and realisation in social life provides the key to explaining what ties knowledge to personal, interpersonal and sociocultural contexts. It is argued that representation explains the diversity of knowledge and opens up the rationality of knowing to symbolic and social logics that go beyond the epistemic.

The idea of knowledge as pure rationality is disputed and an alternative concept of reason introduced: one which is capable of establishing a dialogue with emotional and social logics. The argument is developed through a consideration of key debates and interrelated themes within the social psychology of knowledge. Topics covered include:

- the emergence of social representations in debates about knowledge, rationality and social context
- the relationship between knowledge, community and public spheres
- recognition or denial of diversity in knowledge.

In addition the book covers the implications of the approach presented and how it might translate into an applied research programme in social psychology. *Knowledge in Context* offers a significant contribution to the field of social psychology and will make essential reading for all those wanting to follow debates on knowledge and representation at the cutting edge of cultural and developmental psychology, sociology, anthropology and cultural studies.

Sandra Jovchelovitch is Senior Lecturer in Social Psychology and Director of the MSc Programme in Social Psychology at the London School of Economics. Before coming to England, she trained as a psychologist in Brazil, where she actively participated in the process of de-institutionalisation and restructuring of policies related to the care of the mentally ill. Her research interests are both theoretical and applied and she has published widely in the field of social representations, health, community and development in both English and Portuguese.

Knowledge in Context

Representations, community and
culture

Sandra Jovchelovitch

Routledge
Taylor & Francis Group

LONDON AND NEW YORK

First published 2007 by Routledge
27 Church Road, Hove, East Sussex, BN3 2FA

Simultaneously published in the USA and Canada
by Routledge
270 Madison Avenue, New York, NY 10016

*Routledge is an imprint of the Taylor & Francis Group, an informa
business*

Copyright © 2007 Routledge

Typeset in Times by Garfield Morgan, Mumbles, Swansea
Printed and bound in Great Britain by TJ International, Padstow,
Cornwall
Cover design by Sandra Heath
Cover illustration: *Passante*, watercolour by Miriam Tolpolar, 2006

This publication has been produced with paper manufactured to strict
environmental standards and with pulp derived from sustainable
forests.

British Library Cataloguing in Publication Data
A catalogue record for this book is available from the British Library

Library of Congress Cataloging-in-Publication Data
Jovchelovitch, Sandra.
   Knowledge in context : representations, community, and culture /
Sandra Jovchelovitch.
        p. cm.
   Includes bibliographical references and index.
   ISBN 978-0-415-28734-0 – 978-0-415-28735-7
   1. Representation (Philosophy). 2. Knowledge, Theory of. 3. Social
psychology. I. Title.
B105.R4J68 2006
153.4–dc22

                                                                2006011913

ISBN 13: 978-0-415-28735-7

To Martin and Ana, with love

Contents

List of tables and figures

Tables

Figures

Preface

This book is the result of two sets of experiences that mark both my professional and personal life. The first goes back to Brazil, a place which I never quite managed to leave behind, a place that to this day continues to offer me key references through which I read and understand the world. The second has evolved since the early 1990s, when I arrived in the UK, a place which has given me new lenses to understand cultures, their impact in the formation of the psychological and the difficulties and potentials of processes of communication between very different people. If it was in Brazil that I understood how society, in the form of social inequalities, poverty and exclusion, shapes the psychological, it was in the UK that I fully understood the impact of culture, its claims and hard consequences in the types of beings we are. The continuous line between Brazil and the UK, and the many conversations in between with colleagues, students, friends and the communities with whom I worked over these years, brought together the concerns that shaped this book.

The overall argument and ideas I present here developed through challenging and enriching discussions I have had with students, colleagues and research partners both at the London School of Economics (LSE) and at several other institutions where I was invited to teach and to present my work. I would like to mention in particular the Federal University of Rio Grande do Sul, the colleagues at the Graduate Programme in Psychology at the Pontifical Catholic University of Rio Grande do Sul, the Federal University of Rio de Janeiro, the University of Brasilia, the ISCTE, in Lisbon, the University of Stockholm and the Maison des Sciences de l'Homme in Paris. I am especially indebted to the Maison des Sciences de l'Homme for offering me a congenial and fertile environment in which to work, first by appointing me Visiting Director of Studies and then through the inspiring meetings of the European Laboratory of Social Psychology. I am very grateful for their continuous support. The Brazilian National Council for Research, the CNPq, has supported my research and teaching in Brazil over the years, helping to keep alive my links with colleagues and universities in my home country. For this I am especially grateful. The LSE has been a wonderful academic home, a place from where psychology can be thought, taught and exercised as an integral part of the social sciences. I am particularly grateful to my colleagues at the Institute of Social Psychology who have taken over my responsibilities during my sabbatical leave and generously allowed me to fully dedicate myself to the completion of this book.

Many colleagues, several of whom also close friends, have helped to shape the thinking and the practices that allowed me to write this book. I would like to mention especially Angela Arruda, Cathy Campbell, Soraya Cortes, Uwe Flick, George Gaskell, Marie-Claude Gervais, Saadi Lahlou, Hamid Rehman and Wolfgang Wagner. Rob Farr and Pedrinho Guareschi taught me ideas and more; I continue to draw on their example and inspiration. I owe special thanks to Serge Moscovici for his generous support and time in relation to this project, for listening to my ideas and encouraging me at crucial stages of this project. Denise Jodelet and Ivana Marková have supported me over the years, generously read the manuscript and provided me with invaluable feedback. I am very grateful for their challenging criticisms. Gerard Duveen is present in this book in many ways: our conversations enriched my thinking and expanded my horizons and he will recognise many of his ideas and comments throughout the book. I am also grateful to Bas Aarts for his help and advice during the final stages of this project. As the cliché goes, the faults in the book are solely mine. My thanks to the many people at Routledge, who at different stages have helped to prepare this book for publication, in particular, Penelope Allport, Lucy Kennedy, Kathryn Russel, Tara Stebnicky and Rebekah Waldron. I also should like to express my gratitude to Jacob, Regina and Marlova, as ever.

Finally, I dedicate this book to Martin, for having read every page and for taking care of me, for being there, for me, with me, throughout; and to my darling Ana, who in delaying this project considerably has in fact made it possible, for teaching me every day what foundations matter in my work and in my life.

Introduction

The problem of knowledge does not go away. It was raised some 2500 years ago by Plato's Socrates and again by Descartes at the beginning of the modern era. It persisted throughout the philosophical development of the modern period and it entrenched itself in the emergence of psychology as a scientific discipline. Indeed, it was through trying to respond to this question that all major psychological systems found an identity and a path of development. It is a question that continues to haunt us today as we try to make sense of the legacy we inherited and confront the new challenges presented by the proliferation of knowledge concerns in the contemporary world. Knowledge societies, knowledge economies, local knowledge, global knowledge, the management of knowledge, the knowledge of the other, self-knowledge; it may well be – as our postmodern colleagues once declared – that the knowledge question does not exist, but it certainly insists. From Plato to Descartes, to the very contemporary discussions about who holds and what is knowledge, the question of what makes knowledge knowledge has never really abandoned us.

Throughout this history there is one theme that matters a great deal to the social psychologist: our dominant conceptions about knowledge are underpinned by an ideal that detaches knowledge from its human sources. We can only reach knowledge if we free it from the illusions of our perceptions, the misunderstandings and biases of our cultures, the interests of our politics and the passions of our emotional lives. To free itself from this human substance seems to be the necessary condition for the emergence of 'true' knowledge: no person, no society, no culture. Knowledge, in order to be recognised as knowledge, must rise beyond the context of its production, free itself from the 'impurities' of its producers, from the interests, the passions and the motives that are linked to a human person, to a human polis, to a human culture. While we know that this project has not evolved without antinomies, the basic paradox that marks our relations with knowledge is still very much with us: despite being a human product, our ideal of true knowledge dehumanises it.

This is not a new question for psychology, and indeed, throughout this book I shall be settling accounts with my own discipline. The struggles between psyche and logos, which are constitutive of both, have been largely obliterated by the gradual consolidation of cognition as information processing, a form of knowing conceived as 'pure' rationality, centred on logos as correspondence between knowledge and the reality of the world. This kind of conceptualisation of the knowing subject has contributed to the development and consolidation of an influential representation of what rational knowledge is, and in consequence of how normality and deviation should be conceived. Even those such as Freud, Piaget and Vygotsky who, as we shall see, helped to undermine this view by establishing the emotional, social and historical genesis of knowledge, remained to the very end committed to the idea that true knowledge involves a gradual process of detachment from person, community and culture. The idea of knowledge remained powerfully linked to the impersonal and detached from subjective value, whereas its emotional and relational dimensions have been linked to distortion, deviation and irrationality. From this perspective, to know is to progress from states of emotional and relational entanglement that threaten the rationality of knowing to a state of cool detachment, where the reality of the world can be appreciated as it is. Free from its emotional and relational components, knowledge is achieved at the end of a long ascending process. There, at the top, it stands: objective, cool and impersonal. Left behind is life: subjective, messy, personal and therefore irrational.

This book is partly an analysis of this separation and partly an attempt to overcome it. My aim is to develop a social psychological approach to knowledge that can retrieve its connection to the personal, interpersonal and sociocultural worlds in which it is produced. Central to this effort is the analysis of representation, understood as a dialogical form generated by the interrelations between self, other and object-world. Representation, I shall try to show, is at the basis of all knowledge systems and understanding its genesis, development and realisation in social life provides the key to understanding the relationship that ties knowledge to persons, communities and lifeworlds. It is through representation that we can understand both the diversity and the expressiveness of all knowledge systems.

In turning to the problem of knowledge, via the analysis of representation, I know I am stepping in mined terrain. The weight of the Cartesian heritage in our understanding of representation cannot be easily dismissed and across psychology's many schools and subdisciplinary fields there has been a strong tendency to reduce representation to a purely individual cognitive process deprived of pathos and ethos. Individual mental representations have been theorised as the foundation of knowledge, defined as a quest for certainty and full correspondence between itself and the world outside. This view of representation has held such power that it is to be found not only in the work developed under the umbrella of mainstream cognition but also in the critical work that, under the banner of postmodernism, has dismissed the idea of representation altogether. While I recognise the power of this conception of representation, I do not think that it should dictate how we treat the phenomenon of representation. Disliking a concept can hardly justify declaring the phenomenon to which it refers inexistent, especially if the concept is not the only one available. The theoretical and empirical work of social and developmental psychologists emphasises that the phenomenon of representation is both symbolic and social, going far beyond the idea of a copy produced by a solitary thinker. Representation is social because the human child cannot produce herself as a feeling and thinking self without the participation of other human beings and it is symbolic because it uses arbitrary tokens to invest the object-world with meaning. That the same object can mean different things and represent different aspirations to different people is the simple fact that debunks the idea of representation as copy.

One of my main intentions in this book is to retrieve the dialogical view of representation, reaffirm its symbolic and social character and to connect its dynamics to different forms of knowing. The central argument I shall present is that knowledge must be understood and explained in relation to representational modalities, which in turn relate to the type of public sphere and cultural traditions of a community. The approach I seek to develop is elaborated around three main propositions:

1   Representational processes are both symbolic and social, expressing subjective, intersubjective and objective worlds. They constitute the architecture of all knowledge systems and in order to understand knowledge we need to understand the genesis of representation and the interrelations between self–other–object that make it happen in social life. This involves exploring how the empirical realisation of these interrelations in different public spheres shapes different modalities of representation and the multiple dimensions of representational processes – the 'who', 'how', 'why', 'what' and 'what for' of representation.
2   Different modalities of representation enable different forms of knowledge. Knowledge is a plural, heterogeneous phenomenon that comprises multiple rationalities, whose logics are not defined by a transcendental norm but relate to the pragmatics of contexts. The diversity of knowledge expresses the diversity of subjective, intersubjective and objective worlds represented in its different forms.
3   Understanding the heterogeneity of knowledge involves dismantling the traditional representation that sees knowledge in terms of a progressive scale where superior forms of knowing displace lower forms. Different knowledges coexist, responding to different needs and fulfilling different functions in social life. Diversity in knowledge is an asset of all human communities and dialogue between different forms of knowing constitutes the difficult but necessary resource that can enlarge the boundaries of all knowledges.

The chapters that follow are an effort, no doubt unfinished and tentative at various places, to explore these propositions and bring them together in a coherent approach. The first three chapters provide the theoretical foundations on representation, the diversity of knowledge and communities and public spheres, while the last three seek to take these foundations further by developing frameworks to capture the forms and functions of knowledge, the social psychology of encounters between different knowledges and a programme of research and intervention in the social psychology of knowledge.

In Chapter 1 I set the stage for the book, discussing the main issues involved in the social psychology of representations and exploring in detail the representational form, its relation to the symbolic function and the production of knowledge. I discuss the making of representation in Cartesian philosophy and articulate the dialogical approach to the study of representation, highlighting the genetic and symbolic processes involved in its development. By retrieving the ontogenesis of representation in the human child, I seek to show that as well as being a cognitive structure referring to the object-world, representation is at the same time entangled in the affective and social dynamics of self–other relations, which make it at once a psychological, interrelational and epistemic structure, expressing subjective, intersubjective and objective worlds.

In Chapter 2 I focus on the theory of social representations and its relations to debates, which at the beginning of the twentieth century addressed the problem of knowledge and context, an issue frequently missed in the Anglo-Saxon reception of social representations. This debate coincided in many respects with the very beginnings of the social sciences and it is difficult to separate the psychological, sociological and anthropological arguments, which were produced at a time when disciplinary boundaries mattered much less than today. I trace the origins of social representations, its main presuppositions and the intellectual milieu in which it originated, examining in detail its main ancestors and the legacy they left to the theoretical and empirical programme of the theory. I introduce the concept of cognitive polyphasia and discuss the problem of difference in forms of knowledge and what constitutes human reason. I consider in detail the positions defended by ancestors such as Durkheim, Lévy-Bruhl, Piaget, Freud and Vygotsky revisiting assumptions of linear evolutionism and recasting questions related to how comparisons between the knowledge of adults and children, advanced and 'primitive' peoples, scientists and lay people have been established and treated. These issues continue to matter today because defining who holds rational knowledge is both an unresolved theoretical problem and a political act. Its implications for the valuation and ranking of different peoples and ways of life are vast, and can potentially lead to practices of exclusion and devaluation of specific groups and communities.

Chapter 3 expands the discussion about knowledge and context by introducing a social psychology of community and by theorising the relationship between knowledge, community and public spheres. It offers an approach to community that emphasises the perspective of actors and the symbolic processes involved in demarcating community boundaries: the making of social knowledges, the formation of social memory and the construction of narratives that can give communities identity and produce the experience of belonging, connecting individual persons to a community's trajectory in time and space. I draw on the work of Hannah Arendt and Jürgen Habermas to integrate the conceptualisation of public spheres into a social psychological framework to the study of communities. I review the concept of the public sphere and introduce its social psychology, emphasising the notions of perspective, plurality and dialogue. I then show that there is a relationship between the kind of public sphere of a community and the form of knowing it produces; the analysis of the representational form (self–other–object) is the key conceptual brick for understanding both knowledge and the public sphere of communities. I argue that transformations in contemporary public spheres are related to transformations in social knowledge and while collective representations fitted well in the structure of traditional public spheres, the specific conditions which characterise detraditionalised public spheres today call for new forms of social knowledge, capable of accommodating diversity in perspective and plurality of horizons.

Chapter 4 explores the variation of the representational form and how this variation shapes the form and the function of knowledge. I introduce a framework to study the work of representation that is based on the constituents of the representational process and the intersubjective and interobjective relations that form its basic architecture. These are the actors, the communicative practices, the object, the reasons and the functions of representations, or what I shall call the 'who', the 'how', the 'why', the 'what', and 'what for' of representation. In this framework representation emerges as a social psychological process involving social actors whose identities and emotional lives are co-constitutive of representation, whose interpersonal relations shape what and how they come to know the world, and whose epistemic constructions are intertwined with the logic of self, object and self–other relations. I put emphasis on the 'what for' of representation, identifying five basic functions: identity, community, memory, anticipation and ideology. This framework gives rise to an initial systematisation of how different modalities of representation are related to different forms of knowing. I distinguish two modalities of representation, collective and social, and relate them to different forms of knowing: myth, belief and programmatic ideology, common sense and science. In developing such a framework I am acutely aware of its limitations and difficulties as well as of the fact that I am working with ideal types. My intention, however, is to offer an initial heuristics to consider variation in knowledge and to understand the expressiveness of all knowledge systems, including those that might seem absurd and irrational for the observer.

Recognising diversity in knowledge poses questions related to how different knowledges meet, are compared and communicate in public spheres, which is the problem I address in Chapter 5. How do we encounter the knowledge of others, the representations of others, the reasoning of others? Is there a potential for communication between different representations or do we need to reconcile ourselves with the incommunicability of different worldviews? I address these issues by exploring the perennial ambivalence of self–other relations and the deep psychology of reciprocity and domination. Mutual recognition and perspective taking are necessary, I argue, to establish dialogues between different knowledges and worldviews, a dialogue that in my view is not only possible as it is necessary for the consolidation of democratic and liberal public spheres. On this basis, I propose a framework to identify dialogical and non-dialogical encounters between different knowledges and examine two cases – madness and community interventions for development – to exemplify these two types of encounter. Here, I argue that different forms of knowledge can live side by side, cross-fertilising and undergoing productive transformations on the basis of dialogical encounters. This is a resource for both individuals, communities and for the development of all knowledges.

In Chapter 6 I explore how the approach I develop in the book translates into an applied programme of research and intervention in social psychology and beyond. I consider both classical and more contemporary studies in the field of social representations and identify in these projects at least two aspects of the approach to knowledge that I have developed in the book: the first is the idea that all knowledges are expressive, insofar as they seek to represent subjective, intersubjective and objective worlds; and the second is the idea that different forms of knowing can coexist fulfilling different functions and responding to different needs in the life of communities. These two conceptual threads have guided research in social representations and are essential to research and interventions that seek to establish a dialogical relation with the field being approached. Finally, in the last part of the chapter I bring together the issues I have addressed in the book and summarise the main tenets of the approach I propose.

In writing this book I have used the theory of social representations as a platform from which I could develop further concerns that are at the centre of my research and teaching over the last eight years or so. I consider theoretical traditions as potential spaces that can open up horizons and help us to problematise and better understand the immediate concerns of our present. They are not fixed in stone and it is only by treating them with some scepticism and openness that we can contribute to their development in time. Moscovici's work has reconnected social psychology with the social sciences and offered us the tools to understand the relations between psychological and social processes. His social psychology, as I discuss in Chapter 2, is substantively social without losing sight of the individual. Psychologists who seek the social dimension should not need to renounce the study of mind and psychological phenomena. At the same time, following in the steps of sociocultural psychologists, the theory of social representations has allowed the consolidation of a research programme that seeks to address pressing and urgent social issues. What Luria stated in his memoirs many years ago, still resonates today: 'I wanted a psychology that would apply to real people as they live their lives, not an intellectual abstraction in a laboratory. . . . I wanted a psychology that was relevant, that would give some substance to our discussions about building a new life' (1979: 22). All of the above seem to me 'good enough' reasons to take up this platform and work on its development.

In addition to social representations there are many other sources in this book that have been part of my intellectual trajectory and my grounding in the world – Brazil, Latin America, and in the last 15 years the UK. It has been impossible for me to shake off the deep impact Freud had in my training as a psychologist and the presence of Latin American theorists who kept my generation aware of both our responsibilities towards an unequal and unjust society and our marginal position in the world. Freud, Freire and the experience of displacement are certainly present in this book. Being off-centre has helped me to understand better the position of the centre, and the difficulties I still have in communicating with many of my colleagues in the north. It also made me acutely aware of how deep cultural differences are inscribed in our individual psychology; they are not abstractions but have an existential impact at the level of the subject. In many respects these differences do put people miles apart and prevent them from getting closer to each other. Yet, the recognition of this distance is also a field of possibilities, open to different solutions. One solution is reconciliation with the distance and the experience of solitude; another is the struggle for communication, with all its difficulties and impending obstacles as well as the discoveries and enlargement of horizons it allows. This book makes a clear option for communication and tries to elaborate a model that can both encompass its potentials and understand the obstacles for its realisation.

It was in Europe that I started reading Habermas, and his thought has become a constant reference to my understanding of social psychology and to the approach I have developed in this book. Even if not systematically, there is a clear Habermasian drift in my text. In Habermas I found echoes of Freire and of phenomenological traditions that have put emphasis on the study and recognition of lifeworlds. Ironically, it is precisely where Habermas has been most criticised that my sympathies for him lie. I like Habermas' commitment to the idea of communication, with some ambivalence I like his attempt to recuperate the embattled notion of reason and rescue it through a communicative paradigm, and I like his counter-factual 'idealism', the idea that reaching understanding in an ideal speech situation is at the basis of all human communication. What is called idealism in Habermas for me resonates with the necessity of sustaining a normative and utopian dimension in theoretical constructions, which correspond to the no less necessary emotional experience of hope. What is the point of having theory just to describe what is the case? In this regard I continue to side with the old Marxian view that the task of theory is not only to understand reality but also to transform it. I also think that despite the clear Eurocentric overtones that mark his work and some problems in his readings of Freud and Piaget, Habermas has produced the most comprehensive reassessment of the theoretical traditions that shaped psychology and constructed our views about human consciousness. To read Habermas is imperative for the social psychologist who is interested in pursuing the intersubjective.

Another perspective that is present in this book is the genetic approach to social psychological phenomena, also called developmental or historical. It is a perspective elaborated by psychologists such as Piaget and Vygotsky, who took the development of the human child as an empirical opportunity to observe the historical development of psychological phenomena. In the age of recombinant DNA the term genetic can raise misunderstandings, but in continental psychology it has not needed justification since Piaget spelled out the sense in which he used it: 'genetic psychology tries to explain mental functions by their mode of formation; that is, by their development in the child' (Piaget and Inhelder 1969: viii). I extensively draw on such theories and use the cognitive, emotional and social development of the human child to understand what appear as fully developed phenomena in adult social life. For a long time psychology saw no qualitative change between childhood and adulthood, treating the former as no more than a training ground, a lesser preparatory stage for the real person who emerges in adulthood. That the psychology of adults could ever be considered without recourse to the development of the child is indicative of the difficulties psychology has had to integrate the historical dimension, something convincingly discussed by Vygotsky, Piaget, Winnicott, Erikson and Mead among others. Any analysis of developed forms of behaviour without explaining the genesis of these forms remains partial; this is the main problem I identify in the current cognitive psychology of representation. It will not, and indeed it cannot within the confines of its individualism, explain the genesis of representational phenomena because to explain this genesis would necessarily open representation to its intersubjective and social conditions of realisation. Alternatively, genetic approaches bring to the fore the primacy of intersubjectivity in the constitution of mind, the necessity of dialogue and communication to its development and the redemptive power of both to resolve issues of isolation, domination and exclusion in personal lives and social fields.

In bringing together the sources I mentioned above I have paid little attention to disciplinary boundaries and indeed nurtured the hope that this work can transpose some of the too rigid distinctions that separate them. At the same time my aim has been to highlight the contribution of social psychology to the understanding of issues that constitute a common agenda for the social sciences. Indeed the classical canon of social psychology is not only alive and well but is also being fruitfully used by neighbouring disciplines. Sociologists, anthropologists and political scientists have been able to claim the insights of Mead, Freud, Winnicott, Piaget and Vygotsky to write about self, identity, community, language, communication, intersubjectivity and successfully connect these constructs with social contexts (see, for instance, Habermas' theory of communicative action (1987, 1991), Giddens' (1991) work on self and modernity, Honneth's work on recognition (1995), Benhabib's (1992, 2002) work on self and multiculturalism and Elliot's (1992) work on subjectivity and the unconscious, amongst others). From the late 1980s onwards social psychologists themselves returned to their classical texts as observers and avid readers of a crop of new work concerned with the subjective and the intersubjective in the social sciences.

Inspired and driven by the central problem of modernity, most of psychology saw the growth and development of knowledge as a victory of reason against the irrational, as the gradual process whereby the human child learns how to renounce centration in perspective, and the narcissistic impulses that go with it, to enter the shared world of reciprocity in perspective and the sublimation of narcissism through work, solidarity and cultural creation. This process is a battle fuelled by the contradictory and ambivalent feelings that sustain the tension between self and other, between individual and society, between drive and civilisation. If psychology has taught us anything, it is that the fully rational person does not exist. The so-called sources of irrationality, belief and myth do not go away. They remain with us and to place them exclusively in exotic others, in children, in women, in lay communities, is nothing more than a precarious and self-deceptive defence. It is not a matter of producing an eulogy of these dimensions nor proposing that we should be ruled by them; it is a matter of recognising the logics they express and the rationality they contain, of being able to deal with them for what they are and accepting that they are both inside and outside all of us. It is only in this way that we might aspire to a wiser reason, one that recognises its internal variety and tries to establish a dialogue with its other.

1 Knowledge, affect and interaction

Representation is a fundamental process of all human life; it underlies the development of mind, self, societies and cultures. To represent, that is, to make present what is actually absent through the use of symbols is central to the ontogenetic development of the human child, is at the basis of the construction of languages and the acquisition of speech, is crucial to the establishment of interrelations that constitute the social order and is the material through which cultures are formed and transformed across time and space. The reality of the human world is in its entirety made of representation; in fact there is no sense of reality for our human world without the work of representation. To paraphrase Roland Barthes on narrative (yet another form of representation), representation is just there, like life itself.

Perhaps it is precisely because of this ubiquitous presence that the concept of representation and the processes it describes has generated so much polemic and dispute in the social sciences and beyond. It has generated theoretical battlefields and divided streams of political organisation; it is at the basis of inclusion and exclusion – who is and who is not represented? – and it underlies the very core of our knowledge about ourselves and the world which we inhabit. How do we gain access to what is 'out there' in the world, how well does representation represent whatever it intends to represent? This is a perennial question behind our efforts to know and to understand the world and it becomes a crucial one whenever projects to change the world are at stake. Because the work of representation is open and most of the time an untidy entanglement of human interests and passions it can very easily become controversial. Very few representations, if any, are capable of establishing themselves as verity, as a true depiction of the world. Even when they manage to reach a high level of consensus within a culture, history shows that there will always be some level of dissent, some individual or group prepared to propose alternative representations. In the struggles over representation we can see the precarious and unstable nature of our definitions, of our knowledge, of what constitutes truth and reality.

Much of the dispute over representation can be explained by an underlying tendency to focus solely on its epistemic function, that is, the ability of representation to produce knowledge about the world. Indeed, there is a very strong tendency both in psychology and other social sciences to equate the epistemic function of representation with cognition and to erase from the representational process its connection with persons and contexts. Representation is studied as an accurate depiction of a given state of affairs in the world and disconnected from the human and social processes that make it possible in the first place. Conceived as the sole basis of cognition and knowledge, representation is reduced to a mental epistemic phenomenon, ruled by information-processing mechanisms and a modular computational system that some psychologists call mind. The multidimensional properties of representation, which are clearly visible in its social psychological genesis and societal foundations, are rendered invisible. The power of this theoretical move is such that the notion of cognition, and with it representation, has been almost incapacitated for critical usage in psychology. Much of the work that has engaged in the reconceptualisation of mind and its correlate processes has discarded both notions precisely because of the asocial connotations they have acquired in mainstream psychology: thus the need to reappropriate both phenomena and retrieve the conceptual resources that account for the social and psychological foundations of representation as a symbolic and social process.

In this chapter I shall begin to explore the problem of representation by discussing in detail the representational form, its mode of constitution and its relation to the symbolic function and the production of knowledge. The approach I seek to develop is concerned both with the psychological aspects of representation and the social foundations of its process of production. On the one hand, it is important to retrieve and to consolidate the psychological insights present in the work of developmental psychologists and psychoanalysts such as Piaget, Vygotsky and Winnicott about the ontogenesis of symbolic representation and its relation to self, knowledge and other. All have shown that the ontogenesis of representation involves at once processes of individuation and socialisation that are permeated by the growth and development of knowledge. At the basis of all knowledge, be it knowledge of self or knowledge of the object-world, there is the work of representation and understanding how it becomes possible for the human child to achieve the ability to represent can teach us a great deal about the nature of the representational form and its social psychological foundations. Ontogenetic processes also make clear the link between the work of representation and the symbolic function, something that is central to the understanding of representation I seek to explore in this book. Representations are not a mirror of the world outside and are not purely the mental constructions of individual subjects. They involve a symbolic labour that springs out of the interrelations between self, other and the object-world, and as such have the power to signify, to construct meaning, to create reality.

On the other hand, it is important to understand representation as a social process embedded in institutional arrangements, in social action, in the active dynamics of social life, where social groups and communities meet,

Table 1.1 Representation and its domains

Representation and the symbolic function (produced by and expressive of)		
Self	**Self–Other Relations**	**Object**
Subjective	Intersubjective	Objective
Personal/psychological	Communicative/interactive	Epistemic/cognitive

communicate and clash. The work of representation in social fields relates to the construction of worldviews, to the establishment of systems of everyday knowledge that not only seek to propose a framework to guide communication, action coordination and interpretation of what is at stake, but also actively express projects and identities of social actors and the interrelations between them. Ignoring the social dimension of representation has allowed for the recurrent view of representational processes as purely mental cognitive phenomena, detached from the larger societal constrains that are integral to their processes of constitution. I seek to challenge this tendency by reaffirming the communicative nature of representation and its grounding in concrete contexts. Understanding that representation is social directs the analysis to the consideration of the actual social contexts where representations are formed and to the nature of communication that makes them possible in the first place. The formation of representation is a public affair, a context-dependent process that relies on the social, political and historical conditions that shape specific contexts.

My central aim in this chapter is to introduce the key issues and central problems involved in the social psychology of representations and to offer a detailed analysis of the architecture of representation. Table 1.1 provides an overview of the conceptual scheme I develop throughout the book and brings together the terms I use to discuss representation.

I shall start by outlining the central premises of the approach to representation I seek to develop and the main issues I intend to address throughout the book. After establishing the main issues circumscribing the social psychology of representations, I discuss the making of representation in Cartesian philosophy showing how it has dominated current conceptions of representation and go on to discuss the dialogical approach to the study of representation emphasising the symbolic and genetic processes involved in the development of representation. I retrieve the ontogenesis of representation in the child to show that as well as being a structure that allows the construction of knowledge about the object-world, the development of representation is entangled in the affective and social dynamics of self–other relations. This genetic account will allow a characterisation of representation as psychological, interrelational, and epistemic structures expressing subjective, intersubjective and objective dimensions. The fourth section brings together the main aspects of the architecture of representation substantiated throughout the chapter.

The social psychology of representations

Although the social psychology of representations involves the consideration of several issues, there is one dimension that is central to all others and
that frames, from the outset, the organisation of this field: the problem of
meaning. It is only through a consideration of meaning and the symbolic
function that a truly social psychological account of representation can
emerge. It is the analysis of meaning that can shed light on the fact that
different people, in different contexts and different times produce different
views, symbols and narratives about what is real, and it is only through an
understanding of meaning that we can begin to study how these different
representations relate to each other and the consequences of these relations
in the social world. It is on the basis of the symbolic function of representations – the fact that representation uses symbols to *signify*, to make sense
of the real and at the same time to establish it – that we can understand
both its power to construct reality and the limitations of empiricist conceptions that assume the existence of empirical orders as an a priori to the
labours of human cognition. It is on the basis of the symbolic function of
representations that we can turn away from the idea of knowledge as full
correspondence between representation and the outside world and start to
ask questions that unsettle the old idea of representation as a copy of the
world outside. It is through the analysis of meaning that we can understand
that the relationship between a representing system – an intersubjective
structure between self and other – and the system being represented – be it
objects in the material world or other people – is not a one-to-one but a
many-to-many relationship.

It is only through the symbolic function that we can grasp the work of
representation as going beyond purely epistemic aims to also encompass
expressive aims, which link up the representational form to the logic of self,
self–other relations and contexts. Through representation individuals and
communities not only represent a given object and a state of affairs in the
world, but also disclose who they are and the issues that matter to them, the
interrelations in which they are involved and the nature of the social worlds
they inhabit. Thus it is meaning, its production and transformation by
individuals and communities that occupies central stage in the social psychology of representations and provides the conceptual foundation for an
understanding of representation as both psychological and social.

Understood in this way, the social psychology of representations considers meaning and social context as foundational dimensions of all representational phenomena. Both – meaning and social context – offer the
theoretical lenses through which the field poses and tries to answer questions
related to the production and transformation of knowledge, its relationship
to social and cultural contexts and the diversity of forms it assumes in
contemporary public spheres. They also frame our understanding of old and
new issues that are linked to the construction of representation and

knowledge, from the old and still unresolved problem of subject–object relations to problems related to the social psychology of knowledge and the rationality and/or rationalities that pertain to different knowledge systems. Each one of these dimensions refers back to some of the central problems of psychological science in particular and to the social sciences in general. At the same time, they offer a route for an engagement with issues that, despite being with us for a long time, are still important today and indeed have acquired renewed prominence in our contemporary world. Let me consider each of them in turn.

The relationship between subject–object

This has been a central problem in psychology, it underlies the object of social psychology, i.e. the individual–society relationship, and it is an old problem of the social sciences. How do we, as subjects, relate to the object-world outside ourselves? How do we know it, how do we define it, what is the nature of our engagement with it? Throughout the history of psychology answers to these questions have defined different streams of theoretical elaboration and empirical research. All the classical bodies of knowledge that constitute psychology, ranging from its early formulations in intro-spectionism and behaviourism, to gestalt and psychoanalysis, through to the cognitive revolution of the 1970s, have sought to elaborate a response to the problem of subject–object relations (Brunswik 1952; Wolman 1960; Farr 1996). In all of these responses, with more or less intensity, there has been a tendency to separate too sharply subject and object, a tendency that carries the danger of constructing a full dichotomy between subject and object-world.

In general terms, this tendency can be systematised into two kinds of psychology, which I describe as the 'psychology of the pure subject' and the 'psychology of the pure object'. Both have overly separated the experience of the psychological subject from the reality of the world. The former has taken the subject as the measure of all things and considered the human mind and its activity the full source of what is known, what is done and how engagement with the world takes place. The latter, on the other hand, has given priority to world, conceived as a set of empirical regularities that exists independently of human action and intentionality. Both psychologies rely on the purity of a subject that is seen from its own self-enclosed universe, or on the purity of a world that is seen as devoid of human input. Intro-spectionism, behaviourism, cognitivism, and the form postmodernism took in psychology all belong to one or the other side of this divide. Consider behaviourism, for instance. Its denial of mind, its concern with manifest behaviour and its dependence on the stimulus–response paradigm make it a clear example of an objectifying model that precludes the consideration of subjective structures. The cognitive revolution that followed, while being a forceful response to behaviourism and its denial of the subject, soon developed into a psychology exclusively centred on the subject, considered as the bearer of cognitive processes qua mental functions and studied independently of the social and historical contexts in which persons exist (Bruner 1990). Postmodern forms of psychology have displayed features of both objectivism/behaviourism and subjectivism/cognitivism, as when denying ontological status to the mind and its process or when conferring full subjective independence to processes of meaning production, as if the reality of the world was made of a game of errant signifiers.

Underlying all is a dualist conception of subject–object relations and a failure to apprehend spaces of mediation that constitute the inbetween of intersubjective and interobjective relations. The origins of these conceptions, as I suggest in subsequent pages, are to be found in Cartesian philosophy and its sharp divisions between person and world, mind and body, self and other. Its legacy has produced both an individualist and mentalist framework to conceive of representation and knowledge and a reaction that, in seeking to overcome said legacy, dismisses the concept of representation altogether. This poses a renewed challenge to the social psychology of representation, as it tries to introduce alternative foundations to build a view of representation as a dynamic process centred neither on subject nor on object alone, but precisely on spaces of mediation that lie on the inbetween of intersubjective and interobjective relations. The analysis of the representational form that I introduce in this chapter seeks to show precisely that once we take the 'between' seriously mentalist ideas about representation collapse and representation becomes something other than the isolated intrapsychic process found in mainstream forms of cognitivism. At the same time, a clear appreciation of the 'between' allows for the integration of the object and the other in the conceptualisation of representations, which retains the connection between representation and the materiality of the world. These issues are discussed throughout this book.

The social psychology of knowledge

The analysis of representation is central to understand the social psychology of knowledge as it permits the elucidation of the link between knowledge and context and the representational effort behind all knowledge systems. Representation is not a static entity but a constructed system. I define representation as a triangular form, whose basic architecture is built by the interrelations between subject–other–object. These are at the basis of knowledge formation. Representation is the matter and substance of knowledge, the structure underlying all knowledge systems, the stuff that constitutes all possible knowledge we have of others, our world and ourselves. Yet, most knowledge forms succumb to processes of denial of their representational character, pretending that they are in perfect correspondence with whatever they express and represent. This defensive move, as we shall see, pertains to a long history of defining knowledge as an accurate copy of the world outside and as a certainty provider. Yet all knowledge is made of representation and expresses a desire to represent. 'Who', 'how', 'why', 'what' and 'what for' does knowledge represent? These are questions we can pose to the representational effort linked to the construction of knowledge systems, something I discuss in more detail in Chapter 4 on the forms and functions of knowledge. Each illuminates specific dimensions of the social psychological study of knowledge: its referentiality (who and what knowledge represents), its intersubjective and interactive nature (how knowledge represents), its expressive dimension (why knowledge represents) and its purposive dimensions (what for knowledge represents). These questions can operate as analytical categories that both clarify the desire underlying the representational labour involved in the making of knowledge and the consequential variation that makes knowledge a plural and heterogeneous form.

Indeed, in the detailed analysis of the representational form, both at the ontogenetic and sociogenetic levels, we find a model for the analysis of knowledge production that can go beyond the idea of knowledge as a single and homogeneous form, achieved as individuals and communities reach the top end of a developmental scale. The variation of representational forms poses deep and challenging questions to the conceptualisation of what constitutes knowledge, and in particular to how the knowledge held by specific subgroups and communities compares to dominant ideas about what knowledge is or ought to be. At the same time, this variation brings into sharp focus the connection between knowledge and contexts as it highlights the different communicative arrangements that human communities engage in while constructing representation, and with it knowledge about the world. The variation of the representational form is tantamount with variation in contexts and variation in knowledge. How we deal with this variation is precisely the problem of the third dimension of the social psychology of representations I wish to address, as it considers the rationality of knowledge and its diversity.

The rationality of knowledge and its diversity

The problem of what constitutes the rationality of knowledge and how this rationality is defined is a central problem to the social psychology of representations. Generally, this issue is theorised and empirically studied in two forms: the first refers to the study of different modalities of knowledge and representation expressed in debates about the form and internal properties of knowledge systems held by children, 'primitive peoples', lay people, scientists, etc. This area of study and debate, which has its origins in the work of anthropologists, sociologists and psychologists at the beginning of the twentieth century, seeks to uncover the rationality of knowing by comparing different forms of knowledge. It has been approached by psychologists concerned with education and the development of reason in the child and by sociologists concerned with how the knowledge of 'primitive peoples' compared to the knowledge of 'developed societies'. The second form, which is very much related to the first, refers to conceptions of how knowledge evolves and changes. Developmental psychologists in particular have addressed this issue, although it is also present, if not explicitly, in fields such as the sociology of development and the sociology of modernity. It is an issue that expresses one single preoccupation: how knowledge progresses from simpler to more complex forms, or as it is usually stated in the literature, from lower to higher forms. Is the evolution of knowledge a process of linear development? Does knowledge progress from one stage to another, leaving behind primitive forms? Or do different stages and modalities coexist and/or mix?

Both problems – comparing modalities and looking at the evolution of knowledge – pose questions related to the ranking and valuation of knowledge systems and how the power of different knowledges impacts on their capacity to establish their veracity and impose their authority in social fields. They also open space to bring into traditional conceptions of logic and rationality a pragmatic twist that seeks to redefine the idea of reason through a dialogical and situated approach. The emphasis is put, as I shall discuss later in the book, on the rationality of meaning and the effort is focused on uncovering the different logics that are behind a knowledge system as it tries to make sense of the world and develop strategies to cope with it. These issues, although theoretical in scope, relate to urgent societal problems emerging out of a new regime of encounters between knowledge systems in contemporary public spheres, to choices related to what counts and what does not count as knowledge in social fields, and to the possibilities and limitations of communication between knowledge systems. These issues are discussed throughout the book and in particular in Chapters 2, 4 and 5.

Underlying all the above dimensions is the common problem of representation, be it as a bridging structure between subject and object, when we pose questions related to the nature and efficacy of this bridge, be it as the matter that gives structure and content to knowledge systems, when we pose questions related to how the structure and content of representations shape the internal and external properties of knowledge systems. Thus it becomes necessary to unpack the representational form, map out its process of development and its connection to people and contexts in a way that goes beyond the definition of representation as a mental function. The analysis of the representational form, as I shall attempt to show in the following pages and indeed throughout the book, can generate an effective model to understand both the link between knowledge and context, and the consequences of this link to our understanding of knowledge and its diversity in the contemporary world.

Inventing representation

Traditional concepts of representation have relied heavily on a dualist model of subject–object relations. Dualist models, based on a Cartesian view of mind, see the process of representation as a mental act, where the subject processes the information presented by the object in order to posses a knowledge of it. This may be a simple way of describing it, but any consideration of the work produced under the rubric of mainstream cognition in the last 30 years corroborates this reading. Most cognitive theorists still work in a tradition of empiricism and associationism whose main tenets have not changed much since Locke and Hume. Representation is an affair between a solitary knower who looks into the object-world in order to construct a mental picture of it. There is no consideration of how this knower is located in the world, nor of how it was possible for this subject to become a knower in the first place. The world outside is already there, constituted as a series of regularities waiting to be discovered by the individual subject. There he is, standing on his own, sovereign and without a history, accessing and depicting the reality of the world.

The Cartesian model of the solitary knower is powerful and cannot be easily discarded. It belongs to what Taylor has called 'inescapable frameworks', traditions and streams of thought that circumscribe and shape the ways in which we conceive 'what it is to be a human agent, a person or a self' (Taylor 1989: 3). Whereas there is a general agreement in psychology that dominant conceptions of cognition and representation are directly indebted to Descartes, we rarely spell out why this happens to be the case and what is the problem with this inheritance, the work of Marková (1983) being a notable exception. This is, however, a necessary task not least because the concept of representation we deal with today is a direct product of the worldview that characterised the seventeenth century and it is now, as much as it was then, linked to a set of ideas and practices that mark an age and its preoccupations. From Descartes we inherited the notion of representation as disembodied and asocial. This conception emerged as part of a larger package whose central idea was the separation, in fact the radical severance, between the subject and the world. It is through Descartes that we can understand why it became possible to think about representation and it is only through an understanding of his legacy that we may hope to escape the 'inescapable frameworks' he set for us.

The Cartesian cogito and the individualisation of representation

Cogito ergo sum (I think, therefore I am): if it would be possible to locate a precise beginning for the modern age and its self-interpretation, it would be probably here, in this sentence. No other statement has had such strong impact on how we understand ourselves and its consequences are vast and widespread. It is this sentence and the particular intellectual landscape in which it was produced that inaugurated the representational era. The very idea of representation, of mind, of a distinction between the psychic and the physical as well as between an inner and an outer reality are all linked to the Cartesian *cogito* and to the radical societal transmutations with which these conceptions were intertwined.

The very possibility for the work of representation started with the radical separation between subject and world. This separation, which in itself is a product of the historical transformations that were exploding the medieval orders of European societies, constitutes one of the most important developments of the modern era.[1] It allowed the emergence of individualism as we know it and the appearance of a new vocabulary concerned with the description and understanding of an internal, inner psychological space where the experience of the individual could be located. The new subjectivity of the modern era was made possible by this radical chasm between the subject and the larger order of which previously she was just a part. Sociologists and historians of modernity have described in detail the transformations that made this divide between subject and world possible. They relate not only to changes in the economic, social and political structures of European society, but also to changes in the ideas, worldviews, attitudes and behaviour of the new European public (Hall *et al.* 1992; Micale and Dietle 2000), something I address in more detail in Chapter 3.

If before there was a symbiotic relation between persons and world, where the separation between oneself and the larger social order was inconceivable, the new mentality of the modern age detaches persons from communities and makes possible for the subject to become an *individual person*, to separate himself from the holistic whole of which he was a part and position himself *apart*. With modernity, there appears a new subject, who stands before the world outside as an individual, capable of developing reflexive ideas and thoughts about this world. The new subject of modernity confronts the world from the outside; his location is his own internal world, a new inner space, from which he draws the tools and procedures to confront the world outside.

Descartes was not only a part of this fledging new world; his philosophy became a decisive element in its development and consolidation. More than anyone else he clearly articulated the separation between subject and world by offering to his age a theory that could bridge the new gap between the inquiring mind and the world outside: a theory of representation. Descartes produced a comprehensive theory of representational knowledge based on the new separation between subject and world: once the subject is no longer part of a holistic order, there appears the need to construct a representation of it. Detached from a cosmic order that in a holistic manner kept together people and the world they were a part, the new individual introduced by Descartes is self-bound; he looks at the world outside from within.

Representation of the world outside was, therefore, a function of the new separation between subject and world and, at the same time, one of its conditions: the new consciousness inaugurated by Descartes was based on mental representations about the mind itself, about the individual and about the world. It stands between each one of these new constructs, linking and separating them at the same time.

The Cartesian anxiety and the search for certainty

Standing between mind and world, the work of representation became the centre of Descartes' anxiety: how can we be sure that our representation of the world is not deceiving us? How can I be certain that my knowledge of the world corresponds to the world outside me? In other words, what makes a representation attain the status of true knowledge? Descartes' troubles, as we can see, are still very much our troubles and it is difficult not to identify with the questions he was able to articulate. They were triggered by the interminable doubts that inhabited his mind, by the instability of human knowledge about the world, by a 'malignant demon' he invoked in his writings, whose tricks could deceive the senses and cast the shadow of doubt upon everything. The way he forged to escape from his troubles – presented in a philosophy that strongly tied up representation, knowledge, certainty and truth to the individual mind – may not be as easy to identify with. But when he expresses, at the beginning of his second Meditation, the aspiration of finding like Archimedes 'a point that is firm and immovable', of being 'fortunate enough to discover only one thing that is certain and indubitable' (Descartes 1641/1989: 85), how can we possibly fail to understand him? Who would not want such a firm and secure port today?

Descartes eventually found his Archimedean point and his finding provided us psychologists with a tremendous legacy, if not a total foundation. The psychology of the subject was born out of this fundamental Cartesian certainty: the one fact that cannot be doubted is that my mind is engaged in the activity of doubting. Doubting all in the world outside himself, which included his own body, Descartes (1641/1989: 86) found certainty in the loneliness of the cogito: 'I think, therefore I am.' The mind and the mind alone was the only reality he could not doubt: 'I am, I exist, is necessarily true each time it is expressed by me, or conceived in my mind.'

The Cartesian journey and its main elements – from the anxiety of doubt to the certainty of cogito – were as much part of the challenges that permeated the emerging cultural atmosphere of modernity as an attempt to place inside the individual mind both the labour needed to gain access to the world and the ultimate criterion that could confirm the reality of that access. In placing the work of representation into the mind and in giving to the mind alone the task of achieving truth and therefore knowledge, the cogito provoked a move of great importance and double meaning: on the one hand it took knowledge away from community as the old holistic communion between persons and world, and on the other hand transformed the subject into an individual thinker, the source and the criterion of all reliable knowledge. Tradition, custom and authority were to be challenged by doubt, and the mind, with its own individual resources, became the decisive battlefield between certainty and uncertainty.

Whereas the birth of representation placed it originally between subject and world bridging the new divide, with Descartes's philosophy representation is moved from its 'between' position to an 'inner', internal one. Mental representation becomes the substance of knowledge: it can lead to truth if it is capable of depicting precisely the reality of the world and can offer certainty that this is the case. Here we have the origin of two of the most deep-seated criteria defining what knowledge is and what it can give us – both deeply linked to the psychology of mind developed in the twentieth century: the criterion of correspondence between representation and world, and the criterion of certainty in knowledge. Both criteria of correspondence and certainty, which are at the heart of Descartes's theory of representational knowledge, institute not only the foundations of an epistemology, but also go beyond to produce a comprehensive psychology, one that tries to capture and explain what are the conditions of possibility for the psychological subject to produce representational knowledge.

If in Descartes the construction of representation seems to be mainly bound to its epistemic function – to logos – the process of construction he unfolds proposes and presupposes a certain producer, the subject of representation, and a certain world, the context of representation. The key marker of this process of construction, as Taylor has shown in his commanding study on the sources of self, is disengagement. It requires not only disengagement of the subject from the world, but also of the subject from himself, a project intensified by Locke and his theory of mind and procedural reason (Taylor 1989). The disengagement between self and other that gives birth to Cartesian representation goes a step further and turns to the subject himself as he introduces ideas and practices of self-control, responsibility and distantiation of self from itself.

Knowledge unbound: from certainty to total disengagement

Descartes took the world away from representation and expelled its objective dimension. Locke's theory of mind intensified the process by taking the subject away from itself and thus expelling from representation its subjective and intersubjective dimensions. The double separation between self and world and self from itself operated a double split: it not only deprived representation from its human sources and its context of production but also, and equally important, radically dehumanised the subject of representation. The theory of representation based on certainty and correspondence was constructed on the basis of a double isolation: it isolated self from the world and self from itself.

The double isolation of self put it right at the centre of representational processes and paradoxically gave to it two unprecedented burdens: solitude and self-denial. Self may well be at the centre but it is there alone. New demands of thought, doubt, reflection and self-reflection need to be dealt with in solitude: self must be his own resource to evaluate what is going on and to deal with potential errors, misjudgements and the burden of isolation. At the same time, whilst the centric position of self makes it the one single most important resource for knowledge – indeed, a position that could be seen as privileged – the disengagement of self from itself imposes the need for self-denial. Self becomes its own observer. It takes the identity of a third person rather than expressing its own subjectivity and experience as such. The inscription of a third person right at the core of the I has been well captured by many of the psychologies that attempted to grapple with the problem of self and its identity. From Mead's theory of the I and Me, to Freud's theory of the unconscious, to Lacan's theory of the barred subject, they all identified the presence of an Other at the heart of Self. The Cartesian subject may have been born in isolation but his development and existence were circumscribed and shaped by the presence of the Other, even if this Other was conceptualised as foreign, alien and intrusive.

From the anxiety presented by doubt and the certainty of the cogito to a position of solitude and self-denial, the theory of representation inaugurated by Descartes is in fact more than a theory of knowledge that seeks accuracy in representation and certainty as the basis for the truth of knowledge. It is also a theory about mind, self and their relations to the world. In this sense, it is perfectly understandable why Cartesian philosophy is deeply inter-twined with the history of psychology, and in particular social psychology (Marková 1983, 2004; Farr 1991). In the cogito we find the origins for all the fundamental constructs that shape our thinking about the mind, not only for the individualism, disembodiment and asociality that characterise the dominant development of psychological theory from the nineteenth into the twentieth century, but also for the notions of construction, agency and individual autonomy that guided the social and cultural approach in psychology. Despite the divergence in the present conceptualisations they offer, their origins are not completely disparate. The whole of psychology relies on the idea of the individual person, whose autonomy, agency and power of construction Descartes first theorised.

Deeply engrained in the Cartesian project was an impossible dream: to construct knowledge based on 'a view from nowhere' (Nagel 1986). The extreme isolation of the cognitive subject was an attempt to decouple the processes of production of knowledge, intrinsically linked to contexts and persons, from knowledge itself. By conceiving the bearer of knowledge as a subject in isolation, capable of self-enclosure in the task of assessing the world outside, the dynamic exchanges between knower, others and contexts were erased from the equation. By discarding the psychological and social contexts that produce knowledge and cleansing off its 'human, all too human' sources, knowledge of the world could emerge as a 'pure' construct. The decoupling of knowledge and context is part and parcel of the pathways that instituted modernity and its specific psychology. As mentioned in the foregoing pages, it was made possible by the construction of a radical double separation between self and world and between self and itself. It produced an objectification of mind that, although being at the origin of reflexivity and construction, also led to alienation, the processes whereby previously connected and mutually constitutive entities become unable to recognise each other as such.

In many respects the position of the lonely individual knower betrays a principle that has been essential to the quest for certainty and the self-interpretation that underlies the individual person as the core unit of experience in the west: we know alone and solitude can provide a zone of freedom from the mistakes and habits associated with customs and traditions that blur our vision and capacity to reach true knowledge. In collectives we are prone to error and distortion, something that has been forcefully reiterated not only by the psychology of individual cognition but also by the psychology of crowd behaviour (Moscovici 1985; Gellner 1992). Association with others entails a lethal danger to the project of the cognitive rational thinker because interactions and relationships bring about passions, interests and emotions. They lead subjects into alliances, disputes and power struggles. As soon as we introduce into the model of the solitary knower a partner in interaction things become messy; we will need to consider the vast field of human relations and the webs of complexity that arise from them. These are all potential destabilisers in the quest to produce a true representation of the world out there, something that can be called knowledge. Individuals alone know best and can represent the world adequately; human relationships are too messy to allow for the construction of knowledge.

Descartes and the contemporary dismissal of representation

In discussing the weight and impact of the Cartesian heritage in our understanding of representation I have emphasised the sharp divide between subject and world and the creation of an inner space that gave representation its locus inside the individual mind. Mental representation became the foundation of knowledge, carrying with it the quest for certainty and full correspondence between itself and the world outside, a quest that could only be achieved through a further step of disengagement of self from itself. While emphasis on the representational function qua mental replica or mirroring of the world outside has dominated the field of study of representations, it has also fuelled an anti-representational stance whose most radical consequence has been the dismissal of the notion of representation altogether (Gergen 1985; Ibañez 1991; Shotter 1993). The origins of this view can be found in Rorty's (1980) influential book *Philosophy and the Mirror of Nature*. There the author provides a compelling account of how representation has circumscribed our conceptions of knowledge so that 'to know is to represent accurately what is outside the mind; so to understand the possibility and nature of knowledge is to understand the way in which the mind is able to construct such representations'. Furthermore, continued Rorty, the main concern of philosophy has been the establishment of a general theory of representation that would 'divide culture into areas that represent reality well, those which represent it less well, and those which do not represent it at all (despite their pretence of doing so)' (Rorty 1980: 3).

The critique of such conceptions of knowledge and representation is as understandable as it is necessary. Less understandable, however, is that the critique of representation as conceived by these philosophers should lead to the dismissal of representation altogether. What are the consequences of dismissing representation? Is there no such a thing as a knowing subject? Is our knowledge of the world immediate, i.e. unmediated by both psychic and social processes? Should the critique, and indeed the dismissal, of concepts be followed by the denial of ontological existence to phenomena? These questions have remained unanswered in the work that followed Rorty's assessment of representation. Ironically, throwing away the phenomenon of representation with the conceptualisation it received from seventeenth-century philosophers suggests that rather than attempting to overcome the limitations of Cartesian theories of mind and representation, this work is in fact hooked on what Descartes proposed mind and representation to be. It simply fails to engage with the theoretical streams that evolved in a direct clash with Cartesian theories of mind, streams that demonstrated convincingly that both mind and representation are social and symbolic phenomena (Doise *et al.* 1975; Perret-Clermont 1980; Doise and Mugny 1984; Duveen 1997; Valsiner 2000; Marková 2003).

A full understanding about the making of representation in the modern era and how the process impacts on current conceptualisations about representational processes is necessary to counteract the melancholic tendencies that think we can just turn around and declare the world devoid of representation. We may not like his inheritance and be critical of Descartes, but we cannot undo history as it happened. Without Descartes the frameworks of our debate would simply not exist, and that is why the radical, and in many ways inspiring, critique of representation articulated in the work of Richard Rorty, tried precisely to discard the whole framework and to reset it in different terms. Whether he succeeded, however, I very much doubt. The representational era is still very much part of what we are, from the most intimate and personal to the larger social and political structures that make our historical worlds. Representation still needs to be understood and studied for the simple reason that it is there.

This, however, does not mean that we need to take its past in its entirety, nor that we cannot reconceptualise it. Indeed, this is precisely what has been done by the sociodevelopmental psychologists of the twentieth century. What their work shows is that theories of representation did not develop without antinomies. The ontogenetic history of representation present in the genetic psychology of Piaget, the sociocultural developmental psychology of Vygotsky and the cultural psychoanalysis of Winnicott can provide juxtaposition to the Cartesian paradigm of representational knowledge and bring back to representation the symbolic and social dimensions that make it at once a subjective, intersubjective and objective phenomena.

The development of representation

In this section I shall show that representational processes cannot be understood outside the psychosocial and historical circumstances that make them possible in the first place. Central to this view is a consideration of the ontogeny of the representational form and the symbolic function. Genetic theories of representation have firmly linked the form and structure of representation to both its developmental history and the symbolic function while stressing the connection between the cognitive, the emotional and the social in the developmental trajectory of the child (Piaget 1962, 1964; Piaget and Inhelder 1969; Vygotsky 1978, 1997; Vygotsky and Luria 1994). The construction of the object through symbolic representation – which stands as other and world to the emerging sense of self of the child – is at once a cognitive, affective and social process. The child's knowledge of the object-world does not, and indeed cannot, emerge as dispassionate cognition; the energy behind the construction of all cognitive structures and the consolidation of all knowledge comes from the child's desire for the object-world, or as Furth would put it desire for society (Furth 1996). In order to know the object, the child must invest it emotionally: there must be desire to know. Desire for knowledge is central in childhood and it can be clearly seen in the intensely creative, playful and constructive symbolic action of the child. But it also continues to shape, in culturally sublimated forms, the relationship between adult social actors and the knowledge they produce in social fields.

Winnicott's theory of transitional objects, which led to the concept of the potential space, is particularly apposite to explore these connections, as is the classical Freudian elaboration of the dynamics of libidinal energy on thought activities (Freud 1900, 1911, 1920; Winnicott 1965c, 1971, 1985). The connections between the emotional, cognitive and social dimensions show that while in the genesis and work of representation there is, without doubt, an epistemic function that seeks cognition of the world outside itself, the analysis of representation goes far beyond to involve both the dialogical relations that account for its genesis and the expressive function that makes it into the labour of psychological beings, whose identities and social existence are integral to the representational process. Emphasis on the objective dimension of logos as a mirror of the world has obliterated the intersubjective and subjective dimensions of representation, which are all the basis of the symbolic function. As I emphasise later, this was already clear in the developmental psychologies of Piaget and Vygotsky and in the social psychology of Moscovici. They all showed that the status of representation is at once epistemic, social and personal and it is the appreciation of these three dimensions that can explain why representations are not a copy of the world outside but a symbolic construction of it. Rather than being the replica of a world that stands outside waiting for the labour of cognition, representations are constructive acts of engagement, a mode of relating to the world outside. It is in the social and developmental psychology of self and other relations that we find the genetic account that can put back into representational processes the dialogical and expressive functions that are, as much as the epistemic function, intrinsic to symbolic forms.

The ontogeny of representation

In *Mind in Society: The Development of the Higher Psychological Processes*, Vygotsky (1978) explained the origins of the fragmentation of psychology by its inability to deal with issues of genesis and historical development in psychological phenomena. Unable to produce a genetic account, an increasingly fragmented psychology concentrated on the study of psychological phenomena as attributes that people possess rather than develop (Valsiner 1991; Vygotsky 1997). The problem of genesis is, however, paramount. Without a clear account of how psychological structures evolve we cannot have a full understanding of their mature form. Understanding genetic processes not only sheds light on the mature form of psychological phenomena but also introduces a historical approach to the understanding of human psychology (Scribner 1985).

The historical method is particularly illuminating for the analysis of representation both at the individual level of ontogeny and at the social level where social representations emerge. The consideration of genetic processes is needed if we are to explain representation at all; there is a fundamental connection between genesis and structure that can only be appreciated in the live dynamics of developmental processes, a view that has been equally presented by Piaget in his discussion of the relations between genesis and structure (Piaget 1971; Duveen 2001a). Psychological structures have a history that is both ontogenetic and sociogenetic and with representation it is not different. It is in the developmental history of representation that we can clearly see its social and personal foundations, the processes that link representation both to meaning, to social context and to persons in interaction. These processes are at the basis of a developmental narrative that permits an understanding of the journey of individuation and socialisation whereby a human infant becomes a person.[2] Despite the disparity between their programmes of research and the haste of commentators to identify differences between them, the developmental psychologies of Piaget and Vygotsky have a great deal in common. Both have used the genetic method and both have pointed to processes of decentration as the road to the development of cognitive structures and higher psychological functions.

Both described the emergence of representation as a function of intricate self–other relations that gradually allow the child to develop awareness of itself and the object-world outside. Both expounded and attributed tremendous importance to the symbolic function. Indeed in Vygotsky the use of signs is considered the most important cultural mean for regulating behaviour and it defines the human species. It is these common dimensions – the genetic method, the primacy of self–other relations, and the importance of the symbolic function – that I wish to emphasise to develop the approach to representation I seek to expand here. They constitute the threads that can explicate representation as personal, social and cognitive. At the same time they provide the avatars of a developmental narrative needed to counteract the study of representation and knowledge as attributes without a social psychological history.

The ontogenetic history of the representational form starts with the introduction of the neonate in the intersubjective structure of self–other relations. It is in the context of intersubjective relations that both the body and the psychological life of the infant grow. Neither the physical maturation of the child, nor the tremendous psychological achievements of early childhood can be understood outside this intersubjective context. Entering intersubjective structures is not a choice for the infant but a necessity imposed by the vulnerability of its biological body at birth.[3] The human infant at birth is a combination of biological and psychological potentials that depend, to be fully realised, on developmental conditions. These include, above all, a receptive environment that can give to the vulnerable body of the child the care it needs to develop into a person. Indeed, the reality of the human infant at birth makes the care it receives from the outside world a constitutive fact in its development as a person. Care, as the first response the outside world presents to the immature existence of the infant, is shaped by social, cultural and economic circumstances and constitutes the first social and psychological context of infants.

The primary vulnerability of the infant, which becomes a symbol of all posterior vulnerability, inscribes in the economy of the psyche both the law of desire and the desire for recognition. It throws the human infant in the grammar of self–other relations and opens the way for the love and care that can potentially come from another human being. The drama of this dependency marks the ontogenetic beginning of humans and deeply inscribes the other in the constitution of self. But, and this is crucially important, it also gives infants power: it is because a baby is so extremely vulnerable that her caretaker will hold her unconditionally (everyone who has ever observed a loving relation between a baby and a caretaker knows who is in control; it is not the mother). Psychologically, these primary relations acquire an enormous importance for they contain the elements that will shape all subsequent relations between self and other and the particular manner through which self deals with relations of asymmetry in social life, something I shall address in more detail in

Chapters 4 and 5. The imperative of the other has been widely recognised and it is present in the developmental psychologies of both Piaget and Vygotsky, in the social psychology of Mead and in the psychoanalysis of Freud and Winnicott.[4]

If the imperative of self–other relations marks the beginning of every human life, it is the resolution of this imperative that will shape its development. The gradual resolution of the differentiation between self and other, which evolves as the child goes through the emotional and cognitive labour of working out the relative independence and autonomy of other and object, is the energy that drives the development of cognitive structures. Understanding that the object world has a permanence that goes beyond the action of the child is condition sine qua non for the emergence of representational process and the symbolic function. It is by establishing a relationship with the absent object, understanding that its existence is independent of its presence and allowing it to emerge as a perspective in its own right, that the child will eventually rise to the fullness of ego-relatedness, communication and engagement with the Other. In giving to the other a position in its own right, the child also decentres herself and is able to see her own self as one amongst many others who together share a human predicament. Piaget described these processes through the concept of decentring, which he compared to a 'miniature Copernican Revolution', or the hard-won realisation that self is not the only one and is not at the centre of the world.

Decentration is an essential notion in understanding the ontogenesis of representation and symbolic activity. It captures the process whereby infants open up to the diversity and plurality of the world and charges the development of knowledge with an emotional load derived from the dynamics of self–other relations. Decentration is what brings about symbolic representation, the capacity to represent symbolically that which is not there to be seen and/or touched. Starting from deferred imitation, through play, drawing and image making to a fully established language, the ontogenetic history of representation throws the child into the sociocultural world. With it, comes the birth of time, which frees the child from the present by introducing past and future, the birth of objects, which establishes object permanence and, last but not least, the birth of ethics, which introduces the child in a moral universe where others matter.

From the initial action of the child, in the form of a system of sensory-motor schemes, through to the semiotic function, in all its diverse manifestations, the ontogenetic history of representation is entangled in an interpersonal system that, in relation and decentration, provides the emotional framework within which the child will develop knowledge of the world and of herself. Both through action and the use of symbols the child progressively constructs representation as the psychic structure that at once establishes self, object permanence and society. Let us now consider in more detail the affective dimension of these processes.

Representation as potential space

While Piaget and Vygotsky formulated the basic tenets of representation as a social and cognitive process grounded on the relations between self–other–object, their consideration of the affective dimension was less systematic. Yet this should be seen more as a matter of focus than as a matter of intended inconsideration. They both recognised the importance of the emotional dimension and they both read and appreciated the writings of Freud.[5] In fact, it is difficult, if not impossible to ignore the passionate character of the representations constructed in early childhood, when the symbolic function is at the apogee of its power and the child's constructions are inundated by the emotional life of self and the intensity of the interactions that constitute the first encounters with a world of people and objects that is 'not-me'.

It is precisely this emotional, passionate and constructive dimension of representations that I would like to examine here. I wish to show that the power of the symbolic function of representation rests in its ability to raise above the constraints of the object-world and in a relatively free manner express the intentions, the dreams, the fantasies and aspirations of the subjectivity that puts it in motion. The work of representation is not only social in its formation and epistemic in producing knowledge about the object-world, it is also regulated by the dynamics of desire and the economy of the psyche, which are subordinated to unconscious processes. I shall draw on two interrelated conceptual tools offered by work of psychoanalytical orientation to advance this point: the first is the concept of potential space, a concept elaborated by Winnicott (1971, 1985) to account for transitional phenomena, and the second is the interrelations between the pleasure principle and the reality principle, the two principles of psychological functioning described by Freud (1911, 1920) to account for the exchanges between the general tendency of the psyche to hold on to sources of pleasure and the task of engaging with reality, even if this happens to be unpleasant. Both conceptual tools can enrich the social psychology of representations by introducing the dimension of emotions and unconscious affects in the analysis of representational fields.

The distinction between the pleasure principle and the reality principle was established by Freud to give an account of how the psyche deals with the pressures of both its own unconscious pressures and the external reality. The two principles express the struggles between ego and the outside world: the tendency of the pleasure principle is to avoid the checks and balances of the reality principle and merge the thinking of the subject with the external world and wishes with their fulfilment. In dreams, in play, in daydreaming and in jokes we find instances of the pleasure principle. Freud was clear about the supremacy of the pleasure principle in our mental life. Yet he was no less emphatic about the value of reality and reality testing for the economy of the psyche. In fact, in Freud, the (partial) failure of the pleasure principle is a necessary condition for the very emergence of a desiring subject, capable of confronting and engaging with the limitations, restrictions and frustrations imposed by the reality of world and others. Even though it is tempting to locate in the pleasure principle the energy behind all the creativity and innovation that are present in dreams, play, culture and art, this would be misleading. Without the reality principle, the pleasure principle would condemn the subject to an enclosed reality, unconnected with the world of others and objects, a reality made of solitude and deprived of the wealth of experience the object-world affords to one. Equally, if it were to master alone, the reality principle would transform the life of the mind in a repetition of outside constraints. It is the tensions between the two principles that fuel the potential energies of individuals and communities, creating desire for expressing the inside and engaging with the outside.

Winnicott's account of the transition from absolute dependence to a state of relative independence coincides in many ways with Freud's description of the struggles between the pleasure principle and the reality principle. Winnicott concentrated on the dangers of the reality principle ruling alone, a principle he described as 'an insult'. According to him, 'the Reality Principle is the fact of the existence of the world whether the baby creates it or not, it is an arch-enemy of spontaneity, creativity and the sense of the real' (Winnicott 1984: 236). Since growing, however, involves an acceptance of a world that is 'not-me' and of a relationship to it, how does the infant cope with the 'insult' of the reality principle? Winnicott's answer to this question was the notion of potential space, a concept that is perhaps his most original contribution. The concept deals precisely with this intermediary zone of tensions between pleasure and reality, between the fantasy and omnipotence that are typical of early childhood and the limitations and constrains of the outside reality.

The potential space needs to be understood in relation to Winnicott's discussion of transitional phenomena, an emotional process analogous to the processes of decentring described in Piaget's and Vygotsky's developmental psychology. The concept was developed from direct observation of the relationship between young children, their caretakers and the first object they adopt as their own special possession. This first object – the transitional object – has a particular importance to the child. It is the first 'not-me' possession and it plays a crucial psychological role in working through processes of differentiation between infant and significant others. Transitional objects are located in what Winnicott has called a 'third area of living': they do not pertain to the space of the child or the space of the outside object alone but are a symbol of the union between child and outside object. Through transitional objects young children can evoke the intimacy and comfort of the full union between mother–child that is gradually being challenged by decentration and individuation.

Transitional phenomena deal with the grief of separation and the desire for mastering the outside world, with the troubles of balancing the pleasure principle and the reality principle. They are based on holding and handling, the two key modes of interaction that take the child from a state of absolute dependence to a relative independence. Whereas at the beginning the function of the caretaker is to provide a reliable holding for the immature and weak existence of the infant, progressively she transforms holding into handling and introduces the child to the experience of absence and failure. These correspond to the uncomfortable limits posed by an outside reality to the sensory-psychic experience of the infant. The caretaker is not always there; she or he has an independent existence outside of and beyond her or his relationship with the infant. From the experience of holding, there arises a feeling of omnipotence and a sense of trust in the environment that the caretaker represents, and from the experience of handling the first elements of ego-relatedness, containment of omnipotence and communication in the full sense of the word.

The potential space, or the 'third area of living' (the first is self and the second is the reality of the world) where transitional phenomena are located, merges both holding and handling by drawing on the experience of omnipotence guaranteed by the caring environment and the communication with the outside by the acknowledgement of a 'not-me' reality. It is in this space that reality and fantasy meet and become one: in it the infant has the illusion of creating that which is already there to be found. The illusion experienced by the infant is that of omnipotence, which the holding and handling of his needs in a condition of ego-relatedness permits; omnipotence that, as Winnicott observes, is real for him but an illusion from the point of view of the observer.

The third area of living of the potential space does not end with the transitional object but continues to be expressed in the play of young children and in a sublimated form in all forms of symbolic expression and creativity in adult life. It is also the foundation of all human communication, which in similar vein occurs in the overlaps between potential spaces which transcend the boundary between the 'me' and the 'not-me'. Indeed, if for Winnicott the very essence of growth is the construction of a boundary where the self and the inner reality begin to be one in relation to a shared reality of others, the potential space transcends this boundary. In the potential space people are neither in the world of fantasy nor in the world of shared reality, but in the paradoxical third place that belongs to both these places at once. The potential space is about mediation, about linking up what seems separated forever, joining again what has been separated and creating within its borders a symbolic world that can accommodate self and other, fantasy and reality, art and science, the rational and the irrational.

Symbolic representation is thus the quintessential activity of the potential space; indeed it creates potential spaces. Symbols create the object represented constructing a new reality to a reality that is already there. They fuse the subject and the object because they are the expression of the

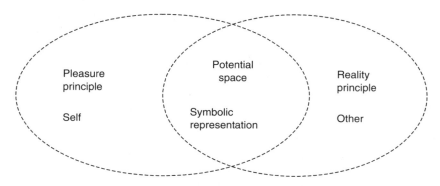

Figure 1.1 Representations as a potential space

relationship between the subject and the object. Through symbolic representation, different things can stand for each other and can converge into similarity; they allow for infinite variability and yet they are referential. Thus, it is of the essence of the symbolic activity – the activity of the potential space – to acknowledge a shared reality – the reality of others. Yet, it is a creative acknowledgement and leads to involvement with others and with the object-world. The reference to the world of others is what guarantees the creative nature of symbolic activity, so one's experience can build upon the experience of others continually creating the experience of a shared reality. That is why Winnicott says that it is out of difference, in every sense of the word, that the human self grows, for 'when one speaks of a man, one speaks of him along with the summation of his cultural experiences. The whole forms the unit' (Winnicott 1967: 99).

Figure 1.1 shows a Venn diagram with the overlaps that constitute the potential space and symbolic representation. The process of constructing these overlaps is developmental, that is, it has an ontogenetic history. It can only be understood if we approach the production of psychological constructs as movement, as entities that emerge out of a historical process, which operates at the individual and sociocultural levels. These overlaps can expand or contract depending on the transactions between person and sociocultural world. It is in the processes of expansion and contraction of the potential spaces of our social lives that we find the workings of creativity and learning how to take the world as a reality that goes beyond our desire to control it.

Finally let me mention two processes that derive from the potential space and are at work in symbolic representation: condensation and displacement. Both can allow us to appreciate clearly the constructive dimension of representational activity and its connections with the life of the psyche. Condensation and displacement relate to a capacity for playing with meaning: they give things a new form, just as the unconscious does (Freud

1900). Condensation refers to the ability of the symbolic function to condense and coalesce different things, events and people so that they can merge and become one in a symbolic representation. Condensation gives to symbols their social, emotional and creative load as it allows for many different things to come together and penetrate each other. Displacement is related to condensation insofar as it allows for things, events and people to be taken away from familiar and natural settings and to be relocated at will, following the logic of meaning and unconscious affects. Both processes are integral to the symbolic function; they are predominant in play and dreams as well as in all work of art and creation, whose psychological origins are directly associated with both ludic and oneiric activity.

Piaget (1962) examined the problem of the unconscious symbol in his studies on the development of the symbol and the mental image in the child. He discussed the work of condensation and displacement in relation to the play and dreams of young children, maintaining that it is pointless to consider an unconscious domain for affects and a conscious domain for thought and intellectual life since 'the unconscious is everywhere, and there is an intellectual as well as an affective unconscious' (Piaget 1962: 172). Further, he argued, the trade-offs between the unconscious and the conscious are incessant in every psychic process, so even the most elementary symbols are at the same time conscious and unconscious. Even the most basic symbols are the outcome of blending images, of contrasts, of identifications that condense, as it were, the variety of objects, affects and significant others at the disposal of the child. In doing so they displace meanings among those various objects, giving to one the reference of the other, evoking in one the presence of the other, mixing in one the image and the sound of the other and so forth.

In discussing the emotional and unconscious processes that are involved in the formation of symbolic representation it is possible to appreciate how the development of knowledge is not restricted to the formation of rational cognitive structures but is also shaped by the multiple feelings and fantasies that constitute the life of the child. The battle between cognition and emotion, between reason and unreason, between logic and illogical thinking, between fantasy and reality, which takes place in the work of representation, continues throughout adult and social life. Despite the theoretical moves that have sharply separated these dimensions, the genesis of representation in the human child reveals it as a cognitive, emotional and social structure. It is this genesis that shapes its internal properties and defines its form as a social psychological construct grounded on the dialogues between self–other–object–world.

Beyond the mirror of nature: representation as social creation

In the foregoing pages I have discussed the genesis of representation as a building block for the overall understanding of representation that I am introducing here. The narrative provided by a developmental perspective brings to light that meaning and context are inseparable from representation: representations emerge out of a context of self–other relations that is always emotional, social and cultural and therefore historically situated. Representations are thus open to the creative constructions afforded by these relations and through the symbolic function they are meaning-making activity.

I now want to conclude this chapter by characterising the representational form in light of the discussion I have introduced in previous sections. Bearing in mind the ground covered until here it should become clear that far from being copy or reflection of the outside world, representation is an active construction of social actors. It expresses in its mode of production, constituent elements and consequences in social life the complexity of the interrelations between internal and external worlds, between individual persons and the collectives to which they belong, between psychic structures and social realities. The work of representation is multifaceted and moves incessantly from the individual to the social and from the social to the individual, constituting thus a privileged focus for the understanding of social psychological phenomena. To close I wish to emphasise the following aspects of representations:

- representation as a mediating and communicative structure
- the material nature of representation
- the polyvalent nature of representation
- the problem of hyper-representation.

Representation as a mediating and communicative structure

Representation emerges as a mediating structure between subject–other–object. It is constituted as labour, that is to say, representation structures itself through the labour of communication and action that links subjects to other subjects and to the object-world (Kaës 1984). In this sense it is perfectly plausible to say that representations are communicative action (Habermas 1989b, 1991): it is communicative action that forms them as it constructs in the same and single process the participants of the communicative process. Communicative action involves language as it involves action of a non-discursive kind; these are manifested in everyday practices, institutions of various kinds and the informal structures of lifeworlds (Schutz 1967a; Habermas 1991).

The communicative work of representation produces symbols whose force rests in their capacity to produce meaning, to signify. Representation puts something or someone in place of something or someone else: this displacement and condensation of objects and people that gives to each and to all a new configuration and meaning is the essence of the symbolic order.

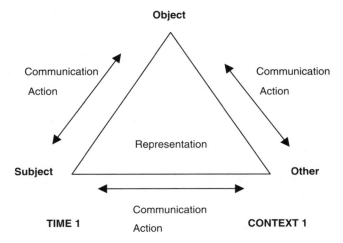

Figure 1.2 The architecture of representation: constituents and mode of
   production

It shows clearly that creation and construction are at the very basis of the
symbolic register, since the operations of the symbolic are ontogenetically
linked to, and involve residuals of, the ability for pretend-play developed in
early childhood. It also demonstrates the connection between the construction of symbols and the production of art and culture, since the latter is the
accumulation of meanings and symbols that stick over time. This conception of representation as a mediating structure belonging to the 'between' is
depicted in Figure 1.2.

This picture represents a slice of the representational process in time.
Bauer and Gaskell have introduced a model that extends Figure 1.2 in time,
adding the crucial dimension of project to the representational process. As
they note 'to this basic triangle a time dimension, both past and future, is
added to denote the implied or espoused project (P) linking the two subjects
and the object' (1999: 170). The problem of time, which corresponds to
the vital problem of history, is thus clearly integrated into the representational process. We have thus subject–other–object–communicative action–
project–time–context as the foundational categories that comprise the overall phenomenon of representation. The triangular conception of representation is derived from Moscovici's basic formula for social psychology
(1984). Representation can be thus conceptualised as a logical function with
seven arguments:

R (S, O, Ob, CA, P, T, C), where

S = self; O = other; Ob = object; CA = communicative action;
P = project; T = time; C = context.

The analysis of the representational form shows that the work of representation involves subjects in relation to other subjects and the communicative action that circumscribes and shapes their relations as they engage in the process of investing an object or a set of objects with meaning. Further, it is a form constructed by the communicative action of interlocutors in context and within a time horizon. This system of intersubjective and interobjective relations is what defines the symbolic shape of objects in the social world and ultimately the set of shared symbolic codes that establish what is real for us in a given context and time. This process takes place over time and becomes institutionalised so that new generations encounter the labour of representation as a symbolic environment organised in cultural traditions and institutional frameworks that, while preceding them, are also open to the new representational labour they will eventually produce. In this sense we can accept the Marxian claim that humans after all do act under conditions which are not entirely of their own making.

The material nature of representation

Within a dialogical conception of representation mentalist views obviously become a limited and limiting view: representation belongs to the between of human communication and societal action and it is not the product of individual minds enclosed in themselves. This view also discards those conceptions that deny the role of objects and objectivity in the shaping of representation. Here, representation is not the act of a subject whose action can shape representation alone. The materiality of the object-world is integral to the representational process and interacts with the subject shaping as much as she or he does the representational outcome. The objectivity of the social world is obviously constructed (fact means made) but no less objective because socially constructed. It is an objectivity that arises out of the constancy and institutionalisation of human practices, which 'thicken and harden' through processes of transmission and grant to symbolic environments their taken for grantedness and factual character. It is against this objectivity that representations are formed.

The polyvalent nature of representation

The status of representation is polyvalent. Representations are ontological, epistemological, psychological, social, cultural and historical constructions. They are all of these at the same time and each of these attributes can only be understood in relation to all others, since phenomenologically speaking they are simultaneous dimensions of the representational system. When people engage in processes of communication, which situates them in a concrete relationship bound to the cultural, social and historical configuration in which they both find themselves and actively (re)produce, they produce the symbolic means to construct a particular representation of an object – be it concrete, physical or abstract – which enters the network of other representations of a given social, cultural and historical framework. This process is ontological insofar as it plays a constitutive role in the emergence of the human subject as a being who represents itself and therefore possesses an identity. It is an epistemological process insofar as it allows (re)cognition: knowledge about the object – both self as an object for itself and the object-world. It is a psychological process insofar as it structures and manifests itself as a psychic process susceptible to the ruses of passion, illusion and desire. It is a social, historical and cultural process because the intersubjective is its condition of possibility and the object matter of representation comes from the intelligibility of history and culture. The polyvalent status of representation reaffirms it as a mediating structure. Representation is not located in any of the corners of the triangle of mediation; its space is in the between of the triangle and the constituent elements that form it. Jodelet's (1985, 1991, 2002) extensive discussion of representation, both in psychology and in the social sciences as a whole, has convincingly demonstrated their polyvalent status.

The problem of hyper-representation

The dialogical conception of representation does not grant to the representational process the absolute power to define completely an object. Let us maintain a distinction that is current in both psychoanalytical and phenomenological thinking, between reality and the real, or *Realität* (reality) and *Wirklichkeit* (actuality) (Erikson 1964; Gadamer 1975). The real or *Wirklichkeit* is the particular horizon constructed by a particular community or a particular person, lived and acted through in the experience of life each day. Representations construct the real but never fully capture the wholeness of reality, even if they desire to do so – science is a form of representation that works very hard to do just that. Since Freud, psychologists have known that there is a disjunction between what is real for one and what constitutes reality, as the sum of all reals, something that always remains partly unknown because nobody has it. This distinction has taught us to listen to the so called hysteric symptom as Freud did, trying to understand what it represented and meant for the women who displayed it. What those women experienced and said was real for them even if not for the observer. So real it was that it could subjugate the body and paralyse it. It is a distinction that allows us to understand, pay attention and grant importance to the truth of a point of view, the truth embedded in the experience and knowledge of individuals and local communities, even if they sound 'mad', absurd and illogical. It teaches the psychologist and the social scientist the practice of listening to as it teaches that there is no representation that can fully apprehend the total reality of an object.

This distinction also alerts us to the dangers involved in 'hyper-representation', the term I use to describe those situations where representations are produced without any consideration to the reality of the object. Representations, put simply, can also distort, tell lies, delude and confuse. Hyper-representation is, of course, part of the power of representation, since the symbolic is a sphere where the law of 'pretend-play' applies. It is a facet of the representational process that plays a crucial role both in the positive and creative dimension of its construction and in the negative and subjugating possibilities of overconstruction. Within larger power relations that operate in any given society these effects can be, and certainly are, used by various social groups at various times to pursue interests and produce effects associated with strategic projects. Racism is one such an instance. Representations about the black person have been historically false, despite being extremely real. They were real to the producers of racist representations and real enough to the black subject at the receiving end of those representations, as Fanon so eloquently argued (Fanon 1967). But we need the disjunction between representation and object to criticise them and to prove them false. Therefore, the distinction between representation and object is crucial and needs to be preserved as the only possibility of sustaining the idea of critique and potential accuracy in cognition. Unless we want to relativise ourselves to death, as it were, it is important to acknowledge that the object-world goes beyond our efforts to represent it. This is the case not only because diversity in society makes this object open to the representational efforts of different others/contexts and the many reals they construct, but also because human knowledge is a form of representation that never fully captures the totality of the object. It is only communication between representations of the real that can lead to a sense of a shared and single reality and provide us with an always provisional objectivity.

The genesis of representation is thus the key to understanding its architecture as a social psychological construct. The dialogical triad self–other–object shapes it as a symbolic construction of persons, self–other relations and world. Understanding this dialogical genesis consolidates the subjective and intersubjective dimensions of representation, which, in conjunction with the epistemic function, are integral to the process of knowledge construction. It helps us to debunk the view of representation as an individual mental construct that seeks to copy the world outside and retrieve to the heart of representational processes the power of human sociality to engage creatively with the world and shape it as a product of human action.

2   Social representations and the diversity of knowledge

At the beginning of *The Order of Things* Michel Foucault (1974) refers to an ancient Chinese encyclopaedia cited in a short story by the Argentinean writer Jorge Luis Borges. The story is 'The Analytical Language of John Wilkins' and the encyclopaedia is entitled the *Celestial Emporium of Benevolent Knowledge*. It contains the following taxonomy of the animal kingdom:

> (a) those that belong to the Emperor; (b) embalmed ones; (c) those that are trained; (d) suckling pigs; (e) mermaids; (f) fabulous ones; (g) stray dogs; (h) those that are included in this classification; (i) those that tremble as if they were mad; (j) innumerable ones; (k) those drawn with a very fine camel's hair brush; (l) others; (m) those that have just broken a flower vase; (n) those that resemble flies from a distance.
>
> (Foucault 1974: xv)

Now consider the following excerpt from *The Child's Conception of the World* (Piaget 1929), where Piaget talks to Roy, age six, about the origins of the sun and the moon. Roy's answers are in italics.

> Roy (6;0) 'How did the sun begin? – *It was when life began* – Has there always been a sun? – *No* – How did it begin? – *Because it knew that life had begun.* – What is it made of? – *Of fire.* – But how? – *Because there was fire up there.* – Where did the fire come from? – *From the sky.* – How was the fire made in the sky? – *It was lighted with a match.* – Where did it come from, this match? – *God threw it away.'* After a moment's pause: 'What is life? – *It is when one is alive.* – What made life begin? – *We did, when we started living.'*
>
> (Piaget 1929: 258)

Finally, consider this shortened version of the DSM-IV-TR (*Diagnostic and Statistic Manual of Mental Disorders*), a classificatory system for mental illness published by the American Psychiatric Association, and widely used by mental health practitioners:

(1) Disorders Usually Diagnosed in Infancy, Childhood and Ado-
lescence; (2) Delirium, Dementia, and Amnesic and Other Cognitive
Disorders; (3) Mental Disorders Due to a General Medical Condition;
(4) Substance-Related Disorders; (5) Schizophrenia and Other Psychotic
Disorders; (6) Mood Disorders; (7) Anxiety Disorders; (8) Somatoform
Disorders; (9) Factitious Disorders; (10) Dissociative Disorders; (11)
Sexual and Gender Identity Disorders; (12) Eating Disorders; (13) Sleep
Disorders; (14) Impulse-Control Disorders Not Elsewhere Classified;
(15) Adjustment Disorder; (16) Personality Disorders; (17) Disorders
Usually First Diagnosed in Infancy, Childhood, and Adolescence; (18)
Other Factors That May Need Clinical Attention.

(APA 1994: vii–viii)

Is there anything in common in the three excerpts above? Each seems to offer
strikingly different ways of thinking, of making sense of what is out there
and developing an account about what is perceived to be the reality of the
world. It is not only that each one of these extracts is generated by very
disparate communities – children, the ancient Chinese and scientists. It is
also that there is an obvious difference in the reasoning they betray, a
different way of explaining, putting in order and connecting different things.
The Chinese encyclopaedia, as Foucault observed, 'shatters all the familiar
landmarks of our thought', and introduces a representation of the animal
kingdom that for us is both ambiguous and arbitrary. It can be funny but it
doesn't work. We find it blatantly illogical. Equally, in children's talk there is
something that is funny and incoherent; in Roy's description of the origins of
the sun and the moon there is confusion between nature and humans and
there is a clear dependence of the natural world on the actions of humans.
There is something that feels *wrong* about his explanation. Finally, the
DSM-IV is relatively well known, at least for psychologists and mental
health practitioners. It is familiar and it makes sense because it expresses a
well-established and quite powerful system of thinking about madness. Its
categories are well delimited and do not appear arbitrary to us because we
know the overall system of knowledge that allows them to hang together.

Yet despite their obvious differences there is something common to the
three excerpts above. They are all systems of thinking about and knowing
the world. They are enabled by representations that allow for sense making
even if, from our perspective as observers, some of them do not make sense.
They show that our understanding of what is logical or illogical in social
life is inextricably linked to what is familiar or unfamiliar to us; we understand what is part of our cultural context and tend to misunderstand what
is not. They take us back to the problem of representation and knowledge
discussed in the previous chapter and invite further questions about the
ways in which social actors, situated in different positions of the life cycle,
holding different social positionings, belonging to different cultures or
different historical periods, come to know the worlds they inhabit and at

the same time construct. They highlight the manner in which societies think and how thought itself is framed by the collective ideas, representations and beliefs that configure the horizons of a community of people. They make clear, by their sheer diversity, the problem of variation in knowledge systems, a problem that arises from the context-dependent nature of the representational processes at the basis of all knowledge. In sum they sharply bring to the fore the question of whether systems of thinking about and knowing the world are social and to what extent the social context grants to them a logical or illogical character.

In this chapter I want to address these issues by examining the theory of social representations and its contribution to the study of knowledge in context. Drawing on the analysis of the representational form presented in Chapter 1, I shall argue that the study of social representations can shed light on the context-dependent nature of rationality and unpack the theoretical building blocks that link knowledge systems to persons, communities, cultures and histories. Indeed, at the origins of the theory is a concern with the relationship between knowledge and social context. Moscovici's research on the reception of psychoanalysis focused precisely on how one system of knowledge – psychoanalysis – changes as it moves away from the context of its production and penetrates different social milieus. This concern was deeply entangled with early debates about the rationality of knowledge and common sense conducted by psychologists, anthropologists and sociologists on both sides of the English Channel, an element that is frequently missed in the Anglo-Saxon reception of Moscovici's work.

Debates about knowledge forms and their rationality expressed two major issues motivating the imagination of social scientists at the beginning of the twentieth century: how to reconcile the assumptions of unilinear evolutionism – the idea of change as progress, the fundamental unity of the human mind and the comparative method – and the realisation that there were tremendous variations in the thinking of different peoples, and in particular, between the thinking of western and non-western peoples. Reports by missionaries and travellers in conjunction with studies of 'primitive man' and of 'savage thought' produced by the emerging discipline of anthropology offered the material for extended analyses of thought processes in 'exotic' societies and of the ways in which they were comparable to western societies. Since a comparison was often made between the thought of primitive peoples and the thought of children, for psychologists this debate took shape mainly, if not only, around issues of child development. How to conceptualise the nature and evolution of children's thought was to dominate the research on child development that took place in the first half of the twentieth century.

Accounting for difference in knowledge forms and for how knowledge forms change was a problem that impacted heavily on Moscovici's work and appears throughout the conceptual programme of the theory of social representations. Central to the theory of social representations is how different communities located in different contexts and cultural frameworks construct knowledge about the world. This connection between knowledge and the life and context of a community has directed the efforts of the theory and pointed to the need to understand the diverse forms knowledge takes and the different rationalities that it sustains. How can we understand this diversity? How do we compare scientific knowledge and common sense? Will common sense ever become 'scientific' if the public is correctly educated? Is there something in common underlying all representational systems or are they irredeemably different? Do children and adults know the world in the same way; is it a matter of qualitative or quantitative change? And what about the knowledge of rural communities in the backlands of Brazil vis-à-vis the knowledge of urban western scientists? Do they all qualify as knowledge, or just some of them? Are they all rational, and if not what defines the rationality of a knowledge system?

These questions are as important today as they have been in the past because in our contemporary global world the claims of culture, to use Benhabib's (2002) apposite expression, are more intense than ever. At the heart of psychological, sociological and anthropological debates we still find the problem of difference in forms of knowing and what constitutes human reason. It is a problem that continues to fuel contemporary points of tension because defining who can pose claims to rational knowledge is not only an unresolved theoretical problem as it is a political act. It carries a string of dilemmas and consequences related to the valuation and ranking of different peoples, different knowledges and different ways of life.

Difference invites comparison, a system of interrelations that can explain and account for how and why things differ. Comparative frameworks are both enlightening and dangerous: on the one hand, they allow for difference to be expressed, for insight and understanding to be gained through the experience of others; on the other hand they can produce hierarchy defining what is better and what is worse, what is high and what is low. Whereas this in itself is not necessarily a problem, it can easily become one when what is at stake is the knowledge and representational systems of communities and individuals. If it is your knowledge and representations that are put at the lower end of a scale this can devalue you as a person and de-authorise your vision of the world vis-à-vis other social groups. It can discredit what you have to say and undermine your chances of gaining access to resources and opportunities. It can shatter your self-esteem and scar you for life. Establishing whose knowledge is rational and whose knowledge is not is an act of tremendous consequences, at the psychological, social and political levels.

In this chapter I shall examine these issues by considering classical work on the problem of diversity in knowledge systems and introducing the contribution of the theory of social representations to this debate. I show that underlying Moscovici's conception of social representations as a form of social knowledge irreducible to any other there is a long tradition that struggled with the dual problem of comparing knowledge systems and constructing a framework to deal with the differences between them. Lurking behind this struggle is the problem of modernity and its conceptualisation of knowledge: on the one hand, a view of knowledge as pure rational cognition, deprived of emotional and social ties, and on the other hand, a view that seeks to acknowledge the entanglement of knowledge with subject and context.

I shall begin by situating the theory of social representations, the tradition to which it belongs and the debates to which it relates. I shall then revisit intellectual ancestors theory and earlier debates about the relations between knowledge and social context through an examination of the works of Durkheim, Lévy-Bruhl, Piaget, Vygotsky and Freud. In the last part of the chapter I introduce the concept of cognitive polyphasia, emphasising its contribution to an understanding of context-dependent rationalities and the plurality of knowledge. This conception of knowledge as plural follows from the premises established in Chapter 1 and prepares the ground for subsequent chapters.

Expanding the boundaries of social psychology

In the preface to the second edition of *La Psychanalyse, son Image et son Public*, Serge Moscovici (1976a: 16, my translation) states the ambitions he had with the original work:

> Je voulais redéfinir les problèmes et les concepts de la psychologie sociale à partir de ce phénomène, en insistant sur sa fonction symbolique et son pouvoir de construction du réel. [I wanted to redefine the problems and concepts of social psychology taking this phenomenon [social representations] as a starting point, insisting on its symbolic function and its power to construct the real.]

Moscovici also enumerated the obstacles that were on the way: behaviourism, individualism and positivism. Each had played a role in the history of social psychology and each had contributed to the narrowing of its focus. To change that state of affairs, he offered what Duveen (2000) has called 'his social psychological imagination'. This was to be a daring imagination, which sought to link social psychology to the big issues of the day, continuously insisting that its resources could shed light on important societal issues. Moscovici's overall writings betray this impetus, for he wrote widely about nature, history, and the sociological masters in a body of work that is as diverse as it is uncompromising in ignoring disciplinary boundaries.[1] Throughout his work he reaffirmed the importance of a substantive social psychology that, as well as being capable of shaking its own internal resources, should be capable of communicating with, and adding to, the general corpus of the social sciences.

The theory of social representations is exemplary of Moscovici's aims towards social psychology, of what it should and could be. Indeed in its conceptual apparatus and trajectory we find all the elements that make it not only a social psychology of knowledge but also a social psychological perspective that can offer answers to more general questions being posed by the social sciences as a whole. There are two interfaces that comprise the dialogue Moscovici established through his theory of social representations. One was with social psychology; the other was with the French intellectual milieu of which he was an active participant, a milieu dominated by battles on at least three fronts – phenomenology and its legacy, Marxism and its suspicion of everyday knowledge, and structuralism and its perceived renunciation of the human presence.

Moscovici did battle on all fronts, convinced that (a) there is no such a thing as 'free' knowledge, produced by a subject 'free' of others, history and belonging; (b) that ordinary people can hold knowledge and know what they are talking about; (c) that history and structures do not exist independently of the subjects that produce them in the first place, or as the humanists once put it 'history has a subject'. He himself has remarked more than once, in the context of debates about subjectivity and the individual in his social psychology, that social representations theory emerged in an intellectual atmosphere where it was necessary to reaffirm the importance of the subject. Ironically enough for a theory that is committed to bringing back the 'social' to social psychology, there is no less commitment to the individual. This commitment is central to understand Moscovici's readings of Durkheim and Weber and the transformation of the sociological concept of collective representations into the social psychological concept of social representations.

The theory of social representations needs to be understood not only as a social psychology of knowledge but also as a theory about how new knowledge is produced and accommodated in the social fabric. This involves theorising the role of innovators and minorities, of individuals who are able to step back and challenge the chains of culture and what they impose on our ways of seeing the world and ourselves. This impetus should not be disregarded as banal individualism because behind it there is a struggle and a desire to see things in a new light, to discover the other side of the object-world and to illuminate parts of it that get hidden by the blindness produced by the assumptions we take for granted and the cultural traditions we inherit. It is by keeping this impetus in mind that we can better understand Moscovici's theory of social representations and the role of individuals in creating new representations in the public sphere, challenging cultures from within and producing heterogeneity in social life. This also betrays his interest in the historical fault lines where individuals, even as a minority of one, confront institutional power and manage to make institutions look silly, redundant and in need of change. Innovators, whistleblowers, dissenters – they were all sources of inspiration for retrieving the dignity of the individual without sliding into individualism.

Social representations

Social representations refer both to a theory and to a phenomenon. It is a theory insofar as it provides a set of articulated concepts that seek to give an account of how social knowledges are produced and transformed in processes of communication and social interaction. It is a phenomenon insofar as it refers to a set of empirical regularities comprising the ideas, values and practices of human communities about specific social objects as well as the social and communicative processes that produce and reproduce them.

The *theory of social representations* is a theory about social knowledge. It addresses the construction and transformation of social knowledge in relation to different social contexts. Social knowledge can refer to any knowledge, but the theory is specially concerned with the *phenomenon of social representations*, which comprises knowledges produced in and by everyday life. In this sense, the theory of social representations belongs to a tradition that I call the phenomenology of everyday life seeking to understand how ordinary people, communities and institutions produce knowledge about themselves, others and the multitude of social objects that are relevant to them. With other neighbouring disciplines, it shares an interest in bringing to light the structure of worldviews, of beliefs and forms of life that can produce a theory of everyday life and the knowledge it produces. This knowledge, which is always plural, is deeply entangled with the lifeworld and lived experience of a community, demarcating its frameworks for thinking, doing and relating. It is a type of knowledge that has been historically questioned; indeed some would not call it knowledge at all. The phenomenology of everyday life, however, is concerned precisely with the legitimacy of such knowledges and the dimensions they express: identities, practices, relationships, cultural traditions and the history of a community, all discussed in more detail in Chapter 3.

In this sense, the theory of social representations militates against the idea that everyday knowledge is distortion and error; on the contrary, it tries to recover the epistemological status of knowledges linked to everyday life and common sense and 'to understand the understandings' they express. To do so, it relies on the concept of representation discussed in Chapter 1 and on the recognition that all knowledge is at once symbolic and social. When ordinary people read the world and develop knowledge about it there is a great deal that goes into those readings: cultural habits, identities, cultural traditions, emotions and practices of various kinds. All these find their way into knowledge systems and allow knowledge to represent at once objective, subjective and interrelational worlds. To reduce knowledge to its objective/cognitive/propositional dimension is simply too narrow: it would severely limit our apprehension of the complexity and richness embedded in the production of knowledge systems. Therefore this tradition goes beyond the isolated cognitive knower and a one-sided monological rationality limited by the ideal (or illusion?) of perfect correspondence between propositions and facts.

The notion of social representations was introduced by Moscovici in his seminal study about the reception of psychoanalysis in France. First reported in a book published in 1961, and again in a substantially revised edition (1976a), the study centres on the ways in which psychoanalysis is appropriated and resignified by different sectors of the French public. What happens to psychoanalytical knowledge when it leaves the original settings of its production, departs from private practices, from restricted centres of study and training, from medical schools and the institutions that control psychoanalysis and penetrates other contexts, other horizons, other communities? What happens when one type of knowledge – scientific knowledge – circulates in the social fabric beyond its source and context of origin? The answer was clear to Moscovici: this knowledge changes. It changes in the same way that it changes the people who have changed it in the first place. Thus, psychoanalysis was not only what its 'owners' would make of it, but became a different phenomenon as it penetrated the lifeworlds of urban-liberal professionals, Catholics and communists, the social groups Moscovici studied.

The original empirical study was concerned with social thinking and how social thinking changes in processes of communication. Usually it is the first part of the study, where Moscovici tackles the representations held by the different milieus about psychoanalysis in interviews and surveys, that receives most attention. However, the second part of the book is no less important. It is dedicated to the analysis of the communicative genres typical of these milieus. Indeed, linking the two parts of the book is crucial to understanding the centrality of communication in the production of representations and how different communicative genres produce different representational systems. The conceptual framework that links representation and communication can be clearly observed in the context of the empirical study. It is resonant of the analysis of the representational form as previously discussed, where representations are the result of communicative triads (self–other–object) in context and in time.

The publication of *La Psychanalyse, son Image et son Public* thus marked the birth of the theory of social representations and inaugurated a tradition that has continued in the work of specific approaches.[2] It is a tradition that sought to contribute to and preserve a distinctive European social psychology by insisting in the societal dimension, its historical substance and its constitutive role in social psychological phenomena (Israel and Tajfel 1972; Tajfel 1984; Doise 1986, 2001; Himmelweit and Gaskell 1990). At the same time, it did not, and indeed it does not, renounce the psychological dimension proper; it continues to pay attention to mind and its phenomena. Social representations theory draws as much on theories of society as it does on theories of the subject and its empirical trajectory has shown that one cannot go without the other if social psychology is to have a specific identity. This double commitment – to the social and to the individual – is present in the original inception of the theory and it can be recognised in the emphasis put, on the one hand, on the symbolic dimension of representations, where particular views of the world, particular identities and particular imaginations are expressed, and on the other hand, on the social dimension of representations, where the power of social reality to circumscribe and frame our individual thinking acquires the force of a symbolic environment.

There are a number of interrelated issues that permeate the theoretical corpus of the theory. These include the role of the social in the constitution of knowledge; the role of the symbolic function in forming representations; and the rehabilitation of common sense knowledge.

The role of the social in the constitution of knowledge

Throughout Moscovici's work there is acknowledgment of the constitutive role of the social in the production of knowledge and a critical engagement with the classical view that the social 'pollutes' knowledge. The task of retrieving the sociality that lies at the origins of all knowledge systems and connecting knowledge to communities has always been made difficult by the idea that whenever knowledge is entangled with the social it falls prey to biases and distortions, it is subjected to a devaluation and a loss of epistemological credentials. In psychology this tradition is powerful. Indeed, it even goes beyond the idea of bias and distortion to propose a full-blown association between sociality and psychopathology. Not accidentally, the first journal of social psychology was called the *Journal of Abnormal and Social Psychology*. Now why should the social and the abnormal be connected? In classical theories of crowd behaviour this connection comes full circle. From Le Bon to Freud the crowd – and even the group – has been a site of irrational behaviour, a place where individuals fall in a territory of uncontrolled emotions, loss of autonomy and depersonalisation. The crowd is a place where individuals become less what they are and more what they are not.[3] The counterpart to this type of theory is to be found in theories of the individual seen as detached and sovereign, whose rational powers and cognitive abilities reside entirely in his self-enclosed, individualised world. In a certain sense it could be said that the cognitive tradition of the individual knower, in detaching persons from social contexts, confirms the view that true cognition is an achievement of desocialisation. This view, as I pointed out earlier, is part and parcel of the Cartesian legacy and the inception of modern psychology. Yet it is a view that did not develop without antinomies.

One powerful antinomy to the decontextualisation of human knowledge has been the phenomenological tradition, to whose legacy the theory of social representations is heavily indebted. As Foucault once remarked, there is no way to understand French thought without understanding the reception of phenomenology in France (Foucault 1991). The phenomenologists showed that before we can even think of possessing knowledge we actually *belong*: belonging, not knowing, is where we all start from. We belong to a culture, to a society, to a family, to a historical time, and this belonging frames the knowledge we construct from the outset. With Merleau-Ponty this belonging to a context was taken to new levels of radicality, for he more than anyone else pointed to the embodiment of knowledge: the subject of knowledge not only belongs to a multidimensional context but is also the subject of a body whose reality cannot be dismissed. The embodiment of psychological and social structures frames perception and thus knowledge (Merlau-Ponty 1986). Therefore, even if we think about knowledge as primarily produced by the individual subject, we need to think of this individual subject as herself a multidimensional context comprising a body and a psychological make-up that are socially, culturally and historically located.

The theory of social representations draws on these insights when it considers the social origins of knowledge and, in particular, when it studies how social contexts and representations mutually constitute one another. Indeed, here the social is not simply an added variable in a piece of research but a dimension that needs to be dealt with theoretically and empirically. It is the social context that provides a key entry point to understanding specific forms of communication, of interrelations, of practices that form and transform the social-psychological processes that shape social representations as well as other systems of knowledge. The theory points to the locality of all knowledge: knowledges are not detached systems; on the contrary all knowledge is dependent on contexts and entangled with a way of life. All knowledge grows out of a social and psychological context.

The role of the symbolic function in forming representations

Permeating the theory of social representations is the acknowledgement of the symbolic function and its role in shaping representations. Moscovici declares from the outset that the power of representations lies in their ability to construct, to shape reality. They are neither a replica nor a reflection of the world: 'representations also evoke what is absent from the world, they form it rather more than they simulate it' (Moscovici 2000b: 154). In pointing to the evocative character of representation, to their relationship with absence, Moscovici reminds us of the constructive dimension of symbolic representations and their world-making capacities, the fact that knowledge systems are not, and indeed should not be bound exclusively to the empirical world: 'In effect, social representations, to rephrase a common expression, are ways of world making' (Moscovici 1988). Understanding the symbolic function of representations is thus central to understanding the plasticity of knowledge and its potential to create and transcend the reality of the empirical world. The requirement of correspondence between representation and reality reduces knowledge to a reading of what is given, to a descriptive task, which is as conservative as it is boring.

Accuracy in cognition is important and should be valued but it is not always the most important, or indeed desirable, aim of a system of knowledge. The rationality of meaning is polysemic and can include reasons that go beyond the engagement with the objective world. Expressing the reality of a community, in its diversity and complexity, social representations are ruled by multiple logics that not only construct objects in the world but also propose states of being, identities, relations and practices that declare the 'who', 'how', 'what', 'why' and 'what for' of knowledge. These dimensions must be recognised in their own right, understood for what they are and put into a perspective that does not betray the original intentions of producers. Without this disposition to listen, to understand and to recognise the expressiveness of knowledge, all we are left with is the attitude of the judge and, in worse cases, of the policeman. There is also a profound ethical dimension associated with this recognition, to which I shall return later.

The effort to rehabilitate common sense and recuperate the wisdom of everyday knowledges

The study of common sense has always been permeated by an attitude of suspicion that systematically deprived it of epistemological status and often equated it with distortion, bias, error and ignorance. Lay knowledge and everyday understandings are usually seen as obstacles, noise and errors to be removed, by replacing the superstitions, mythologies and false beliefs they carry with the truth of expert or scientific knowledge. I shall be discussing this in more detail later in the book but for now it is worth mentioning that whole fields of research and intervention are based on this assumption. Health educational programmes, for instance, have for long operated with the assumption that lay beliefs have to be removed and replaced with scientific knowledge. Development interventions have equally treated local knowledge as an obstacle to the aims of progress and technical achievement carried by development workers. And the whole idea of public understanding of science has been based on the assumption that the public must be educated and taught to understand scientific theories 'correctly'. Behind all these efforts is the underlying premise that be it the public, be it the locals or be it lay people, they must all abandon their existing beliefs and ascend to the superior form of knowing offered by experts and technocrats.

This premise has a considerable history, which I cannot possibly trace in this book. One stream is, however, worth mentioning because of the particular role it had in shaping Moscovici's thinking in relation to the problem. As most intellectuals of his generation in France, Moscovici worked and wrote under the impact of Marxism and the deep suspicions it held in relation to psychoanalysis, common sense and any kind of 'mental', 'idealistic' construction. The Marxist suspicions in relation to common sense are well known. They started with Marx's assessment of ideology as a system of ideas that distorts reality and represents the interests of the dominant class. They took an extreme form with Lenin, whose theories about the vanguard and the role of the party in historical change clearly indicated how unable the masses were to know the true direction of their historical destiny.[4] The idea that elites can propagate their own views to the larger public *ipsis literis* and the former would repeat them unquestioningly may ring a bell or two today, but has been powerfully debunked by studies on mass media reception and the appropriation of ideas (Livingstone 1989; Thompson 1990; Liebes and Katz 1993). No individual and no human community simply copies knowledge and ideas received from others. Rather, they transform them.

This was well understood by Moscocivi, who postulated the wisdom of common sense and its irreducibility to any other knowledge system. Rather than studying how common sense becomes science, Moscovici took the opposite direction and sought to understand how science becomes common sense. Studying social representations of psychoanalysis meant going counter to the ethos of bringing the commonsensical knowledge of ordinary people to the higher stage of true knowledge, i.e. science. The everyday, he showed, is a powerful source of knowledge. It may be a different type of knowledge than scientific and technological knowledge, but no less *wise* in the know-hows and know-whys it contains. What may look irrational or wrong to the observer makes sense to the actors of knowledge, and it is also, if not only, in this sense that a knowledge system must be assessed: in relation to the significance and psychological reality it has for those who actually produce it. Besides, ideas are generative in social life, as much as economic and material processes, and with Weber, Moscovici understood the power of the idea (Moscovici 1993; Duveen 2000). Thus in opposition to the view that common sense and lay knowledges are fraught with error, ignorance and distortion, the theory of social representations attempts to overcome the line which separates a philosophy of knowledge and rationality from a philosophy of experience and sense recognising the relative wisdom (and limitations) of all knowledges.

Revisiting ancestors

The issues discussed above can be better understood if we consider the intellectual ancestors of the theory of social representations and the main theoretical and empirical sources from which Moscovici drew inspiration to construct his social psychology of knowledge. To this end we must turn to the legacy of Durkheim, Lévy-Bruhl, Piaget, Vygotsky and Freud, who are the key sources of the theory (Moscovici 1989). While it is important to retrieve the contribution of each one of these classical thinkers to the formation of social representations, it is also essential to understand that the method of Moscovici is critical engagement: none of them is absorbed in its entirety and without critical reflection.

Émile Durkheim and collective representations

The concept of social representations is a social psychological transformation of the Durkheimian concept of collective representations.[5] But Moscovici owes more to Durkheim than just the origins of his central concept. Indeed, his social psychology is clearly derived from Durkheim's sociology with its emphasis on the social matrix of thought and knowledge, its attempt to understand the formation of beliefs and rituals, and their role in sustaining the social order. In addition, it is Durkheim and his followers that can be found at the bottom of both Piaget's and Vygotsky's psychologies; something that connects the various pieces of the intellectual puzzle that took shape in the first half of the twentieth century when psychologists, sociologists, philosophers and anthropologists were busy trying to determine the roots of the differences between knowledge systems and the laws behind the development and evolution of knowledge.

Collective representations are one of the most important concepts permeating the work of Émile Durkheim and the phenomena to which it refers continues to be central to social theory today. The idea of a society's collective consciousness – its frame of mind as it were – was and still is influential in sociological, anthropological and psychological debates about what holds people together and what shapes the ways in which individuals think and act. Collective representations refer to the habitual, taken-for-granted and homogeneously shared beliefs, sentiments and ideas held by a community. They are pre-established in relation to individuals (by tradition, custom and history) and accepted without scrutiny; they override individual consciousness and provide the moral framework against which all members of the community act. They are re-enacted in all kinds of social ceremonies, institutional practices and rituals of a society (Durkheim 1898/ 1996).

Collective representations offer a response to the main question underlying Durkheim's work: how social solidarity changes in the course of societal development; that is to say, what happens to social cohesion, to the bond between people, to what keeps people together in a community as societies evolve and move from traditional to modern ways of life? Now questions about social cohesion are central to social psychology because they lead directly to the problems underlying the formation of collectives. For Durkheim, as for Moscovici later, the 'collective consciousness' or collective representations of a society were the most crucial aspect in defining social solidarity and what makes a group of people into a community. The mutual relations between the making of community and the making of representations constitute one of the central postulates of the theory of social representations and I shall discuss these relations in detail in Chapter 3.

From the concept of collective representations, Moscovici took central features of social representations, in particular the dimension that refers to their material character, to the fact that they constitute an environment, albeit symbolic. This material character of social representations comes from their being social facts in a Durkheimian sense. When Durkheim discussed the features of collective representations he considered them external and coercive in relation to individuals and stable over time. Collective representations, he argued, have an objective and autonomous existence because they are produced and reproduced through collective action. This gives them a good degree of stability over time and embeds them in the institutions of a community, such as the church, the family, the legal system, etc. Because they are embedded in institutions, change is extremely difficult and they appear to individuals as coercive. While the social psychological concept of social representations lost much of the claustrophobic nature collective representations had in Durkheim, Moscovici retained their character as social facts, their material power and the force of symbolic environments to resist change and make themselves thick and hard through processes of institutionalisation.

It is the Durkheimian idea of collective representations being deeply engrained in the fabric of a community, of constituting the horizon within which all possible readings and interpretations of social life take place that provides the ground for understanding the social nature of logic and classification processes. It is in relation to collective representations, as the symbolic environment and collective consciousness of a community that statements, actions and classificatory systems make sense or not. This basic idea was introduced in 1905 by Durkheim and Mauss in an essay entitled *Primitive Classification*, which dealt with the social and cultural nature of classification and categorisation (1905/1963). In this essay they show that since things do not offer themselves to the human mind in readymade classes and categories and the mind itself lacks the innate ability to classify, the origins of categories must perforce be in the social order. The origins of categories are neither purely in the mind, nor purely in nature. It is society that offers the sources for categorisation and the model upon which large systems of classification and ordering of the world are built. Thus for Durkheim and Mauss all categorisation expresses the social world in which it is generated and, at the same time, the level of evolution of any given human society.

Durkheim's analysis led him to conclude that primitive classification played an important role in the genesis of the classificatory function in general. Indeed for him, primitive classifications were an elementary form of scientific classifications. Studying and isolating the elementary can help to understand the higher: from primitive to scientific systems of classification, it is possible to identify the different stages that societies go through and understand what needs to change if a society is to achieve the stage of scientific classification. That is precisely where the concept of collective representations re-enters the scene, for Durkheim considered that it was only when classification systems free themselves from collective representations based on social and emotional ties that they can become truly scientific: 'the history of scientific classification is, in the last analysis, the history of the stages by which this element of social affectivity has progressively weakened, leaving more and more room for the reflective thought of individuals' (Durkheim 1905/1963: 88).

Whereas Moscovici retained from Durkheim the basic idea of the social origins of classification and logic and the relationship they hold with collective representations, he was less prepared to accept the linear evolutionism inherent in the latter's views. For in Moscovici, so-called primitive thought (and by analogy, common sense) is not an elementary stage of a more developed form of thinking such as science; it is something to be considered and understood in its own right. It was in the work of Lucien Lévy-Bruhl that he found the inspiration to pursue this idea.

Lucien Lévy-Bruhl and the logic of thought

When Lévy-Bruhl published in 1910 *Les Fonctions Mentales dans les Sociétés Inférieures*, translated into English as *How Natives Think*, he opened up an enduring debate about what constitutes logic and to which extent the reasoning found in the thinking of so-called primitive peoples is fundamentally different from the reasoning of western people (Lévy-Bruhl 1910/1985). He continued to investigate the issues raised by Durkheim and Mauss in *Primitive Classification* but gave them a complete new twist. For Lévy-Bruhl primitive thought was neither an earlier stage of scientific thought nor a stage to be replaced; it was a form of thinking that needed to be understood in its own right. He proposed that different forms of thinking could not be explained in terms of linear progression from one form to another. In fact, different forms of thinking coexisted, and this was the case in all societies. So rather than see, as Durkheim did, the evolution of primitive classification to scientific classification as a function of the modernisation of societies and the weakening of social and emotional ties, he maintained that societies never fully discard the social and emotional ties that make up social thinking and originate the 'law of participation'. In short, Lévy-Bruhl not only proposed that there are different modalities of thinking, he also proposed that *all* human communities, independent of being primitive or modern, display different modalities of thinking. He was a universalist without being an evolutionist.

Lévy-Bruhl, as most of his contemporaries, started by asking the question of whether it is certain that the human mind is the same everywhere. His answer to this question was yes, but in such a paradoxical way that obfuscated the deep universalism of his position. To this day he is viewed as the philosopher and social anthropologist that denied the fundamental similarity of the human mind. How was this possible? Perhaps because, as Leenhardt points out in his preface to *The Notebooks on Primitive Mentality*, he saw unity in diversity, and this is counter-intuitive to the law of non-contradiction. Lévy-Bruhl 'wished to demonstrate, through the universality of some primitive aspects of mentality, the unity of the human mind in time and space . . . the mind of men is one in its diversity' (Leenhardt 1975: xix).

The task Lévy-Bruhl set to himself was to 'to find out exactly what are the guiding principles of primitive mentality, and how these make themselves felt in the primitive institutions and customs' (1910/1985: 14). In studying in detail the thinking of primitive people he also pursued the more general aim of expanding our understanding of thought processes, a task in which he was helped by psychologists who, against the dominant tenets:

> aim at showing the importance of the emotional and the motor elements of mental life in general and extending to the intellectual life properly . . . how narrow the limits within which traditional psychology, under the influence of formal logic, sought to confine the life of thought. Mental processes are infinitely more elastic, complex and subtle, and they comprise more elements of the psychic life than a too 'simplistic' intellectualism would allow.
>
> (Lévy-Bruhl 1910/1985: 14–15)

Such a description of mental processes, produced almost a century ago, anticipates a great deal of the work that pushed the study of the 'life of thought' beyond an arid intellectualism to include the emotional, the corporeal and the social. It also gives us some clues as to why Lévy-Bruhl's work was met with such opposition, for his insistence on the entanglement of thinking and psychic life went counter to the main assumptions of evolutionists who saw the progressive development of thought as precisely the abandonment of emotions and sociality.

From his studies on so-called primitive mentality, Lévy-Bruhl established some fundamental features of collective representations predominantly found in traditional societies. His work provided ammunition to challenge the dominant evolutionist conception of his time, which sustained that there was only one type of rationality, and any evidence to the contrary was nothing but a set of early, underdeveloped stages, which were destined to progress towards the 'one type'. In describing the mentality of non-western peoples he pointed to its different logic and content, both ruled by the 'law of participation'. It is the law of participation, in opposition to the law of non-contradiction typical of scientific thinking, that accounts for the mystical and prelogical character of these representations. Let me quote him at length to avoid the misunderstandings that so often characterise interpretations of his work:

> let us abandon the attempt to refer their [primitives] mental activity to an inferior variety of our own. Rather let us consider these connections in themselves, and see whether they do not depend upon a general law, a common foundation . . . Now there is one element which is never lacking in such relations. In various forms and degrees they involve a 'participation' between persons or objects which form part of a collective representation. For this reason I shall, in default of a better term, call the principle which is peculiar to 'primitive' mentality, . . . *the law of participation.*
>
> If we take the content of the representations more particularly into account, we shall call it mystic – and, if the connections are the chief consideration, we pronounce it prelogical. By prelogical we do not mean to assert that such a mentality constitutes a kind of antecedent stage, in point of time, to the birth of logical thought. Have there ever existed groups of human or pre-human beings whose collective representations have not yet been subject to the laws of logic? We do not know, and in any case, it seems to be very improbable. At any rate, the mentality of these undeveloped peoples which, for want of a better term, I call prelogical, does not partake of that nature. It is not anti-logical; it is not alogical either. By designating it 'prelogical', I merely wish to state that it does not bind itself down to avoiding contradiction. It obeys the law of participation first and foremost.
>
> (Lévy-Bruhl 1910/1985: 76–78)

In the above passage Lévy-Bruhl makes clear his conception of the prelogical mentality by stating the particular logic by which it operates: participation rather than non-contradiction. That means to say that there are people in the world that think in such a way as to allow for different worlds to partake in each other. This is what allows the Bororo Indians of Brazil to declare 'the Bororo are Arara'. Declaring themselves as such is not a problem for this is a perfectly valid statement within the context of collective representations where different realms of the world are linked and participate in each other. It is also this logic, governed by the law of participation, which explains much of the usage of holistic complementary therapies, widely present in the western world. Indeed the law of participation, although first described in relation to 'savage thought', is not less present in the industrial, modern world. Lévy-Bruhl knew this well. For him it was clear that 'logical thought will not entirely supersede prelogical mentality'. That is the case because logical thought cannot fulfil the functions it excludes and thus a portion of prelogical thinking will subsist.

The rational unity of the thinking being, which is taken-for-granted by most philosophers, is a *desideratum*, not a fact. Even among peoples like ourselves, ideas and relations between ideas governed by the law of participation are far from being disappeared. They exist, more or less independently, more or less impaired, but yet ineradicable, side by side with those subject to the laws of reasoning. Understanding, properly so called, tends towards logical unity and proclaims its necessity; but as a matter of fact our mental activity is both rational and irrational. The prelogical and the mystic are co-existent with the logical.

(Lévy-Bruhl 1910/1985: 386)

In these final words to his *How Natives Think* is the radical innovation of Lévy-Bruhl's thinking: he considered primitive thinking in its own right and sought to understand it without recourse to an evolutionist framework. He did not see it as an underdeveloped stage or as a stage to be abandoned. And foremost, he did not see it as a modality of thinking held only by 'primitive' people, living in traditional societies. Everyone, at any time and everywhere, can display the logic of participation; it is possible to find it in every human mind. This is a central feature of Lévy-Bruhl thinking, and one he never renounced.

It is generally accepted that towards the end of his life Lévy-Bruhl capitulated to his critics and rejected the characterisation of primitive mentality he offered between 1910 and 1938. Yet, a careful reading of his *Notebooks* shows that it was not so much the characterisation of the mystical and prelogical mentality that he abandoned as the idea that there is a primitive mentality that can be isolated by the mystical and prelogical features peculiar to it. The radical innovation of his position did not go: 'There is a mystical mentality which is more marked and more easily observable among "primitive peoples" than in our societies, but it is present in every human mind' (1975: 101). In this final round Lévy-Bruhl is in fact reinstating the key observations he presented in 1910: the discovery of qualitative transformations in thinking (a legacy passed on to both Piaget and Vygotsky) and the idea of the heterogeneity of human thought within one culture and one individual (from which Moscovici drew inspiration to develop the concept of cognitive polyphasia). These, as Tul'viste (1987) points out, are his fundamental contributions. He allowed us to move from a logic of contrasting 'us' and 'them' to a logic that sought to understand the different types of thought present in 'our' culture and 'their' culture and therefore find out not only what is different between us and them but also what is the same.

There can be no doubt that it was from him, more than from Durkheim, that Moscovici drew inspiration to understand the dynamics of social representations and how science – in his case, psychoanalysis – is transformed and resignified by the different people who appropriate it. Rather than seeing in the social representations of psychoanalysis a vulgarisation and a distortion, Moscovici engaged in an 'understanding of understandings' conceiving of representations constructed in everyday life as a *sui generis* type of thinking. For him, social representations were irreducible to other forms of thinking. They contained a rationality whose logic obeys different rules and fulfils different functions, which needs to be assessed in its own terms and without reference to any absolute standard.[6] What was needed was a theory to produce an account about their genesis and transformation in social life.

Lévy-Bruhl offered valuable insights for the construction of such a theory. He urged us to understand difference and recognise it for what it is. He challenged the assumption of intellectualists and evolutionists that the natural progression of knowledge involves detaching it from the social and emotional ties that constitute it in the first place. He recognised the value of logics such as participation and indeed left us an eloquent defence of those modes of thinking that seek to sustain the fundamental unity between human life and its surroundings. He taught us what is lost with the quest for excessive rationality and what can be gained if we are able to engage in a dialogue with other aspects of our existence that are not guided by the purely instrumental. He helped us to see that development is not only made of gains but also of losses and it is at our own peril that we undermine the value of modalities of thinking and knowing that retain the emotional, social and playful character of representations constructed by traditional communities and in early childhood. Moreover, he insisted that different types of knowing are present in the same society, thus rejecting the idea of a correspondence between the primitive and the prelogical and the developed and the logical. Lévy-Bruhl's views on the discontinuity of logical thinking and on the coexistence of different rationalities gave Moscovici the elements to assess the production of social representations, their irreducibility as a form of knowledge and the functions they fulfil in social life and in relation to other forms of knowledge.

Jean Piaget and the constructive nature of representations

In a recent interview with Marková, Moscovici observed that it was when he became familiar with Piaget's child psychology that he 'had the impression of discovering what social psychology might be . . . a science of development, change, not of reactions to fixed environments' (Moscovici 2000a: 250–251). The impact of Piaget on Moscovici's thinking is vast. He reached Durkheim and Lévy-Bruhl through Piaget and it was in Piaget's work that Moscovici found the notion of representation fully elaborated as a theoretical idea. The study of common sense, through the investigation of social representations, is analogous to the studies Piaget had conducted on the child's conception of the world. Thus from Piaget's psychology Moscovici drew central dimensions of his social psychology: the conceptualisation of representation, the exploration of common sense, the concern with change and development.

And yet, as Duveen (2001a: 170) observed in his illuminating analysis of the relations between Piaget and Moscovici, 'it is not that Moscovici simply adapted Piagetian psychology, but rather he found within Piaget's work some conceptual and theoretical elements or ideas which he could work with (or against)'.

Piaget's research on the development of representational thought in the human child established the specificity of representations in psychic terms, put in evidence the centrality of action (sensorimotor schemes) in the development of representational thought and clarified the genesis and processes of transformation of symbolic representations. In particular, he demonstrated that there are structural differences between the cognitive world of children and that of adults. Contrary to Durkheim, Piaget put emphasis on the creative aspect of representations; representational knowledge of the world involves a process whereby every child must reinvent the world that precedes her. In developing such a comprehensive conceptual scheme to account for the ontogenesis and sociogenesis of representations Piaget offered to Moscovici key tenets to produce a social psychology of knowledge.

One source proved to be especially inspiring: *The Child's Conception of the World*, a book where Piaget (1929) investigates the content and logic underlying children's world through an exploration of the 'theories' children construct about thinking itself, naming and dreaming, life, the origins of the sun and the moon, the sky, clouds, the explanation of night, ice, snow, rivers, lakes and the sea, the origins of trees, mountains and the earth. Considered to this day one of Piaget's most fascinating books, it is at once psychological and anthropological, an attempt to enter the world of the child, to understand its codes, operations, 'to feel with' the child what it is like to see the world from her position. It is in fact, an exploration of collective representations in the child, the most Durkheimian of all Piaget's books and thus not surprisingly the book that led Moscovici to Durkheim: 'it was tempting to regard Piaget's early work as an exploration of our culture through children's discourse, and the material he collected as expressing its folklore, common sense and knowledge, all of that in the thinking of the child' (Moscovici 1998: 411).

Another dimension in Piaget's work that is at the centre of the theory of social representations is the problem of the transformation of knowledge. As I mentioned earlier, the theory of social representations is a theory about the production and transformation of knowledge, and in Piaget Moscovici found the echoes of what could be a theory of how knowledge is transformed as it moves from one structural form to another. In his account of structuralism Piaget clearly defined structures as systems of transformation, permanently changing as the processes of assimilation and accommodation regulate the relations between child and world. In many respects this conceptualisation can be seen in the theory of social representations. Social representations constitute evolving knowledge fields that through processes of communication use anchoring and objectification to make the unfamiliar familiar. How a knowledge field is transformed in social life as it undergoes processes of communication is the problem for the social psychologist; Piaget described such processes in the child. Inspired by Lévy-Bruhl, Piaget showed clearly that development is not a matter of quantitative but qualitative changes. There are substantive differences between children's and adults' thinking; these cannot be seen as just a matter of quantity and accumulation because the qualitative jumps that occur in development presuppose a completely new reorganisation of early structures.

There is, however, an important aspect where Moscovici departed from Piaget and this was in his concept of development and change. For Piaget development proceeded from one stage to another in a course where complex forms substituted elementary forms. The thought of the child, initially constituted as a series of elementary sensory-motor schemes, evolves towards the achievement of complex formal operations. As Duveen put it: 'The child as an epistemic subject may have a characteristic mentality, but it is a mentality identified, defined, and conceived in terms of a movement towards another mentality, that of the adult' (Duveen 2001a: 171). This conception of development towards one type at the end of the developmental scale is part and parcel of Piaget's psychology and it can be found explicitly in most of the papers of his *Sociological Studies* where he discusses the social nature of logic and what are the societal features that need to be present to substantiate rational thought (Piaget 1995d).

Piaget's definition of logic is both social and evolutionist, just as Durkheim' view was: 'Logic is . . . a form of "mobile" and reversible equilibrium characteristic of the end of development and not an innate mechanism provided at the start' (1995c: 140). To explain how logic is constructed, he argues, we need to grasp its processes of constitution and how they reach equilibrium. To this end two essential notions must be understood: 'the functional continuity of development, conceived as a progressive march toward equilibrium, and the heterogeneity of the successive structures that mark the steps in that final equilibration' (1995c: 140). In this conception of logic there are clear indications of how Piaget remained Durkheimian in his evolutionism and yet borrowed from Lévy-Bruhl in his account of the heterogeneity of thought structures. First, he states that logic is not innate but social. Second, he defines it as a state characteristic of the 'end of development', implying that previous stages are prelogical and there is an 'end' to development, a state of equilibrium, which is very important throughout Piaget's thought. Third, there is a functional continuity in development as it is conceived as a progressive march. Finally, the successive structures that constitute development are heterogeneous. In these indications there are echoes of both Durkheim (the first three) and Lévy-Bruhl (the last), of both evolutionism and substantive differences in thought structures. This contradiction testifies to the ambivalence we find in Piaget's work as a whole, which can be seen as part reason, part fantasy, a deep commitment to unpack the raw structure of logic and a fascination with its 'human, all too human' antinomies.

The evolutionism of Piaget's view is ultimately responsible for the difficulties that remain encrusted in an otherwise superb social theory of logic. Piaget's demonstration of the social origins of logic and the variation that social settings can impose on the rationality of a knowledge system remains classical and takes the Durkheimian proposition to a higher level of analysis and interpretation. Instead of treating the social as a generality that constrains logic (an accusation that could be levelled at Durkheim, to some extent), Piaget asks exactly what are the social relationships involved since the social is not an abstraction but a set of relationships between individuals that exponentially construct the social order. These relationships need to be unpacked for they have a quality, a manner of being as it were.

Different social relationships impact differently on the constitution of reason and not 'all action of "society" on the individual is the source of reason' (1995c: 136). Piaget identifies two types of social relationships structurally connected with logic: social constraint and cooperation. The former is typical of societies where authority, prestige and strong hierarchy govern relations. The latter is present in societies where the principle of equality in the public sphere is the rule. Whereas socialisation, or the internalisation of society's rules by the child, is the sine qua non condition for the emergence of logic and the education of reason, not all socialisation has the power to produce logic at the level of collective thinking. The question for Piaget is then 'what kind of socialisation, what kind of society can produce logic?'

His answer is unequivocal: it is cooperation, not social constraint, that produces logic. It is an answer that betrays his unabashed conviction in the superior powers of reason and its constitutive connections with democratic forms of life, based on reciprocity and mutual recognition. It is only in societies where individuation and argumentation prevail that reason proper can be fully achieved. Primitive societies, whose sociocentrism is analogous to the egocentrism of early childhood, fail to produce the type of social bond that is required to the achievement of rational knowledge. So society can give you logic but can also take it away. Traditional societies do not have what it takes to produce rational thought. Their collective representations reveal the same centration of early childhood, which makes it impossible to establish differences between the subjective and objective world. Egocentrism and social constraint, found in the thought of the child and in the thinking of 'primitive men', are two causes of disequilibrium that obstruct the achievement of the logical end of development. They produce thinking structures in their own right; these need to be understood for what they are and recognised as different. But for Piaget they are not logical (Piaget 1995a, 1995b).

This is where Moscovici departed from Piaget. His work does not share the Piagetian enthusiasm for the project of a 'pure rationality' that could be isolated in modern societies and towards which the 'education of reason' would progress. It does not share the idea of a progressive continuum and certainly does not share the concept of evolution underlying the development of rationality proposed by Piaget. Moscovici remains committed to the recognition and understanding of the plurality of reason found in Lévy-Bruhl. Today we can abandon the problem of how a primitive type of representation achieves a developed status and focus on the more real, and more interesting, problem of our contemporary world: how different representations and logics meet and compete in the social sphere. Around this problem lies the potential for developing a social psychology of knowledge encounters and assessing the possibilities embedded in the communication between knowledge systems (which I shall concentrate on in Chapter 5).

Vygotsky and the discontinuities of reason

Vygotsky is not exactly an intellectual ancestor to the theory of social representations; Moscovici came across his work when the theory was fully elaborated (Moscovici 1998). Yet, the work of Vygotsky immediately had an impact on his thinking and continues to inspire research and contemporary work on social representations. This is probably the case because Vygotsky's psychology, as Piaget's, was derived from common ancestry: the French anthropological school and in particular the work of Durkheim and Lévy-Bruhl. Vygotsky's psychology of sociocultural development offers to the theory of social representations elements to theorise change without having to resort to the unilinear evolutionism that was present in Durkheim and Piaget. As in Lévy-Bruhl, Vygotsky's theory of transformation between modalities of knowledge is discontinuous rather than continuous and presupposes coexistence rather than substitution. Despite its clear reference to Hegel and Marx, his conception of development – of which child development is just a case – is free from a messianic understanding of history and reopens the internal structures of knowing to the presence of the subject of knowledge and the context in which she or he is located.

The idea that social changes are followed by fundamental changes in thought processes was central to Vygotsky's psychology and guided most of the research he and Luria undertook in the years that followed the Soviet Revolution of 1917. Indeed, Soviet psychologists were working under the assumption, widely demonstrated by Vygotsky's theoretical work, that the development of higher psychological functions in humans needs to be understood as part of a general theory of sociohistorical development. That, as many of Vygotsky's students and commentators in the west point out, was his most fundamental contribution: culture and societal development shape the development of psychological functions (Cole 1985, 1996; Scribner 1985; Wertsch 1985a, 1985b; Van der Veer and Valsiner 1991, 1994).

This statement derived from a lengthy consideration of what constitutes development. In a less known book entitled *Studies in the History of Behaviour: Ape, Primitive and Child*, Vygotsky and Luria (1993) sought to establish the three lines of development that produce what they call a cultural man.[7] By analysing the use of objects as tools by anthropoid apes, the forms of thinking of primitive peoples and the ontogenetic development of the child they set out to construct a notion of development that unites the evolutionary, the historical and the ontogenetic. As Wertsch points out in his preface to the book, this is one of the most important documents we have for understanding what Vygotsky understood by development, for rather than seeing it as applied only to the periods of childhood and adolescence as it typically is, they argue:

> a thorough genetic analysis must address the ways in which knowledge about all three genetic domains contributes to our understanding of behaviour and mental functioning. Therefore, in addition to considering how a particular form of mental functioning reflects the ontogenetic transitions leading up to it, one must also take into consideration the forces of phylogenesis and sociocultural history that have shaped it.
>
> (Wertsch 1993: x)

It was clear to Vygotsky and Luria that the sociocultural history of behaviour needed to be fully understood if we were to grasp the complexity of its evolution. Phylogenesis alone could not do it. Comparisons of cultured and primitive man show that both are fully human types. Besides, all human communities, cultured or primitive, can speak. They possess a language and thus a semantic consciousness (Scribner 1985; Vygotsky and Luria 1993). Therefore it is cultural and social processes that can explain variation in behaviour and thinking. The influential empirical study conducted by Soviet psychologists in the remote regions of Uzbekistan and Kirghizia sought to determine precisely that (Luria 1931, 1976, 1979). Following closely the insights of Lévy-Bruhl, they set out to investigate whether the huge cultural and societal transformations set in course by the revolution had an impact both on the basic form and on the content of people's thinking. The aim of the expedition, as Luria reported in *Science*, was 'to investigate the variations in thought and other psychological processes of people living in a very primitive economic and social environment, and to record those changes which develop as a result of the introduction of higher and more complex forms of economic life and the raising of the general cultural level' (1931: 383).

The findings of the study were unequivocal: thought changes in structure and content with changes in social-cultural processes: 'socio-historical shifts not only introduce new content into the mental world of human beings: they also create new forms of activity and new structures of cognitive functioning. They advance human consciousness to new levels' (Luria 1976:

163). Luria's description of the context of their research indicates his belief in the potential improvements offered by schooling, economic modernisation, and emancipation from religion and traditional ways of life. In that he did not escape from the general views of his day. Ideas about human progress, development from primitive to modern and the power of science to override religion and backward beliefs were rampant in the first half of the twentieth century and, in line with the overall project of modernity, can be found at the core of the socialist imagination. What was intriguing, however, was that the study provided empirical corroboration to Lévy-Bruhl's thesis of qualitative transformations in thinking corresponding to different societal and cultural conditions.

This insight, combined with Vygotsky's discontinuous view of development, offers the framework to conceive a social psychology of knowledge capable of theorising on the one hand the diversity of knowledge systems corresponding to the diversity of sociocultural settings that make up human life, and on the other the transformation of knowledge as a complex process that goes beyond unilinear evolutionism. In sum, in Vygotsky as in Piaget, changes are qualitative, something that Lévy-Bruhl first proposed. But in Vygotsky as in Lévy-Bruhl, contrary to Piaget and Durkheim, the direction of these qualitative changes is discontinuous: earlier stages are not fully replaced by later stages, but are rather juxtaposed forming layers that change, restructure and adapt as mediating tools between people and their environment.

This belief that development is either continuous or discontinuous constitutes, according to Moscovici (1998) 'the crucial entry point to the theoretical singularity of each of these two great psychologists'. There are thus many parallels between Vygotsky's notion of development and the views proposed by Lévy-Bruhl. They coincided in the fundamental notion that transformation in knowledge is discontinuous and there is no substitution of forms of knowing but *coexistence* (Vygostky and Luria 1993). Rather than conceiving the development and transformation of knowledge within a progressive linear scale that replaces lower with higher forms, they saw each form of knowledge as an entity in its own right. Forms of knowledge relate to each other but not as linear evolution.

Freud and the unconscious

In Freud, Moscovici sought the key for the unconscious processes that shape the production of social knowledge and a view of knowing unafraid of engaging with the psychological proper. He mentions *On the Sexual Theories of Children* (Freud 1908), as a main source providing inspiration to his social psychology of knowledge. In it Freud discusses the 'theories' children construct about sexuality and shows that their origin lies in their cultural environment, in fairytales and legends. He addresses the desire of the child for knowledge and how this desire for knowledge is intertwined with the rituals performed by those who want to know and those who detain knowledge. Freud makes his point describing a situation that is paradigmatic of both our relation to the unknown and the dilemmas embedded in cultural transmission. He considers that point in childhood when young children are invaded by the curiosity and doubts associated with their own origins and start to ask questions of the type 'Where did I come from?' or with the arrival of siblings, 'Where did this "intruder" come from?' These questions, which are not different in kind to the questions asked by every human culture, express the moment when the child is invaded both by the unknown space of the sexual life of her parents and by the mystery of birth and life. To the curiosity of the child corresponds the reluctance and hesitation of adults; and the family, as the primary site and institution of culture, becomes the stage for the intriguing conversation that takes place between the desiring questions of the young audience and the ruses of the grown-up actors, who try hard to hide the rules of the game.

It is in the middle of these interactions, made of a combination of love and hostility, allowances and interdictions, that children start to produce 'theories' about birth, the origins of life and sexuality. These are born out of the relationship between the world of the child and the world of adults and carry the weight of cultural transmission and all that a culture pre-scribes, allows and interdicts. Freud brings to the fore the workings of interiorisation, the processes whereby representations move from the life of all to the life of one, from the level of consciousness to the level of the unconscious. Thus the intense, social and passionate character of the rep-resentations of first childhood, thus the realisation that knowledge entails at once desire and struggle, and thus the evidence that these first battles shape the radical ways in which the grammar of a culture enters the ontology of knowledge and, as a consequence, the ontology of the subject of knowledge.

These battles, Freud showed, never completely desert the subsequent stages of self-development and apprehension of the world. Psychic life is layered and remains so, never completely deleting that which once had meaning in a person's trajectory. Our history stays with us, in sublimated and disguised forms, making its appearance whenever the psyche feels it needs to retrieve some of the 'troops' it deployed along the way. It shows itself in dreams, in lapses, in daydreaming, in jokes, in the uncanny and its hidden connection with the known and familiar. Freud compared this process to the ruins of ancient civilisations that lie buried but do not disappear. His view of psychic development is compatible with Lévy-Bruhl's theory of coexistence of different logics. It allows us to understand the deep nature of our psy-chological and social constructions, whose ambivalent and paradoxical character the quest for a 'pure' rationality never quite managed to erase.

It is also in Freud that we find the acknowledgement of the reality of psychological constructions, the fact that they have a force and an impact that is as solid and material as the gesture, the actual deed. Freud's radical insight, expressed in his explorations of hysteria, was that the imagined or the desired were as real as the actual. To understand that a psychological construction, even if peculiar and bizarre, has a reality and logic of its own and needs to be recognised is central to the theory of social representations; it is central to the study of knowledge in context and it is central to constructing a dialogical theory of what defines the rationality of knowledge and worldviews.

Constructions that do not hold intersubjective validity cannot be just dismissed as irrational. This is what Habermas does when he states that 'anyone who systematically deceives himself behaves irrationally' and when he ties his theory of rationality to a theory of argumentation (Habermas 1991). The exchange of arguments that put validity claims under the critique of others and open those claims to learning and revision presupposes the sharing of a horizon that is equally valid for interlocutors. This cannot be taken for granted and indeed is just absent in situations such as mental illness, radical cultural displacement and childhood, whose subjects not accidentally have traditionally been considered irrational. Habermas fails to capture fully the radicality of Freud: anyone who systematically deceives himself displays a rationality that needs to be understood without being accused of irrationality.

This failure to understand the multiple logics of human behaviour, the reasons behind our self-deceptions and illusions, the sorrows and the hopes that accompany them, leaves Habermas cold to the complex rationality of human desire. It also compromises the need to distinguish the truth of a point of view, always real to the experience of its subject, and truth as a negotiated and worked through consensus, achieved as the multiple reals of human experience struggle to communicate and if possible become one. The importance of this struggle is paramount. But it should not overshadow the importance of recognising the truth of an individual person, her unique universe and her right to have it recognised as such even if it contradicts the reality of all. In this recognition, even if to accommodate crime and extreme error are the sources of all human compassion and the moral imperative of recognising the radical other.

Communicative efforts to recognise radically different logics entail an ethical dimension without which the social sciences would be only judgemental. Indeed recognising the logic and the truth that particular points of view and particular ways of experiencing the world involve is the central legacy of the Freudian insight. This recognition does not lead to acritical acceptance of all statements or denial of the intersubjective space where all propositions eventually live or die, but it does require an attitude and a disposition to engage and communicate with the peculiarity of the Other without the violence of a priori interpretation and intervention. This insight is one of the key contributions of psychoanalysis and the clinical approach to the method of the social sciences and it has been recently articulated as the 'melancholic attitude' in Bauer and Gaskell's (1999) programmatic paper for social representations research.

Exploring the impact Durkheim, Lévy-Bruhl, Piaget, Vygotsky and Freud had on the constitution of the theory of social representations can help to retain the line which links social psychology to the larger problems and theories that shaped the social sciences. Moscovici thought with and against these authors in developing his social psychology. His indebtedness to a tradition much larger than social psychology shows that beyond disciplinary boundaries the social sciences share a set of preoccupations and concepts that it is important to recognise as common. At the same time, the specific synthesis offered by the social psychology of knowledge constructed by Moscovici places the role of the psychological and of the interrelations between the individual and the social at the heart of the social sciences. The position of psychology, and with it social psychology, continues to be fraught with disputes related to the nature of the psychological proper, and whether the discipline stands in the natural or social sciences. It is my view that to leave the study of psychological processes to the neurosciences alone is deceptive and ultimately self-defeating. The social sciences cannot renounce the study of the structures of consciousness and the social and cognitive foundations of knowledge for they have the resources to reaffirm the social and historical nature of mind, the cultural foundations of thought and language and the irreducibility of human consciousness to the brain.

Towards wiser rationalities: cognitive polyphasia and the plurality of reason

In the foregoing pages I have explored the contribution of the theory of social representations to the study of knowledge in context highlighting its main propositions, the tradition to which it belongs and its complex engagement with multiple intellectual sources. I have considered at length the work of theorists who set the parameters within which Moscovici's thinking developed in order to show that the theory of social representations establishes a dual dialogue: one with social psychology, the other with the main issues permeating the social sciences. In the remainder of this chapter I want to systematise the main insights of the social theorists I discussed, point to the difficulties present in their work and develop further the idea of multiple logics pertaining to the same context and even the same individual through the concept of cognitive polyphasia.

As we have seen in previous pages the attempt to establish that to each form of social knowledge there corresponds a fundamental set of social relationships was central to work developed by the intellectual ancestors of the theory of social representations. Piaget, Vygotsky and Freud in psychology, Durkheim, Mauss and Lévy-Bruhl in sociology/anthropology all struggled over the problem of context and its relations to knowing. From different angles they showed that understanding how we think and know in different contexts and situations is central to any understanding of what knowledge and thought themselves are. Durkheim and Lévy-Bruhl concentrated on the sociogenesis, examining systems of collective representations of so-called primitive societies. Piaget and Vygotsky concentrated on the ontogenesis, investigating the development of knowledge in the child and to what extent the thought of the child could be compared to the thought of primitive man. In doing so, they heavily drew on Durkheim and Lévy-Bruhl. Freud concentrated on the ontogenesis in his clinical work and on the sociogenesis in his work on culture, society, art and religion. They all concurred that the development of knowledge is social and that it is society that confers logic to knowledge systems. They all used the concept of collective representations, as proposed by Durkheim, to understand how human communities construct particular mentalities, comprising views of the world and practices towards the everyday. The construction of these mentalities, they thought, could shed light both on the nature of thinking and knowing and on the nature of the societies themselves.

Now accepting the constitutive impact of social relationships on the formation of knowledge requires accepting variation in the forms of knowledge. From the proposition that knowledge is bound to community/social context, it follows that knowledge varies. There are a number of different social formations, which produce different forms of social knowledge. And that is where the real problem begins. To acknowledge variation in, and difference between, social knowledge is not the end of the story. In fact, it is only the beginning. The real problem was not so much that of understanding that psychic and cognitive structures change as social conditions change. The real problem was the old problem of modernity: the quest for an enlightened rationality, that following in the steps of Descartes, dictated the necessity of progress and development as the process of individualisation of knowledge. Free from the bounds of culture, custom, tradition and emotions that usually contaminate it, rational knowledge can emerge as an achievement of the sovereign individual. Their problem then was to understand 'how humans become rational beings, how they master their own behaviour, and how they emancipate themselves from dependence on the environment and on tradition' (Moscovici 2000a: 209). Different answers to this central problem of modernity explain the differences between Piaget and Vygotsky, Durkheim and Lévy-Bruhl and the path taken by Moscovici (Moscovici 1976a, 1998, 2000a).

Variation in forms of knowing raises the issue of how to conceive of this variation and what are the explanatory frameworks going to be used in order to make sense of the difference embedded in the variation. Here we go back to the very questions with which we started this chapter. How do different knowledges compare? How does knowledge change from one form to another? What is the trajectory of the change? Is there a progressive scale whose overall framework encapsulates the development of all knowledge from lower/primitive/simpler forms to higher/civilised/complex forms? To put it in other words: is the knowledge of a child a primitive form of the knowledge of an adult? Or is the knowledge of cultural others a rudimentary form of the logic to be found in western, civilised societies?

In Durkheim and Piaget it was a matter of course that higher forms of knowing, to be found in adults and 'civilised' peoples were bound to displace lower forms, found in children and 'primitives' (Durkheim 1973). Common to their view is the idea that reason progresses from elementary to fully developed forms based on the abandonment of its social and emotional components. Thinking and knowledge that are clouded by sociality and by emotions are not rational and, as the child grows and primitive societies evolve, they eventually achieve the stage of rationality. Durkheim, as Piaget himself stated, 'far from deducing a plurality of mentalities from the social origin of reason, believed that the sociomorphism seen initially simply presages common thought. Logic is singular, permanent and universal, because beneath civilisations, there is Civilization' (Piaget 1995c: 135).

Even though Lévy-Bruhl and Vygotsky problematised this view, they did not escape completely from the idea of progress. Knowledge tends to progress towards a full mastery of the objective world based on logical operations that leave behind all that is myth, belief and superstition. Lévy-Bruhl, despite having turned these issues upside down, was not completely immune to the notion of progress. While examining the functioning of prelogical mentality he stated that logic is the necessary condition for the liberty of thought and 'the indispensable instrument of its progress'. The Vygotskyan research programme was not as explicit as Piaget's but sustained a very similar concern. Socialism was to produce a society based on science, capable of leaving behind myth, superstition, belief and common sense. Comparing the knowledge of peasants in Central Asia, seen as the bearers of irrational and backward beliefs, and the new rational subject produced by the novel societal conditions of socialism was meant to show how social engineering of one particular kind could produce rationality. Intrinsic to the work of these pioneers is the unwritten assumption that public spheres based on argumentation, science and the weakening of tradition are the sites par excellence of all possible rationality. They alone produce knowledge, a knowledge that tends to progress towards the full mastery of the objective world based on logical operations that leave behind myth, belief and superstition.

Yet as much as Lévy-Bruhl and Vygotsky may have valued the development of logic and the progress of reason their work contains the elements to produce a powerful critique of the very idea and to re-set it in a novel fashion. Lévy-Bruhl's conception of plurality of mentalities and Vygotsky's conception of development challenged the assumption of unilinear evolution based on a theory of stages that move from the lower to the higher. They produced a framework to think about relations between stages and between different logics that dismantled the idea of development as progress because stages are not seen as more or less advanced but as structures in their own right. Discontinuity in development and coexistence of difference are elements that elucidate the processes whereby knowledge changes and open the internal structures of reason to a dialogue with the world from which it emerges. This dialogue retrieves the role of self, society and culture in the construction of knowledge and undermines the view of a cold rationality, indifferent to the projects and to the passions that underlie the multiple logics human experience comports.

Moscovici was strongly influenced by these insights (Moscovici 1998, 2000a, 2000b) and the notion of cognitive polyphasia corresponds to a continuation, this time within social psychology, of a debate that had started much earlier and of which Lévy-Bruhl proved to be one of the most important sources of inspiration. Cognitive polyphasia was introduced as a hypothesis in Moscovici's original study about psychoanalysis to describe the sociocognitive heterogeneity of the representational field he uncovered. He was careful enough to present the concept as a hypothesis but the data in the study were unequivocal in suggesting that different types of rationality were involved in the construction of representations about psychoanalysis. In considering whether collective thinking is a Tower of Babel or a well-ordered diversity he discusses the problem of different cognitive styles coexisting in the same individual or group:

> The coexistence of cognitive systems should be the rule rather than the exception . . . the same group, and *mutatis mutandis*, the same individual are capable of employing different logical registers in the domains they relate with perspectives, information and values that are distinctive to each. . . . In a general way, one can say that the dynamic coexistence – interference or specialisation – of different modalities of knowledge corresponding to specific relations between man and his social context determine a state of cognitive polyphasia.
>
> (Moscovici 1976a: 285–286, my translation)

Different modalities of knowledge, he argued, are dependent on the context of their production and intended to respond to different aims. Furthermore, contrary to well-established interpretations of cognitive phenomena, the different forms did not appear in different groups, or different contexts; on the contrary, they were capable of coexisting side by side in the same context, social group or individual. People would draw upon one form of knowledge, or another, depending on the particular circumstances in which they found themselves and on the particular interests they held in a given time and place. Cognitive polyphasia thus refers to a state in which different kinds of knowledge, possessing different rationalities, live side by side in the same individual or collective.

The key theoretical proposition underlying the concept of cognitive polyphasia is to ground the social psychology of knowing in the dynamics of social interactions and cultural contexts. The concept allows for recasting the problem of knowledge: knowing is an act of representation that can only be understood in relation to the social relations from which it derives its logic and the rationality it contains. Knowledge thus must be seen as plural and plastic, a dynamic and continuously emerging form capable of displaying as many rationalities as required by the infinite variety of sociocultural situations that characterise human experience. The process of representation, as discussed earlier, conceptually clarifies the plurality and variability of knowledge and makes possible the state of cognitive polyphasia. People draw on one form of knowing or another depending on the requirements of the social setting and the social psychological configuration of a field. These different forms can coexist rather than exclude each other. Instead of leaving behind forms of knowing socially treated as backwards, primitive or childish, human communities continuously draw on the resources different knowledges offer. In addition to classical studies in social representations, recent research has solidly corroborated this fact, showing that the development of knowledge in the child and the social knowledge held by human communities is made by a coexistence of science, street knowledge, belief, religion, ideologies amongst other forms (Nunes *et al.* 1993; Gervais and Jovchelovitch 1998; Halldén 1999; Jovchelovitch and Gervais 1999; Wagner *et al.* 1999, 2000; Haldén *et al.* 2002;). I shall return to this problem in Chapters 5 and 6.

The idea of unilinear evolution in knowledge ultimately betrays two ideals that have been deeply cherished by the project of modernity: the displacement of the cultural, social and emotional sources of knowledge by the rationality of the self-enclosed individual and the existence of a transcendental standard that operates as the parameter to all others. Yet, as Lévy-Bruhl pointed out, this is more desire than fact. Reason never quite managed to free itself from its human context and is far from being transcendental; the type of knowledge generally described at the top end of the developmental scale is fairly recognisable as based on the social relationships typical of western, industrial societies.

There is also another irony to be considered in examining the work of classical theorists: as much as they provide the elements to understand the plastic nature of knowledge, and as much as they point to decentration as the pinnacle of rational knowledge, they fail to decentre their own perspective. They seem to be unable to accomplish that which they find crucial in the rationality of knowing, that is, a conceptual scheme capable of explaining not only the position of the other, but also one's own, as nothing more than what it is: one, among the many variations which constitute the possibilities of realisation of human experience. Alternatively, the acknowledgement of the diversity of logics embedded in worldviews, and above all the acknowledgement of the coexistence of different rationalities in the same group of people, not only erases much of the deforming effects of centric constructions but also contributes to the enlargement of the wisdom of reason, to producing a reason that instead of denying is capable of communicating with its own differences.

3   Knowledge, community and public spheres

We grow up and live in communities and it is community that both structures our learning experiences and teaches us about life and how to live it. Not as close to each one of us as our immediate family or the various small groups to which we belong, nor as distant as the general rules and codes of practice that govern and structure the larger societies in which we live, community is an intermediate space that offers both the symbolic and material resources within which the dialectics between individual subjects and the social world is lived and played out. It is as members of a community that we become ourselves, grow into competent social actors and learn how to speak a language. It is because we belong to a community that we know how to interpret and make sense of the ways people around us behave and relate to us; our communities give us the framework within which and against which our unique sense of self arises. It would be very difficult, if not impossible, to become a person without community.

But giving to self its ground is not the only task of communities. Whereas community is a central condition for the emergence of the individual person, it is no less important in the development and establishment of those features of human life that originate in what people can do *together*. There is something that is unique to conditions of togetherness, that is, the many and varied instances in the evolution and development of human communities that are characterised by the coordination of action and perspective coming from different individuals. Togetherness is not something that is already there, a priori, or emerges ready-made in social life. Togetherness is a long and labour intensive process that needs to be constructed; it is an *achievement*. When people are together and try to act in concert there arises the need to communicate and to reach understanding, to construct a language, to form groups and divide tasks, to come to know the other and display oneself to the other. At the heart of community thus is the construction of intersubjective spaces that construct not only self but also the set of coordinated interrelations that produce phenomena such as communication and dialogue, social identities, social memory, public life and, linked to all of these, social knowledge.

In this chapter I shall expand the discussion about the relationship between social knowledge and social context by introducing a social psychological framework to theorise community and its relations to knowledge. As I mentioned earlier in this book, once we take seriously the relationship between psychological phenomena and social context, there arises the need to theorise social context, to understand its constitution and the main features it assumes. Historical, economic, societal, political and cultural dimensions form contexts; yet no context can be fully understood without a clear appreciation of its social psychology. Paradoxically, our discipline has turned its back on this task as social psychology has been historically concerned with the private individual (Farr 1991, 1996). Such a concern has shaped a whole programme of research in which attitudes, emotions, cognitive processes and so forth were solely considered at the individual level of analysis. Even those phenomena regarded as produced in social spaces were understood in terms of individual reasoning and the social and the political domains have, most of the time, been considered as 'variables' in the development of social psychology's theoretical and methodological corpus. However, social and political contexts are more than abstractions or added variables in a social psychological research programme. Indeed, understanding what gives form to a social context, what makes one different from another and how these differences produce variety in social psychological phenomena, is central to a substantive social psychology.

Here it is at the level of community that I shall approach the social psychological properties of context. Of course groups, organisations, institutions, nations can all be seen as legitimate contexts possessing a social psychology. Indeed there are so many contexts in social life that it would be impossible to nominate them all. However, my choice of community is related to its being a mediating concept that can easily permeate all others. We can think of organisations as communities, or even nations as communities. As a social space defined by the perspective of actors, community is flexible enough to stretch and entangle itself into other contexts as long as they are *felt* and *experienced* as community. Thus the social psychology of community can be translated to other contexts and lead into fertile applications in a range of settings.

Community

The study of community falls under the umbrella of many disciplinary fields and there has been by now a considerable amount of work from neighbouring disciplines in the social sciences that have specifically dealt with the concept and the revival of the notion (Cohen 1995; Putnam 2000; Bauman 2001). Academics, politicians and policymakers alike are retrieving the notion and its potential to respond to what is perceived as the increasing feelings of isolation, the anomie and the individualism of modern societies. Margaret Thatcher's infamous declaration that 'there is no such a thing as society' has today something of a passé ring to it. After a period in which materialistic values and the power of the individual dominated the social and political scene, there seems to be a new trend emerging: individualism alone will not do. It is not only that communities are crucial in developing resources and contributing to the resolution of pressing social problems; it is also that they offer a new mediating site for the development of participation in the public sphere, something vital to the development, preservation and regeneration of democracies, both in countries of the south and in the affluent north. Community is now identified as an important level of analysis in the field of health, of politics, of education, of crime and deviance, amongst others. We need to understand community to understand identity, social affiliations, rebellion and global conflict. And one of the aspects identified as crucial to the understanding of community is the study of how communities think, how they come to define themselves as a community, how the local knowledge of communities is produced and how it fares and relates to other regimes of knowledge. In this context, theorising community acquires a renewed importance for social psychologists.

In recent years social researchers have shown that community life has experienced dramatic transformations. As Bauman (2001) amongst others has noted, the very commonality that defines community is under question. Increasing contact and interpenetration between communities have undermined that which once constituted the relatively homogeneous and taken-for-granted space of community life. The well-known safety net of community has been shaken to its core as individuals both lose old frames of reference and gain freedom to explore new possibilities of being. Related to this process, profound transformations in technology and communication media have unsettled traditional modes of interaction and production of knowledge, including the knowledge of one's community and one's identity (Thompson 1995). These interrelated issues disturb the traditional idea of a community defined by locale, a relatively small geographical space, where people knew each other well and felt closely related not only to their fellow human beings but also to a landscape, a particular geography and a natural environment.

As important as these developments may be, they need, nonetheless, to be put in historical perspective. Whereas changes shaking sameness and communication today are acute, they are not necessarily novel as historical processes. Studies in the history and sociology of modernity and globalisation have clearly demonstrated that the new dialogue between global and local phenomena that we are experiencing today radicalises processes that started much earlier, at the beginning of the modern era (Thompson 1995). In fact, the history of cultural borrowings between communities can be traced to a past that by far anticipates modernity, probably as old as a distinct human form of life. Human communities have always encountered the other and developed strategies of communicating with them. What is new today is the fast pace of this encounter, the new fuzziness its speed produces in the boundaries between us/them, and the new responses that are constructed to deal with it. Globalisation as a cultural and psychological process has allowed for the simultaneous creation of new virtual communities and the reorganisation of old communities of identity and place. It has allowed for the challenge and, at times, the dismantling of traditional communities and the construction of new projects and solidarities around the globe. These recent transformations pose new questions to community life and communities' survival. However, they have not managed to do away with the fundamental human psychological need for community. The globalisation of the world has paradoxically re-engendered a recrudescence of local identities and people today continue to seek the bonds of solidarity and commonality that are constitutive of community life.

In this context, the perennial dilemma between community and individuality and between belonging and uprootedness continues to provide a fascinating and as yet unresolved panorama for social psychological study. The full grammar of this dilemma, which has been treated for most of the time as a dichotomy, has troubled generations of scholars and remains the one single issue that continues to haunt all the disciplines of the social sciences. Individualism and collectivism have tried to respond to it by constructing worldviews that resolved the tension by denial, i.e. they chose one side of the equation individual–social and discarded the other as if it were not there. Yet, psychologically and experientially this contradiction is there and it will not go away. It needs to be faced and understood as a productive contradiction, one that is part of our condition and shapes to a great extent our experience and the forms of life we construct. It is present every time communities deal with dissent, minorities, strangers and deviance and at all stages in the development of a human person, from infancy to adolescence, to maturity and old age, in which the task of growing poses and imposes the simultaneous clash and reconciliation with the outside world. The social psychology of community shows that the freedom of the human I depends at one and the same time on finding refuge and overcoming the security offered by community. This is because, as we shall see in the following pages, community is itself made by the interrelations between sameness and difference, self and other. Community is neither a homogeneous totality nor an aggregation of individual monads. It is a field of tensions and interrelations that remains an unfinished whole, always open to be changed from within and from without.

Theorising community

In 'Civilisation and its discontents' Freud (1930/2002) left us a legacy to theorise community that is at once daunting and reassuring. Community, he thought, can only come into being if the power and aggressive drives of the individual are tamed by the bonds of identification and love that allow for the emergence of solidarity and commonality. This, he argued, is a perennial struggle, renewed with the birth of every human life and constantly recast by the lessons of history. The battle between Eros and Thanatos is at the root of our condition. Human civilisation is not a given, it is just a possibility. If anything, it is a precarious achievement, reached when the self-destructive and aggressive forces we harbour within are provisionally put under control by the bonding energies of Eros. The following extract captures some of his overall view:

> Communal life becomes possible only when a majority comes together that is stronger than any individual and presents a united force against every individual. The power of the community then pits itself, in the name of 'right', against the power of the individual, that is condemned as 'brute force'. The replacement of the power of the individual by that of community is the decisive step towards civilisation.
>
> (Freud 1930/2002: 33)

Now any attempt to theorise community from a social psychological perspective needs to take into account this tension Freud so comprehensively described. Although it is tempting to think of community as a cosy and comforting concept (Bauman 2001), behind the formation of community there is nothing soft. The issues that are involved when human groupings strive to construct togetherness presuppose an interplay between similarity and difference, between sameness and otherness, that is fraught with both identifications and dissention, recognition and exclusion. Acknowledging these tensions, however, should not prevent us from trying to understand phenomena that, despite being permeated by dissention and exclusion, make identifications and recognition possible. Why and how individuals bind themselves into entities of more than one remains a question at the heart of social psychology, one that takes us directly to phenomena such as the formation of collectives, social cohesion and social solidarity, the genesis of social action and the thinking, knowledges and practices of a community.

Developing a social psychology of community thus calls for a theoretical effort capable of addressing the specific social and psychological processes that are at stake when communities come into being, are sustained and eventually transformed. These processes can also be used to theorise any social context that lies between the small group and society as a whole. In what follows I start by discussing the notion of boundary, and its central role in theorising community. Boundaries can be of many kinds, but a social psychological approach seeks to unravel the processes whereby boundaries are represented and symbolically defined by social actors. In order to understand how boundaries are symbolically shaped by actors so that something like a community can emerge, I shall discuss in turn (a) the relations between social knowledge and belonging that lead to the construction of lifeworlds; (b) the role of social memory in sustaining community and constructing identity; (c) the relations between community and storytelling. Each one of these dimensions plays a role in the construction of community boundaries and together they offer a conceptual framework for the social psychology of community.[1]

The formation of community boundaries

Through relational activities communities produce boundaries. Boundaries can be of different kinds, varying from geographical, physical and administrative to linguistic, religious, ethnic, social and cultural. One traditional way of thinking about communities is through geographical boundaries; imagine the business of map-making for instance and what it carries in terms of power to make and unmake national and ethnic communities. Here defining boundaries is a clear political act, very much related to the exercise of power and the larger historical circumstances in which different levels of power have been played out. We can also think about linguistic boundaries as in the Francophone community, the English-speaking community, and so on. Having a language in common greatly unites people, even if they live in geographically different communities. What could link someone from Mozambique, Brazil and Portugal? Different continents, different ethnicities and different geographies no doubt, but also a great deal of commonality given by the fact that these three countries share a language and all it carries in terms of identity, representations, emotions and cultural practices. In this case the Portuguese language provides the common denominator against which something like a community of Portuguese-speaking peoples can emerge and by the same token differentiate itself from other linguistic communities.

The examples above show that the construction of boundaries is not a process solely defined from within communities. Boundaries are always the outcome of relations between communities. Communities are co-constructed, both from inside and outside their borders. First, they are constructed by those who identify themselves as members of a community from inside its borders. These community members produce the symbolic work and the material resources that are needed to sustain, reproduce and renew the life of a community by perceiving and giving meaning to boundaries as part of the process of constructing a cultural identity. They learn and transmit community rituals and narratives through generations. Through storytelling, institutionalised practices and the construction of projects for the future, community members link the world of predecessors, contemporaries and successors (Schutz 1967a) in an intersubjective and interobjective network that allows for the existence and continuity in time of social memories, social representations and social identities, the social psychological co-relates of history and culture. By engaging in different kinds of relationships and modes of communication, community members help to define the shape of the public sphere and social knowledge that is peculiar to a community, something I discuss in more detail later in this chapter.

Second, and no less important, communities are constructed by those outside its borders. These comprise the multiple others who engage with the life of a community, at different levels of social life and with different degrees of proximity and power. By seeing the community in a certain way, by constructing a set of representations and attitudes about it, by developing practices and expectations about it, the other outside defines as much as the self inside the construction of the community. Understanding how a community is socially represented by other communities is integral to any effort of mapping out its way of life and social psychology.

This is important because boundaries, both symbolic and material, can be defined by actors or imposed on them, they can be negotiated through cultural borrowings and dialogues, sustained through totalitarianism and isolation or violated by external force. Sometimes communities are exposed to totalitarian regimes that close them off to the outside world. Here one does not need to think only about countries or nations. Institutions such as the asylum, or indeed any other organisation that fits into the concept of total institution described by Goffman (1968) conforms precisely to the model of a closed off community, whose contact with the outside world is curtailed by its own internal regulations. In such cases, the establishment of community boundaries is a complex process entangled at the same time in symbolic and dialogical action and relations of power and domination, played out inside and outside community boundaries. All these different modes of establishing boundaries play a key role in how community identities and ways of life are established and evolve over time.

Whereas communities can be studied from many angles, in social psychology we approach a community seeking to understand how it came to think of itself as such, how it constructs social knowledges about itself, others and objects in the social world, how it perceives and gives meaning to the boundaries that define it as a community. We are interested in the perspective of the actors living through the contradictions of the space in between communities and individuals. Much in the same way as in the triangle of mediation, that is the basic unit of analysis of social psychology and constructs representation, the spaces in between account for the genesis of phenomena that constitute community. In what follows I turn to a more detailed consideration of these phenomena.

Belonging and lifeworld

Communities produce a common stock of knowledge that endures over time and gives to community members the points of reference and the parameters against which individuals make sense of the world around them and are able to connect their individual stories with larger narratives of community life. The common knowledge produced by communities offers nodes of connection from which the experience of belonging emerges. Individual narratives and community narratives are entangled in such a way that when a story about one individual life is told it brings about the history, the events, the cultural forms and the ways of behaving of a whole community. Conversely, when events and stories that matter to a community are remembered, discussed or challenged individuals can recognise their part in them, can identify or distance themselves from them, can feel passionately supportive about or passionately reject what is at stake. This experience of connectedness is what produces the psychology of belonging, the feeling that one fits in a cultural milieu, understands the taken-for-granteds and communicates without having to be explicit all the time.

This common knowledge of community has been central to the understanding of what makes community. Common knowledge, common sense, folk knowledge, habitus, thinking-as-usual, collective representations, all of these terms have featured in philosophical, psychological and sociological frameworks that dealt with the problem of what holds social life together (Durkheim, 1898/1996, 1905/1963; Schutz 1944, 1967b; Heider 1958; Gadamer 1975; Bordieu 1994). Phenomenologists have described it as the background assumptions, the 'thinking as usual', the knowledge that constitutes the lifeworld of a community. Schutz's (1944) classical work on the social psychology of the stranger draws on the concept of 'thinking-as-usual' to explain what makes a stranger. The distance between the 'thinking-as-usual' of the community where he arrives and the community he left behind is what gives to the stranger the 'strangeness' of his condition. He has difficulties to interpret the basic rules of behaviour and the unthematised patterns of thinking and acting that are enacted by the host community. For the community, on the other hand, the stranger asks awkward questions, behaves out of pattern. The absence of common knowledge linking up stranger and community reveals with great precision the fundamental social psychological role of common and shared knowledge in linking individual and community life and producing the experience of belonging.

Whereas the common knowledge of communities appears in everyday life as a given, as an already there stock of meanings and resources from which community members draw norms, regulations and patterns of behaviour, its horizon is also constructed through the experience of life each day. The concept of the lifeworld captures well this double character of the common life of communities: of being already there, of providing foundation and ground for community and at the same time of having to be constantly produced and renewed by social actors. In Habermas' theory of communicative action, the concept of the lifeworld is central to define both the context of community and the conditions for all possible communication. He characterises the lifeworld as the space where people communicate in order to reach understanding and in this process come to construct and consolidate the intersubjectively recognised elements of a *shared under-*

standing about the world. The lifeworld takes shape in language and communication and appears as 'a reservoir of taken-for-granteds, of unshaken convictions that participants in communication draw upon in cooperative processes of interpretation' (Habermas 1992: 124). It refers to the unproblematic knowledge that supplements, accompanies and provides the context for communicative action: the traditions, the natural languages, the presuppositions and assumptions that govern everyday life. While seeking mutual understanding actors engage in processes of communication that do not disappear, but solidify in symbolic structures of meaning and understanding that become the matter of the lifeworld.

Thus the common knowledge of communities, or the lifeworld, provide the points of reference, the parameters, the resources against which individuals make sense of the world around them, develop the theoretical and practical competencies to deal with the everyday and establish the communicative relations that allow for the development of bonds of solidarity and cooperation and the experience of belonging. Both produced by, and producer of, communication, the lifeworld involves the bridging of distances and multiple perspectives through an effort that creates the intersubjective. By making possible and facilitating social action, establishing and renewing the interpersonal relations that provide the developing child with a sense of self and giving to social actors a framework for identity and belonging, communities are the privileged site where the lifeworld constructs and reconstructs person, society and culture. Within it, a person can both weave her life experience into a coherent biography and anchor that biography into a larger history. From the perspective of participants, the intersubjectively shared lifeworld is community. From the perspective of observers the intersubjectively shared lifeworld is the space where communities link the past, the present and the future through social memory, social representations and social identities.

Social memory

So far I have characterised how the interplay between sameness and difference that defines community is expressed in the common knowledge held by communities, in the experience of belonging and the construction of the lifeworld. These intersubjectively shared understandings allow communities to achieve some degree of sameness; sameness, as much as difference, operates as a resource that allows communities and individuals to develop knowledge about themselves and others, to recognise a history that is handed down by previous generations and give to self an identity, i.e. a coherent narrative that connects events, actions, people, feelings and ideas in a plot.

Now how can communities sustain a relative sameness and at the same time deal with new points of difference that constantly emerge in time and space? To examine this problem I shall consider the role social memory plays in the life of communities and the relations it has with social representations and social identities. As will become clear, the workings of social memory allow communities both to retain a sense of continuity and permanence and a sense of historical development and change. The capacity to remember opens the future of communities by establishing links between the past and the present through the understanding and elaboration of what has been. In order to consider these processes I shall draw on the work of Halbwachs (1992, 1997) and Bartlett (1932) who extensively studied the social frameworks of memory. Both have demonstrated precisely how the dynamics of the present work through the remembrance of things past, to such an extent that memory is as much about present and the future as it is about the past. The social and psychological elaboration of the connections between the past, the present and the future is what activates processes of remembering. These processes, they strongly argued, are inherently social and based in the patterns and knowledge of communities.

Although Frederick Bartlett is better known by social psychologists, it is the work of Halbwachs (1992, 1997) that inaugurated the study of the social frameworks of memory. When Bartlett wrote *Remembering* he had already read and appreciated the work of Halbwachs, a French Durkheimian sociologist whose work on memory was both a reaction to classical interpretations of the phenomenon and an attempt to shift the understanding of memory from the individual to the social level of analysis. Halbwachs looked at how the relations between subjects and the things remembered are established. For him these relations were not limited to the world of the individual (the relations between body and mind for instance) but were to be found in the interrelational reality of social institutions. The memory of an individual depends on his relationship to a family, a social class, a school, a church, a profession, in short, it depends on the community frameworks that mark the experience of that individual.

By giving salience to the community as the matrix that shapes the individual subject, Halbwachs put into context and called into question the principle that the mind keeps the past in its integrity and autonomy. Memory is not a matter of recapitulation and cannot bring back the past as once it was. Rather the opposite, noted Halbwachs; it is the present that holds the initiative to trigger the course of memory. What has once been lived cannot remain intact in human memory because the standpoint from which the past is evoked is fundamentally different from the standpoint in which it has been lived. If we remember it is because others and the context of our present make us remember. Remembering is a process constructed by the matter that is at one's disposal now, in the stock of representations that circulate and people the current life of a community. As much as clear as a memory of the past can be, it can never be exactly the same image that we have actually experienced in, say, childhood, because we are not the same, because we have changed, and our ideas, values and assessments of reality have changed. The simple fact that we remember the past, in the present, excludes the identity between the images we had then and the images we have now, and proposes to the experience of human communities and social subjects, the dimension of time and history.

Remembering, as total conservation of the past and its full resurrection in the present, would only be possible if social subjects could maintain unchanged the system of representations, habits and relationships experienced in the past. But even the most minimal change in the environment will affect the structure of memory. And it is by this path that Halbwachs ties the memory of the person to the memory of the group, and the latter to the macro-sphere of tradition, which he considers to be the collective memory of a society. The social interpretation that Halbwachs gives to the capacity to remember is radical. He is not talking about an external influence on an internal process; his conceptualisation is not a juxtaposition of social frameworks to images remembered. Beyond that he locates at the very heart of memory, in its structural core, the beliefs, representations and institutional practices carried by the language and rituals of a community.

Social psychology confronted directly the problem of memory and its relation to representations, beliefs and community. *Remembering*, written by Bartlett (1932), remains a classic in the field and coincides in many aspects with Halbwachs' work which, as mentioned earlier, Bartlett knew well. Bartlett's aim was to show that both the process and the content of recall are predominantly determined by social influences. In perceiving, imagining and in remembering proper it is the culture, the interests, the social customs, the institutional practices, the community identity that 'set the stage and direct the action'. Bartlett called this community identity, the group bias:

> every social group is organised and held together by some specific psychological tendency or group of tendencies, which give the group a bias in its dealings with external circumstances. The bias constructs the special persistent features of group culture, its technical and religious practices, its material art, its traditions and institutions: and these again, once they are established, become themselves direct stimuli to individual response within the group.
>
> (Bartlett 1932: 255)

In Bartlett's work we find a key concept to understand the relationship between community and its cultural processes in a given historical time and the workings of memory: the notion of conventionalisation. Conventionalisation studies the principles by which cultural systems moving about from one group to another, undergo change, and finally arrive at relatively fixed and accepted forms in whatever group they reach. It is the process whereby images and ideas, received from the outside by an indigenous group, assume a form of expression that is reconstructed as a function of the technical and cultural conventions of the receivers. Bartlett establishes an analogy between the exchanges of different cultural systems in place and different points in time in the history of a community. The present, as the context from where one remembers, contains a universe of meaning and practices that is different from the context of the past. The lenses of the present conventionalise the past very much in the manner through which communities absorb knowledges and identities coming from other locales. It is in this sense that Bartlett argues that the prime matter of remembering does not emerge in a pure state in the language of the speaker who remembers; this matter is always treated and shaped by the cultural and ideological perspective of the group to which this individual belongs in the present.

Both Halbwachs and Bartlett sought to stress the pertinence of social frameworks, of institutions, social conventions and representations in the process that leads to remembering. Their problem was that of continuity and change in community life through the operations of social memory as a reservoir of social representations and cultural identities. By demonstrating the interpenetration between past and present, remembering becomes an active reconstruction of the past from the perspective of the present. New meanings are added to the experience of the past, transforming it with the experience of the present and the projects held for the future. Predecessors provide the frameworks upon which our knowledge of today develops and our experience of community unfolds. We draw from the past the frameworks of custom, tradition and practice that constitute the system of everyday representations that guide experience, interpretation of what is going on, and schemes of understanding of self and others in the present. By understanding how social memory works, we can also understand the construction of repertoires of knowledge, social beliefs and symbolic meanings available to us in the present, usually organised as the cultural identity and social representations of communities.

Storytelling

It is by telling stories that social knowledge comes into life, and with it, the representations of the past, and the presentations of identity. Through the telling of stories, communities recall what has happened (social memory), put experience into sequence (humanisation of time), find explanations for what is going on (sense making) and play with the chain of events that shapes individual and social life (future making). Storytelling elicits fields of intersubjective reality, fields of cognition and recognition; it lives beyond personal storytelling, growing as discourse in the open spaces of public squares, streets, cities and villages, of social groups, generations and epochs (Bartlett 1923).

Narratives are fundamentally linked to community life. Narratives have the power to bond, to link up events into a coherent history and weave these events to the social identity of any given community. The production of myths, legends and tales can respond to needs related to origins (where do we come from?), to moral predicaments (stories not only amuse, they also teach us what to do); to the resolution of conflicts and the construction of possible futures. Because stories connect the past, the present and the future they are intertwined with both the construction and continuity of communities, the production of the lifeworld and the shared knowledge of a group of people and the possibility of working through and reflecting upon the nature of community life. Narratives teach us the stories and metaphors we live by and at the same time offer the means of reflecting upon, calling into question and criticising our historical heritage.

Storytelling is one of the fundamental media through which communities understand their past and present and project their aims for the future. Freud once famously remarked that a group that does not understand its history is destined to repeat it. It is only experience that is reflected upon and worked through that can change us and retrieve our historical substance. When experience reifies and, in the classic manner of the Freudian trauma, cannot be spoken because it is banished from our consciousness, we feel afraid of history – a history that is perhaps made of too many sorrows and pain. But the trap of this kind of forgetting – forgetting as expulsion and banishment – is that the pain we seek to avoid is a pain that has *already* hurt us. The ability to remember as elaboration, as working through the past that once was, allows for communities to reflect upon, to understand, to revise and if necessary to renew their identities, practices and histories. It allows for the continuation of communities while guaranteeing the renewal that is needed if communities are not going to 'freeze' and compulsively repeat their history. Should the past be frozen in the memory of communities, human life would be subjected to the violence of 'a past that does not pass'. To understand and to elaborate the past from the renewing perspective of the present is what gives to community the possibility of a future that is not held back by the chains of purely traumatic memories. To move on is as important as to remember and the dialectics between the capacity for remembering and forgetting (and forgiving) says a great deal about the health of communities.

This, however, is associated with and depends upon the possibility of free narration and the free circulation of words and symbolic meanings via communication. The struggles between community elaboration and what becomes unspeakable in community life are shaped by the freedom of groups to bring issues into light, to make them visible, to question and to put under scrutiny aspects of community life that are seen in need of consideration. Now this is not a process to be taken for granted for a great number of communities do not enjoy the conditions for such practices. This is the problem I turn to in the second part of this chapter where I consider the public sphere of communities and how the concept of the public sphere can contribute to the understanding of different forms of community life and how these are related to different modes of knowledge production.

Public spheres

One of the most important aspects of community life is that it creates a public sphere, i.e. a space that is common to all members of the community and where community life becomes visible and known to the community itself. Public spaces are meeting points, sites of connection and communication whose main feature is to produce visibility, so that issues of common concern can emerge and the plurality of perspectives that constitute community can be dealt with and resolved. In this sense, the public sphere of a community is a potential space (Winnicott 1971; Jovchelovitch 1995, 2000) where different understandings of self and world can be played out, where projects are negotiated and enacted, where social actors experiment with the openness and unpredictability that is intrinsic to the multiplicity of unique perspectives they encounter. Public spheres are sites of communication and dialogue, spaces where self and other meet, explore each other's identities, construct knowledge and express affects. This public space is the *creation* of a community: it is constructed as the community engenders its modes of communication and interaction, the forms of expression of its rituals and ceremonies and the possibilities and limitations of participation and voice in a forum that is shared by all. Elsewhere I have suggested that a public sphere can be defined as a space that (a) is shared by all members of the community and (b) offers an arena for the debate and the enactment of issues related to the common life of the community (Jovchelovitch 2001). Public spheres, however, are not identical and can take many forms; understanding the type of public sphere a community creates is an important diagnostic tool for understanding the community itself.

In discussing the social psychology of the public sphere I shall begin by considering the idea of the public sphere as developed by both Arendt and Habermas. I discuss the concept as it was proposed by both theorists, explore its social psychological dimensions and offer an account that goes beyond Habermas' strict definition of public spheres as the public developed by liberal democratic western societies. As it will become clear, the definition I propose relies on important aspects of Arendt's discussion and both draws upon and rejects certain aspects of Habermas' account. The interrelated notions of perspective and of plurality are taken up and elaborated upon; both are intrinsic to the experience of community and both come to the fore as makers of the public sphere. Different ways of coping with, and responding to, the diversity of perspectives that makes for the plurality of a community shape the nature of a community's public sphere and define, to a great extent, how the experience of community is felt by individual members and how communities produce knowledge.

Perspective and plurality

In *The Human Condition* Hannah Arendt developed a theory of public life that is fundamentally linked to the phenomenon of plurality, to 'the fact that men, not Man, live on the earth and inhabit the world' (Arendt 1958: 7). Her account establishes the human condition of plurality as the basis of the public realm and introduces the bridging of different perspectives through speech and action as the foundation of a life that is distinctively human. It is in public, in the space formed by the multiplicity of threads that originate in each individual person's story, that human action can face and deal with diversity in perspectives, construct shared understandings and develop its full potential for coordination of acts. 'Acting in concert', as Arendt put it, is the essence of the public sphere.

According to Arendt (1958), the term public indicates two interrelated but not identical phenomena. First it means that everything that appears in public can be seen and heard by everybody. Second, it means the world that is common to all of us and distinguished from our privately owned place in it. The first meaning of the public sphere identified by Arendt is related to our feeling and sense of reality. It constitutes a profound anti-Cartesian statement insofar as it places in the presence of others, who see what we see and hear what hear, the condition for understanding the reality of the world and our own selves. The second meaning of the public sphere is related to sharing, to identifying points of connection that reside between people, are common to all and yet do not coincide with any one individual in his or her own private space. The public sphere transcends each individual's private location and emerges as the space individuals have in common.

However, sharing a common space and being bound to each other through social companionship is not what distinguishes humans from other animals. Sharing alone cannot be considered a fundamental human condition. To live with other people is not enough; rather it is a necessity imposed upon us by the biological cycle of life which includes everything we share with other species – to eat, to sleep, to reproduce, etc. To live among people in a human fashion presupposes the capability of escaping from the realm of mere necessity to construct a quite different domain – the domain of public life in which people realise their capacities for speech and action.

Now the condition for both speech and action is precisely human plurality. Human plurality refers to both equality and distinction, or sameness and difference. It is because people are different – and yet the same – that action and speech become necessary: if we were all identical there would be no need to communicate and to act upon an unvarying sameness; if we had nothing in common at all the very process of speech would lose its basis and action would not justify itself. Hence, what makes individuals' lives unique and distinct are the bounds of a common life constructed by action and speech exercised in public. 'With word and deed,' wrote Arendt, 'we insert ourselves into the human world, and this insertion is like a second birth, in which we confirm and take upon ourselves the naked fact of our original physical appearance' (Arendt 1958: 176–177). To act is to begin, to take an initiative, to start something new, to the extent that 'this character of startling unexpectedness is inherent in all beginnings and all origins'. In acting, argues Arendt, the actor always discloses himself or herself in the act, 'in acting and speaking men show who they are, reveal actively their unique personal identities' (1958: 179).

It is in the human condition of plurality that the most fundamental meaning of the public sphere is to be found. Arendt's philosophy locates in the experience of plurality and in the diversity of different perspectives the sine qua non condition for the disclosure of the individual actor as the bearer of a unique personal identity, the identity of an initiator, someone who can, by virtue of being born and living amongst others, act and speak. Because the web of human relationships that forms the plurality of the public sphere is woven by the unique perspective of individual initiators, the communicative act – in speech and action – is its principal mediator. Through the communicative act, the public sphere of a community can be objectified in stories, in monuments, in narratives and artefacts that survive the natural destruction of time and link predecessors, contemporaries and successors in a 'we-relation' (Schutz 1967b). It is the meeting arena of public life which provides the conditions not only for discovering the common concerns of the present but also for identifying what the present owes to the past and what hopes it has for the future. If people were to be isolated within their own private space in the world, neither history nor political life would be possible at all.

In Arendt's theory of public life we find the philosophical counterpart to the social psychology of G. H. Mead (1934). In Mead, the communicative act is the generative source of mind and constitutes the basic unit of analysis for understanding human life. Communication is about meeting the other, acknowledging her perspective, taking it into account and being prepared to put oneself in the role of the other. It is a process that does not seek to efface differences in perspective but to link up, to connect and to produce, through a creative chain of dialogical acts, what Mead called the generalised other of a community, the shared understandings that express the identity, culture and ways of life of a group of people. The generalised other objectifies, as it were, the chain of dialogical acts that are at the basis of community formation and constitute the public sphere. The concept expresses the norms, the practices and the rules that shape a community's public life. Both the internalisation and the ability to take the perspective of the generalised other are integral to the developmental processes of individuation and socialisation. By being able to establish a reciprocal relationship with the generalised other, individuals grow into a community of fellow human beings, develop the links between their own personal trajectories and the communal trajectory to which they also belong and obtain the frameworks of meaning that allow for self to recognise and to be recognised.

The normative power of Arendt's theory of public life offers a framework within which we can reflect on contemporary forms of community life. Notions such as plurality, action, speech, diversity, dialogue and consensus upon matters of general interest are more than ever present in the context of communities and constitute fundamental issues for the social psychology of community. All of these notions originate in the public sphere and at the same time continue to hold a basic relevance for psychological life. Indeed such categories are in themselves the synthesis of the dialectics between the social and the psychological.

Dialogue and argumentation

If in Arendt's theory of the public sphere the problem of perspective and plurality occupies central stage, in Habermas the emphasis is on the role of dialogue and argumentation as *procedures* to deal with perspective and plurality. Acknowledging plurality and perspective as foundations of public life poses the problem of dealing with the difference embedded in these foundations; different accounts and perspectives need to be settled if members of a community are going to construct togetherness and act in concert. Habermas' contribution to this debate has been seminal. His path-breaking book, *The Structural Transformation of the Public Sphere: An Inquiry into a Category of Bourgeois Society*, became a classic and continues to be the key reference to the debate that picked up in the early 1990s when the limitations and possibilities of contemporary public spheres acquired prominence in the agenda of the social sciences. Although it has been mainly received as an historical and sociological account of the bourgeois public sphere, there can be no doubt that Habermas' book is also a social psychological study, an acute and sharp description of the transformations that occurred in the subjectivity and mentality of a new social class as it tried to assert itself and radically change the social landscape of European societies. Deeply inscribed in Habermas' theory of public life is also a theory about the communication and possible dialogue between self and other, about perspective, reciprocity and role taking in social life, and about the need to justify and validate one's position in relation to interlocutors. Behind the historical account there is a normative proposal about principles related to dialogue and accountability, which heavily relies on the social psychology of self–other relations. These concerns are expanded further in the theory of communicative action and depict well Habermas' attempt to move away from a monological philosophy of consciousness to the construction of a communicative paradigm. Indeed, Habermas' theory of the public sphere cannot be understood outside his theory of communicative action.

Broadly speaking the bourgeois public sphere is a phenomenon created out of the relations between capitalism and the state in the seventeenth and eighteenth centuries in Europe. It is defined as a body of 'private persons' who assemble together to form a public, or to discuss matters of public concern, a space where citizens meet and talk to each other in a fashion that guarantees access to all. The elements that brought into being this new public engaged in critical political discussion evolved in the wake of the development of early modern capitalism and changes in the institutional arrangements of political power. The economic independence provided by private owners of commodities meeting each other freely in the market-place, the discussion flowering in coffee houses, salons and public houses, the emergence of an independent press, and the critical reflection fostered by letters and novels were some of the main factors that contributed to the constitution of the public sphere. Habermas notes that the spread of salons in France, table societies in Germany and coffee houses in England was overwhelming at the turn of the eighteenth century. By the first decade of the eighteenth century London alone already had 3000 coffee houses, each with a stable group of habitués. This is the milieu Anderson (1991) refers to as the imagined communities that created the nation in Europe. He points to the combined emergence of capitalism, the development of print tech-nology and the plurality of languages as the conditions that made possible the establishment of a 'virtual community of readers', who could not see, but could imagine each other, by virtue of the reading act.

This new reading public brought about two novelties that transformed political participation and the relationship between state and society: the principles of accountability and argumentative dialogue. Through the medium of argumentative dialogue, or rational talk, the new public sought a kind of political participation whose main aim was to mediate the relationship between state and society, by making the state accountable to society via publicity. Accountability meant, at first, the requirement that information concerning the actions of the state should be subjected to scrutiny by the force of public opinion. It also meant that the general interest of society was to be transmitted to agents of the state via insti-tutional channels such as legally guaranteed free speech, a free press and freedom of assembly. In this context, the development and transformation of the media became a key element in the consolidation of the public sphere. The rise of literacy and journalism to give an account of the intense debates occurring within literary circles soon gave way to a fully developed press. The public sphere, therefore, comprised institutional mechanisms aiming at a rationalisation of political life by rendering the state account-able to its citizens. At the same time, argumentative dialogue became a central procedure of the public sphere and its practice was guided by a number of ideal features:

- debate in the public space must be open and accessible to all
- the issues at stake must be of common concern; mere private interests were not admissible
- inequalities of status were to be disregarded
- participants were to decide as peers.

The results of such a public dialogue would be public opinion considered as a consensus reached through free debate about common life. The public sphere and its ideal principles produce a social space where argumentation and rational dialogue are the entry points to deal with difference in perspectives. In it, participants are recognised by the quality of what they have to say and not by the authority or wealth of their position. The use of arguments and reason as the guide for public debate was thus another substantial novelty in the liberal model of the public sphere; through it society as a whole would create a knowledge of itself.

Critique of the public sphere

Habermas' theory of the public sphere has been extensively criticised, mainly for its heavy idealisation of the phenomenon (Landes 1988; Fraser 1990; Eley 1992; Thompson 1995). At the core of these critiques is the view that the bourgeois public sphere never came to actualise its presuppositions and its utopian potential was never fully realised. Although the public sphere was constituted by the principles of accessibility and publicity, its actual constitution rested upon a number of important exclusions, of which gender and class were the most important ones. In addition, Habermas has also been criticised for failing to recognise and examine other types of public action which were present at the time of the formation of the liberal bourgeois public sphere. Fraser (1990) has pointed to the multiplicity of public arenas competing with the bourgeois public sphere; these various publics have always been in conflict with one another.

Habermas (1992) has reflected on these critiques and very much to his credit has recognised the faults of his early work. However, neither Habermas nor many of the theorists who criticised him would be willing to deny the importance of the public sphere as a guiding normative concept. Whereas it is obvious that the assumptions that constitute the public sphere have never been fully realised, it would be dangerous to rely on theories that only describe what is actual. Unrealised principles are not necessarily unrealisable principles and the importance of normative ideals lies precisely in their function of guiding and constraining action and historical change. The ideal principles of the public sphere, although never realised, carry a utopian potential that must be retained as today we still struggle to sustain and renew our contemporary public spheres. The public sphere thus remains a paradigmatic idea for thinking about the nature of community life, the limits and possibilities of a common space for dialogue and the political project of establishing a radical democracy (Calhoun 1992).

While the importance of the principles of the Habermasian concept of the public sphere as normative ideals should be taken seriously, it is important to recognise that there are public spheres that do not conform to them. There are other 'publics' which also need to be recognised. It would be incorrect to call a public space 'public sphere' only if it is guided by the mostly unrealised principles described by Habermas. Think, for instance, of a marketplace in traditional societies or of ritualised ceremonies such as carnivals and other types of religious celebration. Insofar as these spaces constitute, as suggested above, a space shared by all members of the community and a stage for issues related to the common life of the community, they are public spaces. They bring out and make visible the common life of a community and act as a forum of engagement and participation in its common life. The principles that organise the sharing of that space and the location of people in it are other than the ones adopted by the liberal model of the public sphere, but this does not make them 'less public'. They are just different from the liberal model dominant in the west.

Comparisons between the public sphere of western and non-western societies show that there are a number of important differences that need to be taken into account: the impersonality of law and the universality of principles can be enacted with greater acceptance in public spaces that remain relatively free from personal issues and kinship relations, to cite just the most obvious ones. In western, liberal, public spheres, patterns of communication tend to be less hierarchical and the production and circulation of knowledge is less attached to sources of authority. Yet it would be too facile to dismiss the public sphere of more traditional societies because it is penetrated by emotional and personal relations, and the authority of tradition guides the rules and procedures. Differences between public spheres need to be acknowledged and recognised for what they are; rather than constructing a theory of public spheres that relies on one specific, and ideal for that matter, model of public life developed in the west, we need a more encompassing theory that is capable of taking into account the variety of publics different human communities construct. Such theory also needs to be sensitive to the social psychology and culture of a community.

No public sphere can escape from its social psychology; social, historical and economics processes are interrelated with the subjective dimension and the psychology of communities accounts in equal footing for the constitution and genesis of public spheres. Understanding how communities construct representations about themselves and the world, their modes of communication, the rituals and practices that govern their internal and external relations is part and parcel of any theory of public life. Such theory also consolidates a societal understanding about the production of knowledge as it provides valuable insights on the connections between the transformation of public spheres and transformation in social knowledges, a concern has been at the centre of the theory of social representations from its inception as seen in Chapter 2. Understanding the transformations of knowledge in relation to social contexts is one of the avatars of the theory. Indeed, social representations themselves are forms of knowledge that rely on a specific kind of public sphere, which in turn they help to form and consolidate. This is the issue I turn to next.

Knowledge and public spheres

When Moscovici transformed the sociological concept of collective representations into the social psychological concept of social representations he provided the means to capture how the symbolic knowledge produced by a community of people changed as a function of larger transformations occurring in the public sphere. He noted that in contemporary public spheres representations were contested and open to scrutiny, sprang from different sources of authority and needed arguments as sources of legitimation. It was not possible to sustain knowledge just by appealing to some recognised centre of authority because there were new forms of contestation in social fields. Active minorities, for instance, were imposing a great deal of innovation by challenging dominant and relatively homogeneous views; in many respects Moscovici's theory of active minorities is deeply connected with his theory of social representations. But the move from collective to social representations betrays a deeper concern of Moscovici, one that is visible in his commanding analysis of Durkheim and Weber and the implicit social psychologies that lie behind their work; one that is to be found not only at the core of the theory of social representations, but throughout his writings: the concern with social innovation, or how to break up and transform the order of things. It is this concern that makes Moscovici indebted to Weber as much as to Durkheim. Although it is to Durkheim that commentators grant the source of inspiration for the theory of social representations, Weber is no less present in Moscovici's social psychology. It could be said that social representations are born out of a contrast between Durkheim and Weber; out of the struggle between a perfect theory of social conformity provided by Durkheim and a theory of innovation and minority influence provided by Weber (Moscovici 1993). In fact, it is in the sociology of Weber that Moscovici locates the issues that drive the move from collective to social representations: innovation, the importance of individuals and the transformations active minorities can impose in the shape and nature of a public sphere.

Collective representations: conformity and tradition in the public sphere

The central issue underlying all of Durkheim's work is the analysis of social cohesion. What keeps a community together, what constitutes social solidarity? The concept of collective representations addressed precisely this problem and it became a generative notion for capturing the role played by knowledge in the formation of community. As discussed earlier in this chapter, collective representations belong to a string of concepts that refer to the habitual, taken-for-granted and homogeneously shared beliefs, sentiments and ideas held by a community. Conceived by Durkheim as the 'collective consciousness' of a community, collective representations are, in conjunction with the social division of labour, the source of all social solidarity. The analysis of changing forms of social solidarity in the course of a society's evolution implied the understanding of changes in collective representations and in the social division of labour. There are a number of features in Durkheim's notion of collective representations that are worth considering, in particular because these features make clear how collective representations both concur and differ from social representations as defined by Moscovici. These features also show clearly the connection between collective representations and the public sphere of communities where they are found.

Collective representations can be defined as a framework for thought and action that is homogeneously shared by a community. They comprise the ideations, emotions, rituals and customs enacted and carried by individuals but upon which individuals have little control. Considered by Durkheim as social facts, they confront individuals as an external force and have coercive power over them; fixed in the thought and rituals of social institutions, collective representations are resistant to change and social scrutiny. They exist in, and are handed down by, tradition, authority and institutions, which provide the centres of legitimation for what is known and what is not, what is acceptable and what is not, what defines the community and what is made pariah, alien to the community. Collective representations guarantee cohesion and homogeneity by circumscribing the social bond and making communities spaces of sameness. They protect communities from internal and external difference and constitute a resource for the preservation and survival of identities and ways of life. Indeed, of all forces and mechanisms which integrate and preserve the whole against fragmentation and disintegration perhaps no other phenomena is so powerful as collective representations, a social system of knowledge, emotion and action that is unquestioned by the members of a community as well as shared by all. Here the link between collective representations and conformity in the public sphere is clear. Collective representations mould, and in turn are moulded by, public spheres where the power of tradition and the emotional component of the social bond predominate, where it is difficult to dissent and to propose alternative views, where strong inequalities in status organise and govern the display of opinion and worldviews, where the authority of a few sacred people defines the access of others to knowledge and the legitimacy of worldviews. Strong hierarchies between interlocutors shape communication and the transmission of knowledge.

In this type of traditional public sphere, collective representations emerge as a type of everyday knowledge which all members share and which operates as a full binding force: they are produced through conditions of strong asymmetry between participants; they are strongly bound to, and dependent upon, ritual, and the conditions for their change are minimal. Collective representations are a type of knowledge resistant to experience, argumentation and logical proof, which relies mainly, if not purely, on the social bond and its subjective value. They have the force of a social fact in the Durkheimian sense, and fulfil functions of social integration and reproduction while guaranteeing a strong solidarity between those who share them. Here, the social knowledge constructed by a community in the form of collective representations constructs, in the sense of fully defining for participants, all reality. It is the social world that shapes and circumscribes all that exists, and the community, with its peculiar hierarchy, is the fundamental source of authority. In this type of community the social bond and the feelings of allegiance and obedience it entails have primacy over what happens to be the case and there is very little scope for individual variation. Here one can understand why Durkheim has been criticised for his tendency to speak of society as a homogeneous unity (Giddens 1971; Moscovici 1988). The claustrophobic nature of his over-totalising conception of the social is evident; the notion that society can also be conceptualised as a system where there is tension and contradiction between different groups, or collectives, is quite absent from his sociology (Giddens 1978).

Now it is obvious that this account of representations and the public sphere to which they correspond is no longer capable of capturing the complexity of most communities today. Whereas it would be plainly wrong to assume that collective representations and traditional communities have evaporated from the contemporary landscape, it is undeniable that very few communities, if any, live only by their collective representations. We know there are some few indigenous tribes in the Amazon that still live in total isolation; yet they are a very specific case in a world where new patterns of communication and exchange have redefined the production of knowledge and the understanding communities have about themselves and the world as whole. As mentioned earlier in this chapter, the dynamics of globalisation has redefined the nature of communication between human communities, the pace of change and the introduction of novelty coming from distant, remote others. In this context, traditions cannot remain impermeable; they are put under scrutiny, revised or fiercely defended and through this process precisely lose the unshakable and unquestioned form that defines them in the first place. This has been called detraditionalisation (Beck *et al.* 1994; Heelas *et al.* 1996), a process that blasts open the public sphere of communities to practices of contestation, argumentation and debate. In this type of detraditionalised public sphere, collective representations cannot survive intact and undergo processes of transformation. They become one amongst many other forms of knowledge.

Social representations: innovation and de-traditionalisation in the public sphere

As we have seen in Chapter 2, in elaborating the concept of social representations, Moscovici thought with and against Durkheim. With Durkheim he understood the power of representation to constitute an environment, to confront social actors as an external force, as a social fact. But Moscovici reached Durkheim via Piaget and from Piaget he drew the inspiration of what social psychology might be: a science of development and change rather than of reactions to fixed environments. In social representations therefore we find the struggle between tradition and innovation, between conformity and the rebellion of active minorities. As he recently wrote:

> when a new idea of scientific knowledge penetrates into the public sphere, the cultural life of a society, then you have a real *Kulturkampf*, cultural struggles, intellectual polemics and opposition between different modes of thinking . . . There is a drama involved in the process of transformation of knowledge and the birth of a new social representation.
>
> (Moscovici 2000a: 229)

Moscovici paid detailed attention to this drama, as did many other theorists of modernity. It is a drama that refers to the loss of traditional forms of knowing and behaving and the pains and gains associated with the birth of the new. It is a drama that presupposes a historical and sociological process and a social psychological one. How do societies move from a dominant traditional way of life to the increasingly open communicative patterns of modern societies? What makes the transition from the closed, sacred and ritualistic interrelations of traditional communities, to the open, secular and individualistic features of modern societies? This drama became widely known as the disenchantment of the world, a term proposed by Weber to designate the process whereby communities lose their close ties with the heavens above and the sacred nature of hierarchies below. Ceasing to look up to the skies – indeed Pascal famously remarked how arid had become a world where all the skies had to offer was silence – human communities sought in their own agency and resources, in their ability to communicate and act and in the resourceful and innovative character of their individual members, the responses to their needs and aspirations.

Disenchantment of the world: in this formulation rests the whole formula of the modern world, a world where reality contained no mysteries and became increasingly open to the scrutiny and rationality of the human mind. It is a particularly apt formulation for social psychological analysis as the idea of disenchantment contains a subtle and dual meaning: on the one hand it refers to the loss of magic and on the other to the loss of belief, utopias and hope. To become disenchanted is to be left without any recourse to the transcendental and at times healing powers of the mystical; it means to lose the ontological security offered by hierarchy, authority and belief. The counterpart of such loss is the experience of autonomy and the awareness of one's own power to make decisions and act.

Weber's view about the disenchantment of the world was unmistakably pessimistic – for he saw in the end of magic a concomitant increase in instrumentality and bureaucracy, and the modern world as incapable of replacing the old superstitions with anything that could offer meaning and unity to life. Moscovici, however, offers a redeeming reading of Weber's sociology by identifying in his account of modernisation three features that would also provide a basis for social representations: the problem of innovation, the importance of the individual and the power of active minorities. In addition, he puts processes of communication at the origin of representations and their transformations, which inserts the theory of social representations in a communicative and dialogical paradigm. Here modernity is seen as a contradictory process, open to utopian potentials that derive from the possibilities open by communication, innovation and the individual impetus.

Now this redeeming vision of modernity lies at the centre of Habermas' project and it is extensively discussed in the theory of communicative action. Habermas too is concerned with the drama between tradition and innovation and the changes in social solidarity. If social solidarity, or community, is not guaranteed by tradition and collective representations as before, will it disappear? Or can we find another source of social solidarity? Contra Weber, Habermas devotes his energies to demonstrate that in communication lay the potential source of social solidarity. While struggling to reach understanding in a world where taken-for-granted knowledge and rules come under scrutiny and are open to problematisation, social actors construct the dialogical bridges that are embedded in the structure of speech acts. Theoretically, Habermas' journey is strikingly similar to Moscovici's while transforming the concept of collective representations into social representations: he starts with both Mead and Durkheim as ancestors of a communicative turn and he resolves the critique levelled at Mead about the unaccounted origins of the generalised other by stating that the concept of collective consciousness/collective representations provides just that. In other words, at the origins of the phenomenon of the generalised other are collective representations as the archaic core of a community's collective identity.

Collective representations, however, have changed and thus there is a shift in the generalised other of communities in the modern world. Habermas calls this shift the 'linguistification of the lifeworld', a rather obscure term that probably suffers from the limitations of translating German into English. While the term might be obscure, the process to which it refers is well known: the linguistification of the lifeworld is not too different from what Weber called the disenchantment of the world; a gradual shift from religious symbolism and sacred rituals to the communicative practices that institute dialogue and criticisable claims to validity as the norm. That is to say, instead of accepting unquestioned social orders and reproducing them through sacred rituals, communities rely on dialogical communication sustained by principles of parity and equality in the public sphere. What is different in Habermas, however, is the genetic role of communication and language in the disenchantment of the world; the linguistification of the lifeworld is not only made of loss and bureaucratisation, but emerges as a redeeming process of communication. He sees in the very structure of speech acts the learning process that leads communities to rely less and less on the pre-established rules and norms of traditional lifeworlds. It is because interlocutors need to explain themselves and be accountable to each other that arguments and not authority acquire predominance in communication. Arguments in turn imply scrutiny and questioning of what is said; they expand the scope of interpretation and increase the need for justification. The sphere of personal autonomy and the differentiation of personal identities increase as the a priori power of traditional lifeworlds decreases.

It is thus in the disenchantment of the world and in the linguistification of lifeworlds that we find the larger contextual transformations that, in changing the everyday of communities, also change their processes of communication and the representational systems that circulate in their midst. Very few, if any, remain traditional in the sense described by Durkheim. Most communities today are permeated by the principles of detraditionalised public spheres where, at least ideally or in the word of law, members meet as peers and discuss and decide in conditions of equality, access is open to all and the procedures transparent and the legitimacy and subsequent authority of a proposition is established by argument and dialogue. In such detraditionalised public spheres social representations tend to replace collective representations insofar as they are a type of social knowledge formed by the mobility and diversity of social groups and by the reflexivity propitiated by the multiple encounters of different traditions. Representations in detraditionalised societies become social because communities today must handle the diversity of realities that constitutes their life horizons and find new symbolic strategies to make sense of them. Sense is attained, sustained and transformed in a manner which transcends the limitations traditionally imposed by tradition, where most communities have escaped from unquestionable historical orders and belief in a pre-given order of things has declined, or at least, lost some of its authority, and where voices of authority become themselves decentred and multiply, resting either on a variety of voices or, as in the case of most western industrialised societies, on self (Jovchelovitch and Gervais 1999; Wagner *et al.* 1999, 2000). The diversity of worldviews that circulates in communities today renews the symbolic content of representational systems and brings to the fore the expression of variety and its concomitant phenomena. This makes clear that social representations are as much about shared and consensual symbolic codes as they are about contradictory and unresolved ones.

This is especially important in social representations theory. In opting for 'social' and dropping 'collective' Moscovici was guided by the problem of plurality and the renewed importance of communication in modern societies, where worldviews and practices are contested and negotiated, and the space for a homogeneous, unquestioned and single view of the world is very limited indeed. In 1988 he wrote:

> it seems an aberration, in any case, to consider representations as homogenous and shared as such by a whole society. What we wished to

emphasise by giving up the word collective was this plurality of representations and their diversity within a group. . . . In effect, what we had in mind were representations that were always in the making, in the context of inter-relations and actions that were themselves always in the making.

(Moscovici 1988: 219)

Moscovici's acute observation came full circle some 25 years after the publication of *La Psychanalyse, son Image et son Public*. It is an observation made possible by the development of his theory of active minorities in the 1970s and his superb study on Durkheim and Weber in the 1980s. It allows us to go back to the thread that unifies Moscovici's work and provides the foundation for his social psychology of knowledge: how communities change and how this change becomes incorporated into the social representations that sustain our relationships and our lives.

4 The forms and functions of knowledge

What makes knowledge knowledge? This is the question that Plato addresses in Theaetetus, the dialogue in which Socrates uses his 'midwifery'[1] skills to extract from the title character the features of what constitutes knowledge. Plato never offered a full-blown definition of knowledge in the dialogue, even though he did expose with great clarity his method – maieutics – for seeking knowledge and constructing his epistemology. Socrates' famous disavowal of knowledge – I don't have that which I am pursuing, 'I myself am barren of wisdom' – still resonates today as we struggle with definitions of what constitutes knowledge and who is comfortable declaring it as a possession. From Plato to Descartes, the question of what makes knowledge knowledge is still very much with us. As Habermas stated at the very beginning of *Knowledge and Human Interests*:

> if we imagine the philosophical discussion of the modern period recon-
> structed as a judicial hearing, it would be deciding a single question:
> how is reliable knowledge (Erkenntnis) possible. The term theory of
> knowledge or epistemology was coined only in the 19th century; but the
> subject that it retrospectively denotes is the subject of modern philo-
> sophy in general, at least until the threshold of the 19th century.
> (Habermas 1987: 3)

That Habermas should use a legal metaphor is indicative of how contested this history is. Yet some themes have been constant throughout and there is one that matters a great deal to the social psychologist: for many the trick behind the construction of true knowledge seems to be the progressive detachment of the internal structures of knowing from the subjects, com-munities and cultures that give knowledge its substance and its *raison d'être*. While we know that this project has not evolved without antinomies, there remains a paradox in our relation to knowledge: on the one hand there is knowledge, objective, rational, cognitive; on the other hand there is life, subjective, emotional, at times, irrational.

It is out of this paradox that the idea emerges that there is only one 'true' knowledge, which we achieve after many years of development and study, as we learn as individuals and as societies, to leave aside the noises of affection and belonging. In our contemporary societies this 'true' knowledge, a Platonic/Cartesian knowledge capable of describing and understanding the world as it is, tends to be considered a prerogative of science and is usually separated from contexts of everyday life. If you are a housewife, a five-year-old child, or a peasant living in a rural community in the Peruvian Andes you are likely to hold lay beliefs, ideologies, myths, or superstitions, but not knowledge. The notion of local knowledge, which has recently emerged to describe the knowledge of communities and local peoples is an exception, but as I discuss later why does it need the adjective local? The fact remains that it is science, and science alone, that has been able to claim the authority and power associated with true knowledge.

There is of course a problem with this view. As soon as we start researching knowledge as a practice, the ideal of a 'true' knowledge deprived of its life content fails to survive. Agencies such as motivations, emotions, unconscious affects and social interests that are usually considered deficiencies in knowledge irretrievably find their way into knowledge practices and show that under the search for the objective there are other layers of meaning linked to subjective, intersubjective and cultural worlds. These, rather then being pathologies or noises in the system, are in fact utterly routine occurrences, which need to be understood and unpacked as integral to the formation of knowledge. The separation between knowledge and life does not withstand the empirical examination of knowledge practices and remains, to use Lévy-Bruhl's apt formulation, a desideratum, not a fact.

In this chapter I seek to counteract this separation by developing a framework to understand the different forms and functions of knowledge in social life. My starting point is that knowledge is a plural and plastic phenomenon whose genesis and transformation need to be understood in relation to the social psychology of contexts of knowing and the concomitant variability of representational processes. The analysis of the representational form shows that its architecture rests on intersubjective and interobjective triads (self–other–object) whose realisation in social life gives texture and form to both community and representation. These triads constitute, in their most elementary form, contexts of knowing; these contexts vary as different communities, holding different types of public spheres, produce different representational processes. Thus the social psychology of knowledge contexts can say a great deal about the different forms of knowledge that circulate in social life.

While self–other–object relations constitute the architecture of representation and community, it is representation that constitutes the architecture of all knowledge. Our reality has no smooth and direct passage to knowledge – it must be represented and communicated in language. Representation, language and communication are the only path to knowledge we have. The representational, linguistic and communicative resources of knowledge systems are intrinsically intertwined and show that acts of knowing cannot, however much one tries, be completely disconnected from their human source. Our knowledge of the world depends on representational processes; as mediating structures bridging the world of subjects and the world of objects they deeply affect the structure of knowledge. Knowledge in this sense is neither a copy of the world nor is it the world but it is in the world. Knowledge systems are proposals of the world – literally, representations – whose processes of construction we need to understand and to unpack if we are to understand their complexity and variability in social life.

Exploring the variability of knowledge systems and defining them as proposals of the world does not entail equating all forms of knowing or failing to appreciate their differences and their capacity to grasp the object-world. Let me say again that bringing context back to the study of knowledge and interrogating its connection with persons, communities and cultures is not synonymous with a wild relativism where all knowledges become accepted and relevant. What I am proposing here is to engage in an exercise of recognising diversity for the sake of understanding that what seems to us as 'the one and only ideal type' is in fact just one amongst many types. Decentration of perspective is what I propose here by identifying the ways of knowing persons and communities deploy in different situations and depending on the psychological, social and cultural circumstances in which they find themselves. This of course does not preclude our capacity of being critical towards different knowledge systems, allowing comparisons to be established and hopefully constructing productive dialogues that can alter and expand the boundaries of a system of knowing. Recognition of diversity does not mean blind acceptance of all there is; it does, however, imply an ethical commitment to recognise others and engage in a dialogue with what they propose, even if what they propose is eventually unacceptable.

In order to address these issues I shall begin exploring the social psychology of contexts of knowing through a consideration of the different dimensions of representational processes, the 'who', 'how', 'why', 'what' and 'what for' of representation. I examine these dimensions in some detail, linking them back to the threefold architecture of representational systems: the subjective, interrelational and objective. I go on to discuss the different functions knowledge systems fulfil in social life – the 'what for' of representations – exploring identity, social memory, community, anticipation/future-making, and ideology. I then elaborate further the social psychology of collective and social representations, relating these different modalities of representation to different forms of knowing. These steps intend to shed light on the problem of variation in the forms of knowledge by (a) using the analytical categories of the social psychology of contexts to identify different forms of knowing; and (b) considering what a form of knowledge wants through the analysis of its representational aims, or responding to the question 'what does this type of knowledge want to represent?'

Dimensions of representation: 'who', 'how', 'why', 'what' and 'what for'

In order to explore the different forms and functions of knowledge, let us start by considering the social psychology of contexts of knowing and how it is related to different modalities of representation. Having accepted that the work of representation frames knowledge we need to go beyond this general formulation and ask under which particular conditions of representation a knowledge system is produced and sustained. To this end, we need a framework capable of giving an account of how the work of representation is actually realised in social life, that is, what is the particular architecture of self–other–object relations that gives rise to different representational processes. Interrelations between self–other–object are not always identical, nor are the types of communication that define how partners in interaction take each other on board while engaging with the object world. There is a diversity of issues to be considered including the status and positioning of partners, the emotional bond between partners and how partners establish symmetries and asymmetries in dialogue. All are part of the social, emotional and communicative bricks of the representational processes that structure the social psychological properties of communities and ultimately define the form of a knowledge system. These are also bound, as seen in Chapter 3, to the type of public sphere of a community.

In examining the architecture of self–other–object relations that forms representation I draw on the notion of 'architecture of intersubjectivity', found in Rommetveit's (1974, 1984) work on language and communication. Rommetveit makes clear that beyond the propositional content of utterances there is a social psychological dimension – an intersubjective architecture – that is ultimately responsible for the meaning and form they take in social life. The manifest, objective content of speech acts rests on the subjacent communicative strategies that are used by interlocutors within particular social psychological contexts of interaction. Utterances communicate more than content; they have pitch and intonation, they are uttered within circumscribed social relations where it matters if they who speak are a child, a teacher, a parent or an elderly person. Rommetveit's analysis provides an illuminating account of how these intersubjective relations at the micro-level are intertwined with the very structure of language at the macro-level. He shows that the intersubjective and the particular form of the relations it entails constitute the architecture of communication and language. We need to unpack the former to understand the latter. His analysis is particularly apposite for the purposes of my discussion here. It is consistent with the understanding of representations as threefold structures and calls for the analysis of the three dimensions of representations: the affective or personal dimension, which corresponds to the emotional bond between partners; the intersubjective dimension, which corresponds to the status and position of partners as well as to the nature of the dialogue they establish; and finally, the objective dimension, which corresponds to the construction of the object-world.

The framework I suggest in the following pages seeks to capture how the work of representation is realised in social life by asking questions about the constituents of the representational process and the intersubjective and interobjective triads that form its basic architecture. These are questions referring to the actors, the communicative practices, the object, the reasons and the functions of representations, or what I call the 'who', 'how', 'what', 'why' and 'what for' of contexts of knowing. In this framework representation is not purely the content it proposes about the object nor is it a purely cognitive and mental act. Representation emerges as a complex and rich social psychological process involving social actors who hold identities and emotional lives (which are indeed constructed in the act of representing), who engage in relationships with others (whose nature shapes what and how they come to know the world), who have reasons to do what they do, and in so doing enact the purposes of what they do. Representation here is a practice, which implies relation and communication and in this way imprints on the heart of knowledge the same relational and communicative structures that make it in the first place. In the 'who', 'how', 'why', 'what' and 'what for' of contexts of knowing we find not only the dynamic components of representational processes but also central social psychological categories: identity and intersubjective structures; communication and practices; attribution, justifications and functions. The very diversity of these processes explains the diversity of knowledge and offers insights into the different 'desires to represent' behind a knowledge system.

Identity and the 'who' of representation

The question of who is doing the representational work and in relation to which significant others this work is taking place is central to define the conditions of representability of a knowledge system. The 'who' of knowledge takes us back to the problem of identity and to the process whereby actors represent both themselves and others as they engage in acts of knowing (Jovchelovitch 1996; Duveen 2001b). It relates not only to identity, both individual and social, but also to the positioning and the status of subjects in the social field. Representations are always constructed by someone in relation to someone else (Jodelet 1989, 1991) and this dynamics is fully present in the representational outcome. Every representation is linked to the effort of persons and communities to represent *themselves,* even if this subjective representation is intended to be actively withdrawn as in the case of science. Representations bring together the identity, culture and history of a group of people. They inscribe themselves in social memories and in narratives and frame the feelings of belonging that reaffirm to individual members their grounding in a human space. There is no process of knowing that does not project the identity and the project of the knower and this constitutes a central social psychological dimension of contexts of knowing.

It is in this sense that we can see that knowledge also seeks to represent the persons who carry it and put it into use. Understanding how much a knowledge system seeks to do just that is one of the key indicators of what type of knowledge is at hand. Some knowledge systems are heavily dependent on the identity of knowers and desire more than anything else to project this identity in the social field. In this case, the predominant representational aim is related to identity and the desire behind the epistemic act is to represent the persons or the communities involved. At times representations have more to do with representers and less to do with the object being represented, a case of preponderance of the 'who' over the 'what' of representations.

Traditional knowledge systems, such as myth and collective representations, are good examples of that. What these systems of knowing seek to do, for most of the time, is to represent the object-world through the lenses of identity, so that the identity of the community is projected, sustained and reaffirmed in the dynamics of representational processes. What matters in these cases is to guarantee the continuation of traditions and the knowledge of 'who we are'; it is a logic ruled by the force of the subjective.

Other knowledge systems, alternatively, make strong efforts to bracket out the identity of knowers, and produce a representation of the object-world that can go beyond its dependence on locale and the subjectivity of knowers. The clearest example of this type of knowing is science, whose method of operation is entirely devoted to the process of distanciation between knower and knowedge, or what Bachelard (1938) described as breaking away from one's first and immediate experience. Scientific knowledge makes a tremendous effort to exile the subjectivity that produces it, even if it consistently fails to achieve this aim (Knorr-Cetina and Mulkay 1983; Latour 1987; Latour and Woolgar 1996). While social studies of science have convincingly shown that scientists are far from being the dispassionate operators they want (or pretend) to be, nevertheless there remains the desire, the systematic effort to withdraw identity. Between what science wants and what it manages to achieve there is obviously a gap, but there can be no doubt that processes of distanciation between subjects and the object-world for the sake of a better approximation are at the heart of the scientific enterprise.

Thus the position of actors in the representational process and how they engage in the representational effort allows comparison and understanding of the different textures of systems of knowing and the weight of subjective dimensions in processes of knowledge construction. It also shows that investing knowledge with emotional dimensions and the identity of knowers does not necessarily disqualify a knowledge system. It just gives to it different functions and aims in social life while demonstrating the importance these have. Indeed when knowledge systems relate to affect and identity they are usually fulfilling functions of identity maintenance, social integration, cooperation and reproduction of cultures.

Communication and the 'how' of representation

As much as the 'who' of representation provides insights on what a system of knowledge wants to do in social life, the 'how' of representation can inform the different manners in which actors communicate and interact to produce the representation in question. Communication and interaction are thus the 'how' of representational processes; representations are always produced in communicative action and the analysis of communication is central to define modalities of representation and the form and functions of a knowledge system. In Moscovici's original formulation the study of social representations was conducted as a study on how different communicative strategies shaped social representations of psychoanalysis; diffusion, propagation and propaganda were the communicative genres he considered when investigating representational outcomes (Moscovici 1961, 1976b). It can be said that without communication there is no representation and representational processes are an achievement of communication. Acknowledging communicative action as the central unit of analysis in the representational form is an important theoretical step to link knowledge and context and reveal its social and psychological underpinnings. At the same time, the analysis of communication mediating the triads that form representation shows with great clarity the malleability of knowing and its dependency on processes of interaction.

Issues related to the 'how' of representation have been examined in detail by anthropological, sociological and psychological traditions concerned with differences between knowledge systems. As discussed before, these different disciplines were very much unified around this concern at the beginning of the twentieth century when examining the differences between 'primitive and civilised', 'adult and children', 'individual and crowd', 'sane and mad'. Whereas today we can spot a clear normalising ring to these types of comparison, the theoretical problem they sought to address then continues to matter now and is at the core of the approach I am seeking to develop in this book: how patterns of communication and interaction can shape a certain outlook and knowledge of the world. Thus we need to understand the position of the child and her patterns of communication and interaction with both peers and adults if we are to understand the shape and developmental trajectory of the knowledge she constructs (Doise *et al.* 1975; Perret-Clermont 1980; Doise and Mugny 1984; Piaget 1995a). Equally, can we identify a specific type of interaction and communication in the aetiology of madness? Freud thought we could. And what is the architecture of intersubjectivity in the crowd that makes it into a distinctive site for the production of knowledge, even if it is of an 'irrational' kind, as it has been usually described? In studying these exemplary cases social scientists thought they could demonstrate, as discussed in Chapter 2, the intertwinement between a system of knowledge, the type of representation underlying it and the specific self–other relation that produced it. How do people talk to each other, within which kind of context and with which powers? Are dialogues symmetrical or asymmetrical, do they involve turn taking and recognition of perspectives or the imposition of one voice over another? From mutualities to asymmetries in dialogue, from face-to-face communication in conditions of everyday life to large communication systems, from social constraint to cooperation, from propaganda, to persuasion and to diffusion, different styles of communication shape the representational outcome and the form of a knowledge system.

Whereas there is little doubt that communication and social interaction shape representation, the real question in this discussion remains that of how different kinds of social interaction lead to different representational outcomes. What features need to be present in social interactions to produce the type of representation at the basis of science? And what features of social interaction lead to representations at the basis of belief? Piaget has considered at length the impact of two extreme types of social interaction – social constraint and cooperation – on the formation of knowledge, an issue that Duveen and his collaborators continue to explore systematically in a diversity of studies ranging from how the structuration of the classroom shapes children's knowledge of the curriculum to how specific patterns of interaction and communication between children and between adults and children frame learning and knowledge production in childhood (Duveen 1997, 2002a, 2002b; Leman 1998, 2002; Leman and Duveen 1999; Ivinson and Duveen 2005; Psaltis and Duveen forthcoming). Piaget's analysis of these two kinds of interaction locates the genesis of creative knowledge and the genesis of an autonomous personality in the establishment of cooperative relations based on the gradual construction of reciprocity of perspectives and reversibility. That is to say, the child learns that her interlocutor is another person in their own right and that rules and obligations apply reciprocally to partners in interaction, and it is only in learning this that the child comes to know at all. Equally, it is when the child realises the reversibility of operations – that, for instance, if she has a brother, her brother also has a sister – that she starts to understand the relational nature of all that exists and develops a form of knowledge that is able of escaping from the restrictions of imitation to co-create the world that is being discovered. Cooperation implies mutuality in dialogue and reciprocity of perspective while social constraint implies asymmetry, unidirectional communication and imposition of perspective, which may or may not be linked to lack of recognition of the position of the other. That is why Piaget argued so eloquently that logic and rationality are fundamentally social.

Rommetveit's (1974) detailed observations on the architecture of intersubjectivity in autistic and schizophrenic thought constitute another instance of how communication and interaction shape the representational outcome, a point stressed by Marková and her collaborators in their studies of dialogue (Marková and Foppa 1991; Marková *et al.* 1995). Rommetveit's argument draws on the work of family analysts such as Bateson and Watzlawick, who studied the world of autism and schizophrenia and found a sociality made of ambivalent interactions replete with contradictory I–you relationships. They named these types of interactions 'double binds', marked by messages that are given together despite being contradictory and mutually exclusive. Classical psychological examples of these double-bind interactions are situations between mother and child where there is verbal invitation for expression of affection without a correspondent bodily gesture and facial expression. The words communicate what the body does not, and the reaction of the interlocutor – here the child – is bound to fail: if they connect with one of the binds, they cannot connect with the other. It is a no-no situation, which leaves the child without a way out. These interactions shape the possible outlook towards the outside world and explain why in this situation the very connection between person and outside reality is compromised: what comes from the other does not reassure my assumptions, it confuses me and makes me doubt at every step what is really going on. Without the ontological security the other provides, the knowledge of self withdraws to a world of her own and 'he does not know what is real anymore because the very foundation of intersubjectivity seems to have broken down' (Rommetveit 1974: 53).

Hsu's (1999) study on the different styles of knowing in Chinese medicine is yet another example of how the form and content of knowledge are directly linked to the manner in which actors relate to each other in the process of knowing. She identifies at least three different modes of transmission – secret, personal and standardised – describing relations between masters and medical practitioners and their apprentices. Each mode of transmission leads to a different set of practices and knowledge, all comprising what is known as Chinese medicine. These different modes indicate that, rather than being a homogeneous field of notions, Chinese medical knowledge is made of the different styles and modes of transmission that vary according to the different social settings in which Chinese medicine is enacted and taught. In her study we have strong evidence that even in systems of knowledge deemed traditional there is variation and plurality of styles.

Common to the examples above is the consideration of symmetries and asymmetries in the self–other dialogue, how these lead to different communicative patterns and are dealt with in the interaction. Horizontal and vertical patterns of communication constitute prototypical forms to consider self–other interactions. Indeed, the pyramid has constituted a classical architectural metaphor to describe intersubjective contexts made of asymmetry and unidirectional transmission of knowledge. Patterns of communication marked by asymmetry tend to be associated with social constraint and modalities of representation that provoke 'closure' in knowledge.

Belief, myths and ideology, albeit not identical, can be described as knowledge of this kind. Belief systems tend to be transmitted by deep-seated cultural practices, have little malleability and openness to change and strongly resist variation arising from plurality of perspective. Myth, while being open to marginal variation (Blumenberg 1985), also keeps its core unchanged, as it moves through time and space. The asymmetry in self–other relations that produces them arises from recognition of the social bond and commitment to the tradition that frames the unequal position between self and other, which can be based on gender, age or recognised wisdom, amongst others. Here the asymmetry is not necessarily linked to abuse of power, violence or domination; rather it is an asymmetry recognised and legitimised by the power of the social bond that gives to some social actors authority over others. This is internalised by all actors and translated into the relationship between self and other.

Ideology is yet another form of knowledge that relies heavily on the systematic use of asymmetry. Yet, in the case of ideology systematic asymmetry in the power of interlocutors is used to dominate, and it is domination that frames and determines the relations between self and other. As Thompson (1990) argued in his reappraisal of the concept, the study of ideology focuses on the connections between meaning and relations of power, and in particular on how meaning is used to establish and sustain relations of domination. Through a style of communication (or miscommunication) systematically distorted by domination (Habermas 1992), ideology is a form of knowing that bends knowledge towards the perspective of the oppressor and tends to distort the object world (through hyper-representation) using legitimation, dissimulation, unification, reification and fragmentation as strategies. Ideological narratives such as the ones contained in the James Bond films, analysed by Eco (1966), can entertain and at the same time convey a precise reading of the world that relies on the power of certain actors over others to be sustained. The ideological texture of the Bond films relies on a narrative where the same distorted discourses are repeated again and again: there are a number of moves, where Bond, M, the villain and the women appear to each other, check each other and pose challenges to each other. These are resolved in terms of a number of simple binary oppositions, where Bond is tempted by woman, as he consumes and saves her; is challenged by a villain, a foreigner who went uncontrolled by his own government, with a menacing accent and an army of robotic people ready to follow, as he first succumbs and eventually conquers him; and a final move where all the properly instituted powers of the world unite, dissolve differences and restore an idyllic situation where Bond consumes woman. As funny and as entertaining as they may be, these narratives have nothing innocent about them: they represent the power of some over others and use meaning to make this state of affairs stick.

In examining these different possibilities it is important to note that not all asymmetry involves coercion and domination and truly symmetrical relationships are rare, indeed very difficult to find, in social life. Constructing horizontal communicative patterns is usually an action that requires resolve and determination to bracket out asymmetries, and in this resolve we find again the issue of recognising the position and perspective of the other who is different from us. Symmetry in the dialogue between self and other, where the perspective and position of interlocutors are recognised by partners in interaction, is associated with cooperation and tends to produce modalities of representation that 'open' the structure of knowledge, leading to awareness of differences and alternatives. Social representations and science constitute knowledge systems of these kind[2]; in the case of social representations, because it is a form of common sense that is made of different modalities of knowing, which are mixed and combined in polyphasic representational fields, and in the case of science, because it is aware of its own lacunae and relies on doubt and verification to establish its propositional content. Here, the very symmetry between partners in communication is indicative that there are no monological understandings of the world; if the intersubjective architecture recognises and takes into account plurality of perspective, this plurality finds its way into the very structures of the knowledge produced.

The architecture of intersubjectivity and the type of communicative action it involves constitutes thus an essential dimension of contexts of knowing and is essential to understand how representations are shaped. Understanding how self and other interact and communicate reveals yet another facet of knowledge structures. Through different styles of communication and interaction representations produce different systems of knowledge, which express in their very form the nature of communication and interaction between self and other. Symmetrical and asymmetrical architectures can open and close knowledge systems, defining the content and functions they pursue in social life.

Reason and the 'why' of representation

Representational processes, as I have been arguing, represent much more than the object-world. They invest logos with a polyvalent structure containing subjective and intersubjective dimensions. In this sense, the 'why' of representation goes far beyond its cognitive function, to include the symbolic function and all it allows in terms of representability: it represents the logic of subjectivity and intersubjectivy and in this sense it is always open to express motives and intentions that are ruled by unconscious processes and affects and the dynamics between partners in interaction. The 'why' of representations indicates first and foremost the rationality of meaning and the desire invested[3] in that meaning, something I indicated in Chapter 1 while discussing representational processes as potential spaces. The symbolic function of representations opens knowledge to the logic of the unconscious and the work of condensation and displacement that goes with it. In this sense we can speak of an epistemic drive where desire to know is propelled by personal and emotional logics that may be more or less identifiable within knowledge systems.

Let us consider science in this regard, for it is a type of representation normally thought capable of avoiding subjectivity. It is perhaps to Bachelard (1938, 1971, 1987) that we owe the best characterisation of how the logic of desire and unconscious affects penetrates the formation of logos in science. He shows that the development of epistemic structures, and the construction of science, cannot be sharply separated from the affects, memories and existential grounding that make up the life of the mind and lead to scientific creativity. There is a psychoanalysis of scientific discovery to be written out of the hidden motivations that are behind technological and scientific advances: traces of our desire to fly, to enter forbidden territories, our feelings of control and omnipotence in relation to nature, and indeed in relation to the very creation of human life, not to mention the darker desire to destroy and to eradicate, these are just some of the emotions sublimated in the work of science. Whereas it is in other modalities of representation that we tend to find the emotional component of representational processes clearly dominant, a more in-depth analysis of scientific representation shows that it is not immune to the investments of our feelings and unconscious desire. Science uses sublimation to subordinate emotion to the needs of a more detached episteme, but it does not fully escape from it. Indeed, lurking behind its achievements are old human wants and logics that the logic of science itself should learn to understand.

Whereas even the logic of science betrays the hidden logic of symbolic processes, in the rationality of myth they are fully exposed and reveal, usually in dramatic ways, the unconscious grammar that institutes communities and individual persons. Myths are systems of knowing the world that can account for the genesis, development and characteristics of families, communities and nations, firms and organisations and the very trajectory of individual persons. Caring nothing for the literal, myth is a form of knowing defined first and foremost for its intentions (Barthes 1973). The 'why' of any mythology is to produce a system of signification that can invoke and teach the motivation that put it into motion in the first place. In doing so, myth distorts or even disregards altogether the reality of the world outside, which rather than diminish its force constitutes the main source of its power. The power of myth as knowledge lies precisely in its capacity to provide lenses to understand and to maintain those dimensions of human life not so easily captured by other systems of knowing in a way that is comforting, reassuring and imaginatively liberating. The theory of the 'big bang' or the meeting between the sperm and the ovum are not quite the answer for the curiosity of five year olds about the origins of the earth or the more pressing question of 'where did I come from?' Mythologies, tales and legends can fulfil needs that belong to a register where accuracy is not required.

It is thus the symbolic function of representations that houses the underlying reasons and logic that contribute to the specific rationality of different knowledge systems. Using symbols to give meaning, representational labour carries in itself the complex dynamics of processes of signification and all they entail as mediators between persons and the object world. Symbols can retain a measured relation to the object, as in the work of science, or invest it with excessive signification, as in the case of myths and religious traditions. In both cases, however, their mode of operation invests the construction of knowledge with the logic of affects and desire, whose traces are left behind even when there is active effort to exclude them from the process of representation. This rationality not always conforms perfectly to accuracy in cognition, nor can be assessed by its internal connection to argumentation and doubt. It is a rationality based on different logics that vary from commitment to the knowledge system itself, as it is the case with most belief systems, specially mythological and religious ones, to the need to sublimate and work through the dynamics of unconscious affects.

The recognition of multiple rationalities behind symbolic representation invests the constitution of knowledge with the positive value of imagination and the productive impact of potential spaces. An excessive conformity to what is the case interrupts the labour of creativity and closes the development of knowledge to dimensions of the not-yet-conscious or not-yet-become (Bloch 1986, 1988). In dreams, play, art and narratives lies the unrealised potential of human knowledge and the need to acknowledge the shadows and gaps of what is known. Without opening the analysis of knowledge to its as yet unrealised dimensions, expressed in projects and the formulation of futures, we fail to capture the human inspirations that are incubated in the anticipatory function of representation, which I address later in the chapter.

The object and the 'what' of representation

The 'what' of representations refers to the construction of the object, the content ascribed to it, and the solidity of symbolic environments. Whereas there can be no doubt that the object world is always a product of human action, this does not make it less objective and 'hard'. Our human reality is socially constructed not only because we want, but also because we have to: the world in itself exists only as empty ideation. The world needs to become *for* us and through our own labour and representation it is *made* into our human reality. That it is made, however, does not make it a less objective reality. Controversies that oppose the permanence of the object-world to the idea of a socially constructed reality simply fail to appreciate that these are not mutually exclusive. Berger and Luckman (1966) made this point convincingly some 40 years ago. Indeed it is ironic, to say the least, that some of the views on social constructivism that emerged during the 1990s are combined with the denial of an objective world, as if that which we humans construct could not lead to a solid outcome. Constructing solidity in the world is, however, a major task of human cultures, one that only our species fully engages in, a tremendous achievement of both our psychological, social and cultural lives.

The solidity of the object introduces into representational processes the materiality of the world as an objective reality, instituted in time and space as the provisional, and yet stable, set of coordinates against which and within which we act. Without the solidity of the object, representations would be a game of wondering signifiers; without the checks and balances that come from the social world as instituted reality the very production of meaning would be compromised. It would be a situation analogous to the pre-objectal child whose actions are seen as the sole maker of the world and who sees the object as a function of her own behaviour. Understanding the 'what' of representations helps to understand that there is a history and a trajectory belonging to the issues we engage with and the objects we try to capture and that other people before us and around us have engaged in similar efforts. This history constitutes an environment that, in its turn, captures us and throws into our self-interpretation the endurance of the social fact. It shows that the object has the power of fact to the psychic subject; it imposes itself and demands recognition. All knowledge systems deal with the solidity and historicity of the object, albeit in different ways.

Objects are always represented in conditions that presuppose previous stocks of representation as there are very few objects in the social world that have not been represented before. Everyday forms of knowledge such as social representations draw on previously established content through processes of anchoring, which is an attempt to connect the object with the past and its significations. Anchoring expresses a certain tendency to retrieve and to conserve meaning since it is a return to a familiar signification that can help the unfamiliar to be made familiar. The content of the first representations about AIDS defined the then new phenomenon as a plague, revealing in a single theme the array of fears and practices that were to come in the wake of the disease. By calling it a plague, AIDS was connected to the history of epidemics, and to the practices, ideas and sentiments pertaining to their trajectory. It matters a great deal if representations are about peace or about AIDS, if they are about an ethnic community or about a dominant group, if they are about the cosmos or about suicide, if they are about friendship or about the Israeli–Palestinian conflict. In each one of these objects there is a whole reality to unpack; it is a reality made of knowledges, people and practices that came before and which, gradually, solidify themselves in the texture and reality of the object. This is what objectification is about.

Whereas one of the main tasks of the object is to express the resilience of the objective world, it also serves as a platform against which new points of departure are constructed and imagined. Without acknowledgement of the object there is no innovation and radical departure. In all forms of representation there is a battle between the history of the object and the intention of capturing the object anew, to entangle what has been in an altogether new network of signification. The object as it is now provides the material against which representational processes develop over time constructing projects and new representational possibilities, the world of the not-yet-known. In the shadow of the object is the impetus that propels social actors to know more and to find out more about either unseen or badly understood angles. It is this shadow that moves scientific representation and its desire to capture the object in its entirety, to 'cannibalise' it as it were, and it is the same shadow that puts the construction of social representations into motion when social actors try to make the unfamiliar familiar.

The understanding of content and its importance in the configuration of a knowledge system is another dimension related to the 'what' of represen-tations. Content matters because the themes, ideas and significations expressed in a representation reveal the symbolic links that are established by social actors and the resources that are brought to bear in the formu-lations they construct about the object-world. The 'what' of knowledge is symbolic: it is grounded on representational processes that use symbols to signify, to convey meaning. There is a long tradition that dismisses content in favour of processes in the understanding of representational systems as if what people have to say about something mattered less than how they say it. In fact the 'what' is related to the 'how' and it is in conjunction that they need to be understood. Systems of signification, which express the content of the object, are intertwined to processes of constructing signification.

Understanding the object is thus central to the understanding of repre-sentational processes and how they define a knowledge system. In the 'what' of representation we find the double-edged character of meaning construction: on the one hand, representational processes actively construct the object-world, are an instituting energy that creates the object. On the other hand they are constrained by their very creation, i.e. by the historicity and solidity of the object, expressed in the institutionalisation of represen-tations and in the ability of certain meanings to stick and perpetuate themselves over time. Both are integral to the process of signification and reveal themselves through the content of representations. Processes of institutionalisation are themselves intertwined with the dual, and frequently contradictory, manner in which representations operate: they are instituting and instituted. They create representational orders and at the same time stabilise them, 'thickening' and reproducing symbolic worlds.

Making the unfamiliar familiar: function and the 'what for' of representation

The most fundamental function of all representation is to deal with the unknown and make the unfamiliar familiar. Representations bridge the distance between social actors and the world by creating sense, tools and understanding; they tame the object world and make it known. They create familiarity and respond to old and deep-seated needs of feeling at home in the world. It can be said that the drive towards logos, the epistemological drive, is fuelled by psychological energies associated with return, with making an inhospitable world homely and secure again. In all representation and in all knowledge, be it science, belief or myth, amongst other forms, there is desire to capture, to encompass and to understand the unfamiliarity of the world.

Out of this desire arise more specific functions of representational processes, which correspond to central dimensions of our social and personal worlds. As instruments of knowledge and communication, representations construct self and reality proper without which we would be unable to develop either a personal identity or the social worlds in which we live. As systems of shared understanding of the world, representations offer the patterns of cognition and recognition, dispositions, orientations and conduct that make a social environment home for individual actors and allows them to know the rules of the game. Solidified in cultural practices and in institutions, they provide resources for the construction of social identities and for the reproduction and renewal of societies. They allow us to recognise the effectiveness of what we say and what we do and are the source of the 'already-there' rules and roles that make possible the development of personalities and individual initiatives. Both the general and specific functions of representations are an outcome of the symbolic function and involve the power to name, to identify and to categorise. In constructing what is real for a group of people, representational orders express identity, frame thinking and action, allow communication and social integration, create the memory of social groups and institute projects. The general functions of representations respond to fundamental social psychological problems and make human life, as we know it, possible.

These general functions of representations translate into social psychological dimensions that are constitutive of contexts of knowing. They are directly related to the other dimensions of the representational context and underlying each we find indications of the aims and objectives of different types of knowing in social life, of what a knowledge system wants. The dimensions I want to emphasise here are identity, community, social memory, future making/anticipation and ideology.[4] As discussed in previous chapters, they are all present in knowledge systems, as there is no system of knowing that does not seek to represent identity, community, past and future as well as to hold enough power to institute itself over time. In previous chapters I have considered in more detail the dimensions of identity, community and social memory. Let me add here a brief word about the future-making and ideological function of representations.

Representations seek to construct knowledge of the future cognitively, socially and emotionally. Cognitively they do so through the construction of projects, which correspond to cognitive anticipations of things to come; socially, through the construction of utopias, which correspond to the projection of visions about how things should be in times to come, and emotionally through the experience of hope, which corresponds to the emotional field in which anticipation operates. Project, utopia and hope are the constitutive elements of the anticipatory function of representations and are present mainly in knowledge systems open to the future and to the unknown. Whereas a great deal of knowledge construction is driven by backward energies linked to the past and to trajectories that remain active in the present, there is a dimension of the process that is disposed forwards, towards the not-yet-conscious and not-yet-become, the categories Bloch described when examining anticipatory consciousness (Bloch 1986). Valsiner (2003) has examined this function at considerable length. His theory of enablement seeks to capture precisely the role of social representations in adjusting present–future transactions. It is because representations operate forwards that social actors are enabled to act and to recast the constraints of the past in such a way that the dynamic of personal, societal and cultural change can be observed.

Representations fulfil ideological functions when they intersect with power struggles in representational fields. It is clear that not all representational systems hold the same power; unequally equipped social actors use the different levels of power they hold to exert influence and achieve goals. When there is a systemic use of asymmetry in power to dominate others, we can say that a representational system becomes ideology and there is a preponderance of the ideological function. This is the case with representational systems such as racism. Racism cares little for the reality of the object it seeks to represent, as its main representational purpose is segregation, exclusion and defamation of the other. Racism is a knowledge system dominated by the ideological function and in this sense it can be called ideology. All representational systems can be permeated by the ideological function and be used to dominate, but that does not mean to say that all representations are ideological. When representations contribute to distort and obscure what is going on in order to dominate, they become ideology, but there is more than domination and distortion in representational fields.

In making the unfamiliar familiar, all representations draw on the identity, community, memory, anticipatory and ideological functions. These are intrinsic to knowledge and are at the heart of the symbolic function itself. They show that all knowledge is made of representation and aims at representation. They allow us to relate forms of knowing that are usually considered utterly apart and to understand that there is no form of knowing that can escape from the workings, the expressiveness and the ruses of the symbolic function. There are differences, however, which are related to how these functions are used and how preponderant they are in representation. This is because different modalities of representation use the functions of symbolic forms in different ways, something I shall examine in more detail in the next section of this chapter.

Modalities of representation and the forms and functions of knowledge

In the foregoing pages I have introduced a social psychological framework to analyse the different dimensions of contexts of knowing. These dimensions are related to the architecture of the representational form and encompass the 'who', 'how', 'why', 'what' and 'what for' of contexts of knowing. In discussing each of these dimensions I have used examples of different representations, collective and social, and mentioned different forms of knowledge such as belief, science, myth and ideology. My use of these different forms was somewhat random; I drew on one or the other for purposes of exemplifying how the different dimensions of contexts of knowing and different representational aims can shape the form of knowledge. Whereas it is not my intention in the present work to construct a detailed typology, I wish to propose an initial systematisation of how different modalities of representation are related to different forms of knowing and how these can be understood and unpacked through the consideration of the analytical categories I proposed above.

The modality of a representation is defined by the manner in which it is constructed. I distinguish two modalities of representation, collective and social, which are treated here as ideal types. However, there are various levels of continuity between them, not least the theoretical one. In what follows I explore further the contrast between these two modalities and systematise some of the main elements that characterise each. This is intended to show that what explains the plurality of knowledge is the diversity of the representational form, whose architecture is open to manifold actualisations. After having established the diversity of the representational form, I suggest an initial typology of different forms of knowledge, constructed on the basis of the different representational modalities that underlie them. Let me stress again that it is not my intention to present here a fully fledged typology of social knowledges. What I seek is to identify the main elements, the potential contours of a framework that can be developed and enriched by further work on the social psychology of knowledge.

Two modes of representation

While discussing the distinction between collective and social representations in Chapter 3, I considered the development of the concept of social representations in Moscovici's work and its connection with a particular type of public sphere. I argued that the social psychology of community and public spheres is inseparable from the processes and dynamics of representation. I have shown how these interrelations are at the basis of the work of classical theorists and how the type of social interaction typical of traditional and detraditionalised public spheres can explain the difference between collective and social representations. Let us now explore this in more detail.

Collective representations are formed in the context of traditional public spheres, where the community exercises strong pressure on individual members and the power of the social bond can greatly define how people come to develop knowledge about the world. The social psychology of traditional public spheres imposes itself with constitutive power on self–other relations, and it is in turn reaffirmed by the way in which these relations are realised in everyday life. Collective modalities of representation, however, are not exclusive to this type of community. They are also produced in any interactions that retain the features of traditional communities. In collective modalities of representation, the personal, intersubjective and objective dimensions are closely connected and interlocutors privilege the emotional and social bond to regulate their interactions. Collective representations tend to be cognitively homogeneous and strongly shared because the self–other interaction that produces them is marked by low levels of differentiation and strong levels of compliance, usually obtained through asymmetries in social positioning and/or cognitive ability. Relations of this kind are widespread in all types of communities and make collective modalities of representation a constant feature in the production of knowledge systems. Equally it would be equivocal to think of them as relations of domination or oppression because unequal and asymmetrical. Domination and oppression are not the only possible responses to asymmetry in social life.

In collective representations self–other relationships can be characterised by asymmetry and social constraint. In social constraint there is authority and submission marking the interaction between self–other and communication is unidirectional, with direct transmission and imitation being the main outcomes. We can see here why collective representations tend to be homogeneous fields of knowledge: there is little space for differentiation between partners, a constraint that is sustained by a structure where recognition of authority and tradition with submission to its power is paramount. This power derives its force from the content of the traditions it conveys and from the emotional bond that links partners. Self obeys and follows the other because it recognises the authority it upholds and because of the strong emotional entanglement between them. In this modality of representation there is a tendency to remain unaware of alternatives outside the boundaries of the relationships involved. The force of the social bond between self–other is such that it obfuscates differentiation, maintaining wholeness, strong social integration and preventing distantiation from the social field that constitutes the self–other interaction. It is a modality of representation that tends to close the horizon of knowledge, circumscribing it to the realm of what is known and already there.

While this kind of intersubjective architecture obviously presupposes a great deal of asymmetry and evokes images of oppression and domination, it is important to recognise its nuances and the ambivalence it contains. Indeed, no relationship in social life is fully symmetrical and social constraint, being at the basis of collective representations, has a number of positive potentials that need to be taken into account. Its totalising and all-encompassing nature produces a circumscribed lifeworld that can, despite appearing limited to observers, provide existential grounding and strong feelings of belonging. Relations of this kind are akin to what Winnicott called 'holding', a type of interaction where the vulnerability and dependency of one partner make the other attend to her needs with total devotion and self-donation. The relative powerlessness of a partner in interaction can command feelings of care, understanding and recognition; the paradigmatic case here is the mother–infant interaction to which I shall return in Chapter 5. Other examples of unequal partners in communication include the teacher–pupil relationship, all relations between adults and children and the therapeutic attitude. They all share, at least ideally, the potential for communication that derives from recognition of the vulnerability of the other and a desire to care for the other. Trust and existential security derive precisely from interactions of this kind. Indeed, questioning, differentiation and distanciation would be impossible without the secure basis provided by this modality of relating and representing the world. In the formation of knowledge social constraint has costs and benefits; it would be misleading to assess it only from the perspective of an argumentative and reflexive rationality that values differentiation and questioning. Collective modalities of representation need to be considered in relation to the functions they fulfil in social and personal lives: the perpetuation of identities, community integration and social cohesiveness. These functions are indispensable for societies and persons.

In collective representations the representational outcome underlying knowledge systems usually privileges the subjective and intersubjective dimensions of representation over the objective dimension. In this kind of representational work there is a predominance of the subjective functions present in knowledge systems; they tend to frame the content and logic of knowledge. Thus in collective modalities of representation the subject of representation is fully projected into the content of representations; it is possible to identify who is doing the representational work by the analysis of what the representation conveys. Equally it is possible to identify how the representational outcome came about by the analysis of the communicative strategy used by partners to construct the intersubjective architecture.

What are these representations for? What do they want to achieve and what is the problem they are trying to solve? In collective representations such as myth, belief and political ideology, representations seek to frame thinking and action by consolidating and solidifying the identity and memory of a community. Since these systems of knowing are particularly apt to close worldviews, they are able to achieve a great deal of stability and cohesiveness while guaranteeing conformity and the allegiance of knowers. There is a clear preponderance of functions related to identity, community and social memory, which maintain social integration and the cohesiveness of social fields. The anticipatory function of these representations is used to reaffirm the present and the past and the very construction of futures is irredeemably subordinated to the now and then. Collective forms of representation are produced to maintain and to coalesce, to encompass and to contain, to avoid the unfamiliar and to reassure the worldview of participants. These are purposes deep-seated in old human fears of the unknown and in the angst related to dissolution and the exploration of the new. They offer comfort and existential security and that is why these types of knowledge will not die. Despite the illusions of the replacement hypothesis, that sees the evolution of knowledge as the gradual abandonment of myth and belief, there is a logos in these forms of knowing that is fundamentally connected to the human. For this sheer reason, they have survived and will endure.

Social representations are formed in the context of detraditionalised public spheres, where communities are confronted with diversity of worldviews and practices that constantly challenge the structures of taken-for-granted realities and make the new a common feature of everyday life. In this context there is less reliance on knowledge traditionally acquired and social actors are propelled into a stream of open symbolic spaces manufactured 'on the go'. Social modalities of representation presuppose a strong awareness of alternatives and heterogeneous social fields where different communities and individuals compete and clash in the public sphere. Representation in this context becomes a more open and unstable symbolic form, tuned to the very diversity of perspectives that constitute it in the first place. Representational fields in social modalities of representation are usually patchworks made of different knowledges and different traditions, expressing states of cognitive polyphasia.

In social representations the personal, intersubjective and objective dimensions are differentiated and actors are usually aware of the distinction between them. The social psychology of detraditionalised public spheres, by imposing awareness of plurality and perspective, produces an intersubjective architecture where partners are recognised as independent actors, each with a project and perspective of their own. It is the plurality of perspectives, to return to Arendt's basic formulation on the meaning of the public sphere, that shapes discourse and action as a field of open possibilities and therefore opens the representational outcome to the mobile interactions of this type of community. In social modalities of representation the emotional bond between interlocutors tends to compete on equal footings with considerations of a different kind, in particular the assessment of the link between the representational effort and the object-world. Thus, knowledge that represents specific social objects through the lenses of strong emotional elements also absorbs other components that change emotional readings and alter representations of what is going on. Examples include the development of social representations of diseases such as AIDS, where the fear and social anxiety that shaped these representations ended up coexisting and even being supplanted by other knowledges coming from science and social movements related to the groups most affected by the disease. The exposure of the representational process to the dynamics of a social life replete with alternative accounts and encounters between actors holding different experiences and degrees of contact with AIDS shaped the formation of social representations from the start. It is such dynamics that accounts for the process of development and transformation in representations of AIDS.

In social modalities of representation self–other interactions tend to be based on cooperation, the other type of extreme interpersonal relationship described by Piaget. This kind of interaction implies equality and autonomy as well as reciprocity between distinct personalities. Cooperation opens representational processes and produces differentiation between the personal, intersubjective and objective dimensions. Cooperation is what allows the construction of the other as a person in their own right, someone who, just like me, holds a position and a view that need to be recognised as legitimate. In cooperation, action is reciprocal and through it actors come to develop knowledge of themselves as selves and of others as beings who, although related to me, stand as autonomous selves with rights that are similar to mine and needs that may be different from mine. Cooperation not only constructs knowledge of self and other but also the knowledge that self and other are not identical and the difference between them needs to be dealt with procedurally. Because of the diversity of perspectives and the differentiation processes it entails, cooperation tends to produce less imitation and more innovation in the processes of formation of representations. Transmission of knowledge is not as closed as in collective representations; here learners are less dependent on the authority of knowledge holders and more inclined to explore their own sense-producing and sense-making capacities. The possibility of autonomy imposes its own range of emotional experience and tends to overtake feelings of respect and conformity that are at the basis of collective modalities of representation.

Social representations deal with the new and are aware of it; they appropriate novelty through processes of anchoring and objectification and novelty becomes part of the very structure of the representational fields involved. Social representations tend to open systems of knowing and are particularly linked to innovation and change in social fields, be it at the level of identity, community or social memory. Awareness of the unfamiliar, and engagement with it, implies the use of a great deal of social psychological energy. The unfamiliar shakes identities and communities, challenges traditional views, the taken-for-granted. It can propose radically new ways of proceeding. The unfamiliar opens fields of representation and in the response it receives we can find indicators of what modality of representation is at hand. The anticipatory function of social representations is used in the construction of projects, whose relationship to the past and present is open to scrutiny and assessment and whose central commitment is with the future itself. The social mode of representation is produced to maintain and to change, to open up spaces of unfamiliarity that can be controlled and tamed by adjustment and internal transformation. These are purposes linked to the human impulse for discovery and exploration, to the reasoning of navigators, to the curiosity of the child who touches fire despite being well advised not to do so.

The analysis of collective and social representations shows that, on the one hand, they are related to social constraint and cooperation, and on the other to traditional and detraditionalised public spheres. These homologies demonstrate how the study of representation implies a consideration of its social and psychological genesis as well as of its structural connections with micro and macro levels of analysis. The public sphere of communities at once relies upon and produces a particular type of intersubjective architecture, which in turn produces a specific mode of representation. Modalities of knowledge therefore are established by the societal patterns that shape the interrelations between members of communities and how they construct representations about themselves and the world. Public spheres, self–other relations and representations are genetically linked; the link that is clear in the ontogenesis is sustained in the sociogenesis.

Table 4.1 summarises the contrast between collective and social modalities of representation. The table shows that the characteristics of each can be grouped under the threefold architecture of representational processes: the objective, which involves the types of public sphere of a community and the cognitive structure of knowledge fields; the intersubjective, which involves the nature of the interaction and communication between self and other; and the subjective, which involves the emotional and personal dimension, including some patterns of conduct. Collective and social representations comprise different ways of representing, which express the different representational commitments that are at the basis of knowledge formation. To understand these different representational commitments it is necessary to take into account the social psychology that underpins the effort to represent undertaken by individuals and communities when they construct knowledge.

In distinguishing between these two modalities I do not wish to suggest that all representational processes will conform perfectly to each one of these or indeed that collective and social modalities of representation exhaust the potentiality of forms that are open to the representational structure – rather the opposite. Most representational fields involve features of both and produce multifaceted knowledge fields – they express a state of cognitive polyphasia and are hybrid in character. Research in the social psychology of knowledge suggests that, in accordance with Moscovici's

Table 4.1 Modalities of representation

Collective	Social
Traditional public sphere	*De-traditionalised public sphere*
Unawareness of alternatives	Awareness of alternatives
Tendency to closure	Tendency to opening
Recognition of authority: highly centred processes of legitimation	Diffusion of authority: decentration of legitimation
Subjective–intersubjective–objective	*Subjective–intersubjective–objective*
Low differentiation and wholeness	High differentiation and individuation
Self–other relations	*Self–other relations*
Asymmetry in dialogue	Symmetry in dialogue (actively constructed)
Non-reciprocal	Reciprocity and recognition of other
Hierarchical	Non-hierarchical
Social constraint	Cooperation
Psychological holding	*Psychological handling*
Symbiosis, ontological security and origins of trust	Ego relatedness, introduction of absence and frustration
Attention centred on the subjective	Attention turns to objective
Homogeneity in knowledge	*Heterogeneity in knowledge*
Heteronomy	Autonomy
Conformity	Innovation
Closure	Openness

hypothesis, most, if not all, epistemic fields are made of myriad knowledges, each expressing different representational modalities. Science, myth, social and collective representations appear intermingled and deeply connected in the knowledge practices of the contemporary world. There is no pure form, and all knowledges interpenetrate and mix in the process of making sense of the world. Figure 4.1 seeks to capture some of this dynamic.

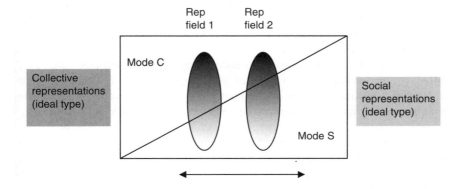

Figure 4.1 The inter-penetration of modalities of representation

Modalities of representation and forms of knowing

Let me recapitulate the theoretical argument I have been developing in this chapter. I have proposed that knowledge is a plural and plastic form because it relies on representational processes. The analysis of representation shows that its architecture is connected to objective, intersubjective and subjective dimensions, expressed in the 'who', 'how', 'why', 'what' and 'what for' of representational processes. I have called these dimensions the social psychology of contexts of knowing. I have explored how these dimensions vary and produce different modalities of representation, collective and social. Now I want to link these different modalities of representation to different forms of knowledge. The typology I propose is based on the main features of collective and social representations I have discussed and on how the different dimensions of contexts of knowing shape the form of a knowledge system.

Table 4.2 shows how different modalities of representation are connected to different forms of knowledge. Myth, belief and ideology are forms of knowing that typically use collective modalities of representation whereas common sense and science draw on social modes of representation. While these various forms of knowing share features of collective and social representations, the differences between them can be identified through the functions they fulfil in social life and the nuances which characterise their deployment. The analysis of these functions permits recognition of the internal plurality of knowledge systems and the manner in which communities and individuals put them to use. Rather than operating with an ideal and transcendental form as the standard against which all others are compared and judged, the social psychology of contexts of knowing brings to the analysis of knowledge the multidimensional processes that constituted it and make it a plastic and malleable form.

Issues of identity, community, time and ideology penetrate knowledge systems and impact on the plurality of forms they assume. Let us consider collective modalities of representation. Myth, belief and ideology fulfil functions of identity, community and social memory through the strong preservation of patterns of signification and action. They seek to maintain and reproduce the traditions they uphold and draw on the past for that purpose. However, there are some differences that can explain how they differ, which are related to the use of both time and power. Whereas myth and belief are directed towards the past, myth has a strong presence in the anticipation of futures and allows for marginal variation in representation, something belief tends to resist. Ideology, equally, can challenge social memories and open itself for the future depending on the project it wants to impose. It is typical of all political ideologies to play freely with the past in order to propose a future. Of course, there is no knowledge that can conserve the past in its integrity. This, as Bartlett has shown, is impossible. Belief systems, however, work hard to conserve it and put more emphasis

Table 4.2 The forms and functions of knowledge

Modelform	Collective representations (homogeneous)			Social representations (heterogeneous)	
Functions	Myth	Belief	Political ideology	Common sense	Science
Identity	Present – tend to constancy	Present – tend to constancy	Present – tend to constancy	Present – mobile	Attempt to withdraw
Community	Present (constancy)	Present (constancy)	Present (contingent)	Present – mobile	Attempt to withdraw
Memory	Conservation	Conservation	Conservation or manipulation	Working through	Working through
Anticipation	Past/future oriented	Past oriented	Future oriented	Past/future oriented	Future oriented
Ideology	Present contingent	Present contingent	Present	Present contingent	Attempt to withdraw

backwards than forwards (Blumenberg 1985). Myth and belief draw power from recognition rather than systematic domination; mythologies and beliefs are powerful because they are recognised by communities and individuals. Yet, they can be easily permeated by the ideological function, when there is a mobilisation of mythologies and beliefs to fulfil purposes of domination. The presence of the ideological function in myths and belief systems is contingent; there is more to these forms of knowledge than just domination. Ideology, on the contrary, is a knowledge system that seeks to exert effects and pursue projects through the use of domination.

Common sense and science are forms of knowledge linked to social modalities of representing. As with all representation, they fulfil functions of identity, community, memory, anticipation and ideology. Yet, as open and heterogeneous fields, they open these dimensions to change and innovation. Common sense comprises hybrid epistemic fields, whose internal structure brings together patterns of signification and conduct that clash and challenge each other. Thus internal multiplicity leads to transformation and mobility as well as an orientation towards the future. The case of science constitutes a special one because of the active efforts of this knowledge system to overcome its 'representational' status and establish a direct link with 'what is' (Latour 1993). Of all knowledges, science is the only one that actively tries to withdraw identity, community and ideology from its modus operandi. It does so through the methodological quest, which comprises an attitude, tools and procedures that seek to bracket the subjective and intersubjective dimensions of representational systems for the sake of better understanding the object.[5] Both forms of knowledge can be permeated by ideologies and used to dominate. This is very clear in the case of science in the contemporary world.

Finally, let me note that in assessing forms of knowledge it is important to keep in mind the distinction between what a given form of knowing wants and what it manages to achieve. No intention can be realised in full and perfectly. The gap between the desire to represent behind knowledge and its representational achievements is part of the very constitution of knowledge; in the imperfections, losses, errors and unrealised potentials of knowing lies the faulty history of all human attempts and the possibility of all human learning. That is why the analysis of knowledge as action, as practices of knowing rather than a finished and closed-off phenomenon can lead to a richer and more comprehensive understanding of what knowledge actually entails.

From one to many: knowledges in the plural

The analytical framework elaborated above is certainly not comprehensive and much remains to be done in tracing the moving patterns of representational work in our contemporary world. What I tried to offer is a heuristic to consider the social psychology behind knowledge practices and how they relate to the context of persons and communities. The predominance of symbolic goods and the widespread penetration of mass communication media redefine the production of symbolic forms and present new challenges to social psychologists interested in their operations at the individual–society interface. If there is any value in the framework suggested, it lies in its analytic potential and in how it can stimulate further work towards the identification and understanding of different ways of knowing in social life.

From this perspective, knowledge is a system of symbolic representations organically linked to the social psychology of contexts and entangled productively in a way of life and its culture; it is always carried by community and therefore must be understood in the plural. There is not only one form of knowing, there are many. This variation corresponds to variation in the forms of social relating that constitute both knowledge and community: to know is an act dependent on who knows, from where and when one knows, what, why, what for one knows, and in relation to which significant others one knows. Knowledge is thus a heterogeneous and malleable form whose rationality and logic is not captured by a transcendental norm but must be assessed in relation to the social, psychological and cultural context of a community. Empirically the locus of enquiry on knowledge moves from an apparently final product to the fundamental relationships that constitute the 'between' of knowledge formation. These relationships and their empirical actualisation as community/context become the focus of the investigative effort. In studying a diversity of representations in contemporary public spheres we social psychologists want to unravel how different contexts and communities produce knowledge about themselves and others as well as about the issues that are relevant to their way of life. The key concern is to understand how local knowledge is produced, sustained and defended by communities as well as how these processes are entangled with key social psychological categories such as identity, community, conformity, resistance and innovation, social memory and the construction of futures, dialogue and intergroup relations.

It is my conviction that the recognition of the diversity and fundamental locality of all knowledge has been one of the key outcomes of this particular stream of research. This recognition has a number of consequences that recast the problem of knowledge and moves theoretical and empirical efforts away from the hypothesis of linear progression and displacement of one form of knowledge by another. First, it shows that forms of knowing linked to self, emotion and culture did not, and will not, disappear as the grand narrative of the Enlightenment dreamt of. The functions they fulfil and the problems they address continue to be part of human experience, and this is what guarantees their survival. Different forms of knowledge coexist in social life. Second, it allows the rehabilitation of so-called local knowledges and other forms of knowing often dismissed as error, superstition and ignorance. These knowledges are not necessarily irrational nor wrong; they are different and need to be understood in terms of what they express and achieve in social life. Third, it helps to challenge hierarchical conceptions of knowledge that overvalue some at the expense of others, reducing some knowledges to the local while granting to others the status and legitimacy of universality. Finally, it sheds light on the relations between different forms of knowing and the possibilities embedded in the communication between knowledge systems. To recognise that there is difference in knowledge does not mean the blind acceptance of all knowledges, the romantic valuation of some and the deification of others. All knowledges involve representation and all are fallible at times. Science has been quite hopeless to resolve sorrows of the heart and belief alone has not entirely helped in the promotion of public health strategies. But it would be foolish to deny the contribution each could potentially have for both problems. Rather than putting knowledge in a hierarchical scale, the understanding of its different forms and functions sheds light on the resourcefulness of its diversity. It is in dialogue and communication between different knowledges that lies the potential for deciding what is right or wrong, true or false, acceptable or unacceptable and to enlarge the boundaries of all knowledges.

5   Encountering the knowledge of others

What is at stake when we encounter the knowledge of others, the reasoning of the other? Sartre once said that hell is other people and, to a large extent, the turbulent history of western civilisation has confirmed his dire onto-logical assessment. Recognising others is a thorny issue and even a brief look at the history of our relations to otherness will show that it has provoked fear and segregation, domination, exclusion and violence. Our tendency to construct the other in negative terms is evident in social practices, in every-day life, in the media, in institutions, some of which built exclusively to segregate and discipline the other: think about the trajectory of our relations to the mad, to deviants, to remote peoples; think about the nature of extreme intergroup conflict, the conquest of the Americas and the colonial experi-ence. Behind all these cases, we find a set of representations, attitudes and practices that consistently fail to take into account the perspective of the other; we tend to snigger at, belittle and even dehumanise people who fail to be just like us. It is a state of affairs that betrays not only the amount of negative value in the knowledge self holds *about* different others; it also reveals how self, by the same token, devalues, rejects and in extreme cases sets out to destroy the knowledge *of* the other.

Yet, despite the overwhelming empirical evidence of the destructive tendencies that mark the social and historical relations between self and other, the relationship self develops with others is the basis of selfhood, knowledge and social life. Without others there is no human life properly so called and it is in our relationship to significant others that we find both the ontological and social resources to become what we are. Knowledge is itself a construct that requires the other and the vast majority of psychological systems that conceptualised the development of the person and the emer-gence of cognitive structures in the child relied on the relations between self and other. Groups, institutions and communities are about engaging and living with others. Cooperation and communication, without which human life would not be possible, presuppose recognising the other and learning how to take into account the perspective from where she proposes her psychological, social and historical truth.

This double-sided nature of our relationship to others is a permanent reminder of the complexities embedded in processes of communication between self and other. While intersubjectivity and sociality are at the core of self-constitution and knowledge formation, the tragic history of failures that has permeated self relationship to others, and in particular, radical others, shows that moving towards the other is not smooth and it is not a choice; rather, it is an imperative of our biological and social constitution fuelled at once by loving and destructive energies and fraught with underlying psychic forces that struggle to preserve the omnipotence of self and its narcissistic programme. This ambivalence is present in the genesis of our psychological lives, substantiated and expressed at both individual and social levels, fostering a range of possibilities that vary from attempts to communicate, understand and take into account, to practices of classification, exclusion and in the most extreme cases, sheer extermination, of the perspective and body of the other.

In this chapter I want to return to the social psychology of self–other relations to consider processes of communication between knowledge systems. My main concern in previous chapters has been to demonstrate that knowledge is a plastic and plural phenomenon, originating in subjective, intersubjective and objective worlds, which it seeks to represent. Having established that knowledge varies, I now want to reflect on how different representations, and the knowledge systems they enable, meet and communicate in public spheres. What happens when scientists talk to lay people, or doctors with patients? What takes place when technocrats working in developing countries meet local people? What is at stake when policymakers discuss how to educate children, how to treat people with mental illness, how to accommodate the claims of diasporic communities? How do global firms establish common practices across the divide of culture, nation, lifeworld? All these situations involve meeting points between knowledge of self and knowledge of others, between competing representations, practices and views of the world that both recast the communicative dynamics between self and other and bring to the fore the nature of the dominant representations self holds about the knowledge of the other. Underlying the social psychology of knowledge encounters is thus a dual and interrelated problem: communication with, and representation of, the other.

Today, perhaps more than ever before, this problem matters. The chances for self to meet and communicate with the knowledge of others are greater than ever and whereas there is nothing new in the fact that knowledge systems communicate, it would be misleading to assume that this process has remained unchanged in the contemporary world. The last two decades or so have witnessed dramatic examples of new self–other encounters, expressed in the battles of multiculturalism, the plight of asylum seekers and the insertion of new diasporic communities in national states (see for instance, Honnig 1991; Taylor 1994; Benhabib 1999, 2002, 2004; Chryssochoou 2000a, 2000b). Ours is a world of social rather than collective representations, where the knowledge of others travels relatively free from the constraints traditionally imposed by geography and time, class and culture, penetrating locales that are psychologically and geographically distant with relative easiness.

Whether in mediated or in face-to-face interactions (Thompson 1995), the imagined other, whoever they might have been, is much closer to home and presents his force and reality in immediate and concrete ways: he enters everyday lives in a multitude of arenas, ranging from work, schools and families, consumption, art and leisure activities, to the negotiation of resources and policies; he proposes different interpretations and readings about what is the case, redefines personal and national identities and shakes our ability to sharply define the boundaries of what happens to be reality and what can be called knowledge. Difference loses a certain idealised and abstract character to become real and something to deal with, upsetting usual parameters of self-understanding and the enactment of social practices. It throws self, individual and collective, into uncertain directions, offering new models for its identification project while by the same token hardening its defences and narcissistic tendencies.

This new regime of otherness within and across cultural communities intensifies encounters between knowledge systems and transforms social arenas into terrains for testing and confronting cultural practices and the knowledge systems they carry, for experiencing contestation and conflict associated with the clashes between self and other. It raises questions about the potential for communication and dialogue between radically different people and the nature of the obstacles that undermine such efforts. It brings to the fore issues of perspective and plurality, which are central to the formation of communities and the social psychology of public spheres. It puts in sharp evidence the assessment and valuation of knowledge systems in social life and the claims and tribulations of communities whose knowledge, culture and way of life do not command the status and recognition present in more powerful locales. It recasts the old problem of how knowledges change as they move from one context to another and how transformations in the public sphere of communities relate to the transformation of knowledge.

In this chapter I want to address these issues by suggesting a social psychological framework to examine encounters between different knowledges and their possible outcomes. I define a knowledge encounter as the meeting between two or more representational systems, expressing different subjective, intersubjective and objective worlds. The approach I shall develop draws on two central and interrelated concepts of the psychology of self–other relations: perspective-taking and recognition. Both are complex social psychological achievements that depend on the paradoxical communication between self and other and on the societal context where particular representations and practices about others take place. It is important to ground perspective-taking and recognition on societal contexts for self and other are concrete social actors, positioned in social fields from which they also derive the status, the resources and the power needed to be recognised. Both processes are always already permeated by the dominant representations and practices that societies hold about specific others. These come to play a crucial role in defining whether knowledges can communicate or not.

I shall start by considering the problem of communication between different knowledges and discussing the ambivalent social psychological dynamics which underlies recognition and perspective taking. These processes, I suggest, are the key entry points to understanding the dialogical and non-dialogical possibilities embedded in the meeting of different forms of knowing. I go on to discuss the dominant representation of knowledge that permeates processes of recognition, retrieving the debate already initiated in Chapter 2. I suggest that the hierarchical representation of knowledge, present in classical theoretical models about knowledge and its development, betrays an illusion linked to the omnipotence of self and difficulties to take the perspective of the other. I shall then characterise dialogical and non-dialogical encounters and consider some of the outcomes they produce: displacement and coexistence, segregation/destruction and hybridisation. In the last part of the chapter I explore these issues discussing the case of madness and community interventions based on Paulo Freire's literacy method. I conclude by suggesting that dialogue between different forms of knowing is a resource for individual people and communities.

Difference and communication

Dialogue and communication between knowledge systems is a complex and difficult task. Some doubt it is possible at all. Needham's (1972) superb study on belief, language and experience is perhaps one of the most incisive pieces on the incommunicability of worldviews. Drawing heavily on Wittgenstein and Lévy-Bruhl, to whose memory he dedicates his monograph, he argues that given the perpetual variation of representation, our attempts to establish common parameters for human life are in vain. There is no hope for the quest of discerning an understandable overall order that could encompass our many particular orders. All that remains are 'shifting relativities' because:

> the phantasmagoric variegation of the collective forms of significance, in grammar and in classificatory concepts and styles of thought, reflects the essential relativity that marks all ideas about the meaning and determinations of human experience. . . . Once outside a given form of life, man is lost in a 'wilderness of forms'.
>
> (Needham 1972: 244)

Needham was not alone in thinking that once we step outside our own representations, our language and our culture all that remain are senseless forms. His position is akin to a spectrum of theoretical views whose common denominator is the assumption, often unacknowledged, that the divide between self and other is unsurpassable. The intense debate between followers of Habermas and Foucault that started in the 1990s and to some extend still continues today (for an overview, see Ashenden and Owen 1999) roughly expresses this opposition between belief and disbelief in communication with others. Habermas concentrated his efforts on the conditions of possibility for genuine communication while Foucault produced a comprehensive account of the history whereby self struggles for sameness and sets out to classify, segregate and exclude the other. Habermas' theory of communicative action has been consistently accused of being idealistic as if the idea of reaching understanding, which he claims is the universal foundation of communication, expressed an unachievable aim (see Thompson and Held 1982 and Calhoun 1992 for an overview of such criticisms). Some theorists of qualitative methods seem equally inspired, even if unconsciously, by the idea that self and other cannot communicate and understand each other: they propose that researchers should match gender, ethnic background and whatever other features possible when working with human participants as if difference between researcher and researched infringed an ethical requirement for sameness (for a good account of this debate see Smith 1999).

While these positions are in many respects suggestive and at times real enough, in my view they remain partial because they are unable to relate back to the role of the other in the ontogenesis and understand the dual and contradictory nature of self–other relations. The psychology of self–other relations shows that while communication between self and other is indeed a difficult process, fraught with contradictory and destructive energies, it also contains a positivity without which there would be no person at all. Recognising the other, establishing a relationship with the alterity he proposes as a person in his own right and learning how to take his perspective are not only central processes in the development of the child; they are absolute requirements if this child is to become a person. The problem with Needham's view, despite his excellent use of Vygotsky, is that which it leaves aside. It does not realise, because it does not consider, that in more than one sense, it is outside a form of life that we all start from. Becoming human is precisely the process whereby we start to recognise, to know, to understand the wilderness of forms that the world presents to us. The child must enter the world in which she was born as an outsider, constructing resources to relate to it as she moves along, experiencing and trying again, learning how to accept frustration and eventually recognising by co-construction the variety of signs, codes and perspectives that constitute the order of significations in which, and of which, she will be an actor. Notwithstanding the rudimentary structures that allow the non-conserving child to navigate the new world in which she is born, the psychodynamics underlying the perspective of the infant points precisely to a phantasmagoric variegation of forms and movements (only gradually forms stabilise and movements will become recognisable action). The idea of a phantasmagoric variegation is in fact an excellent psychological metaphor for the angst that accompanies the process of having to co-construct an order out of the initial chaos. This is a formidable task, one in which the child, however, is not alone.

The encounter between child and world is from the start grounded in an intersubjective dyad that gives the infant ground and ontological security to invest in the strangeness outside – as Winnicott remarked there is no such thing as a baby: there is a baby and a caretaker. The chaos, which is real enough from the perspective of the infant, is a responsive chaos: as the mother holds and feeds her newborn baby she and many others will also be travellers in the long journey whereby the infant will come out of the wilderness. The child will rely on the emotional scaffolding provided by the other who recognises and sooths her needs. The other *is there* and if the child is fortunate enough, this other will be able to give and to love the child.

I use the ontogenetic argument to show that the very process whereby a child becomes a person is about establishing coordinates with a form of life that is utterly alien at first. The ontogeny of human experience is about encountering and communicating with the other and succeeding in this encounter is paramount for human life. Moving towards the other is as intrinsic to the survival of the child as is breathing and eating; it is not a choice but an imperative, and in order to remain alive the developing infant will need the other not only as a holder and carer but also as a psychological field where she can project and play with the task of becoming a self (see Spitz 1945, 1959; Stern 1974, 1985). In more than one way we are all well trained to engage with the wilderness of the other, with the phantasmagoric variegation of human knowledges and cultures, because we all had to do it at first in relation to our own way of life.

That we *can* and *need* to do it, however, does not define *how* we do it. The manner through which self and other establish their relations and if possible engage in dialogical communication is open. Intersubjective relations are empirical events in the social world and depend on a number of psychological, social, cultural, economic and political considerations. Not all encounters between self and other manage to establish communication, even less a dialogical relation of mutual recognition; this is the case both in individual and social histories. As I mentioned earlier, there is nothing cosy in the relations between self and other; it is a contradictory process made of erotic and destructive energies, with both potentially contributing to its shape and outcome. In this sense, encounters between self and other can produce different outcomes, which depend on whether interlocutors can communicate and mutually recognise each other as legitimate partners in interaction. Out of the contradictory potentials of self–other relationships, communication and dialogicity between self and other as well as domination and the concomitant potential for destruction, are permanent possibilities.

Both of these outcomes, despite their tremendous difference, have a common root in the core conflict between assertion and recognition that permeates the development of self and the simultaneous process of coming to know the other. Both processes have been extensively discussed in the social psychology of Mead and in the psychoanalysis of Winnicott. I shall turn to both to consider the role of perspective-taking and recognition in the dynamics of encounters between different knowledges.

Perspective-taking and recognition

Perspective-taking and recognition are central processes in the approach I seek to develop here because both refer to the territory between self and other and are at the core of a dialogical social psychology (Marková 2003; Jovchelovitch 2004). Understanding the role of recognition as well as its complications and uneven realisation is a key entry point to assess the social psychology of knowledge encounters and, in particular, to establish whether such encounters are of a dialogical or non-dialogical kind. To this end it is crucial to appreciate both the foundational role of recognition in the constitution of persons and social realities as well as the deep psychic duality involved in the process of recognising and being recognised by the other. The former has been extensively demonstrated in the social psychology of Mead (1934); the latter in the psychoanalysis of Winnicott (1965c). The distinctiveness of Mead's social psychology is that he traces the development of self and the emergence of self-consciousness back to the moment in which self is able to recognise itself by taking the perspective of the other (Farr and Rommetweit 1995). Without the capacity to see itself through a decentred perspective, which is the perspective of the other, self cannot conceive of its own position. Winnicott's theory of development is equally dialogical and provides the elements to understand the emotional struggles that permeate the establishment of recognition and intersubjectivity from the start. Both reverted the monological psychology of a self grounded on its own centre and gave primacy to the space of the 'between', which is precisely where recognition and the intersubjective lie. Both emphasised that recognition is intertwined with a full appreciation of the perspective of the other in its own right, that is, with an understanding that intrinsic to the formation of self is the understanding of plurality of perspectives. Self is not alone; it is one among many others whose different perspectives and positions in social life are as legitimate as its own.

In Mead, taking the perspective of the other and recognising it is at the basis of mind, self and community. Recognition and perspective taking are intrinsically connected: recognition is about recognising perspectives, the different locations from where people speak and in which people stand, perspectives that exponentially increase as the child moves from playing with a limited number of significant others to the more demanding task of recognising the rules of the game and internalising the perspective of the community, or what Mead calls the generalised other. Decentring one's perspective goes hand in hand with recognising plurality in perspectives and being able to take them into account so that self can become an object for itself. These processes are inscribed in the very structure of self through the instances Mead called the 'I' and the 'me'. Each corresponds to the tensions expressed in the space between self and other, where processes of recognition and perspective-taking give to the structure of self contradictory elements: the I can only be an I as long as it is also Me, i.e. if it is able to symbolically represent itself from the perspective of the other.[1] Mead's model of intersubjective recognition flows from the personal to the sociopolitical and back, connecting the spheres of person and community formation. It emphasises that recognition of the other is about recognising the difference of the other and the legitimacy of this difference. At the level of the person, this recognition of perspectives allows for the establishment of self; at the level of community, recognition of perspectives allows for the establishment of a democratic and moral public sphere (Mead 1932).

While Mead's theory of perspective-taking and recognition is able to retrieve their foundational role in the formation of both self and societal experience, it remains silent in relation to the emotional forces that permeate both processes. Winnicott's theory of infant maturation, partly exposed in Chapter 1, is particularly suitable to remedy this gap as it renders intelligible the psychological forces that operate in processes of recognition and perspective-taking while equally emphasising the acknowledgement of the reality of the other in her own right as central to the constitution of self. In the context of psychoanalytic theories of development, Winnicott's view is radically dialogical: his unit of analysis is not the baby in isolation but the dyad infant–caretaker. His starting point is the primary symbiosis between the radical vulnerability of the biological body of the infant and the total devotion of a loving caretaker, which creates the conditions for the fantasies of omnipotence the infant derives from maternal care and for the mother's fantasy that her baby continues to be an extension of herself. This circle of psychological undifferentiation obliterates the dependency that marks the beginning of all human life; because the caretaker holds her baby with total devotion and acts as an extension of its needs the symbiosis of intra-uterine life is partially continued in a psychological sphere. Winnicott called this stage holding.

How to break free from symbiotic ties and move towards differentiation, i.e. towards the establishment of identity for both self and other, is the question to which Winnicott tried to respond throughout most of his work (Winnicott 1965c, 1971; Davis and Wallbridge 1981). He always considered the process of identity formation as a task of both self and other: both infant and caretaker must renounce the fantasy of oneness and gradually recognise each other as independent beings. How can the child and the mother start to recognise each other as independent beings? How can they accommodate the pains of separation with the gains of full ego-relatedness between two persons? The answers Winnicott provided to these questions constitute a full narrative of how recognition of perspective evolves and take us back to the discussion of transitional phenomena I have introduced in Chapter 1 (Winnicott 1965a). The process of recognising perspective is painful for both child and caretaker because it involves separation from a state of fusion and the need to renounce the omnipotence derived from holding. It requires from the caretaker to move towards a stage that Winnicott called handling: she must be able to return her attention and focus to a world beyond her baby and gradually act as an empirical obstacle to the fantasy of indifferentiation and omnipotence.[2] In ceasing to be an extension of the I, the caretaker creates frustration and disillusionment and introduces the 'insult' of the reality principle to which the child, of course, will respond.

Winnicott argued that the nature of the psychological conversation that accompanies the transition from holding to handling is paramount to how the perennial tension between self and other is resolved and continues throughout a person's life. It is a conversation real and imagined, which offers a space for trying out and testing the limits of what self and other can do to each other. The introduction of a reality that resists the child triggers feelings of aggression and deep angst, which are directed to the immediate representative of the outside. The caretaker becomes a target for the fantasy in which the child seeks to 'destroy' the limitations imposed on her. The reality of a child who kicks and bites, throws tantrums and tries by all means to do what she wants is expressive of an imagination that is attempting to see how far one can go and how to demarcate the imagined and the real: what the child really wants is to test the 'reality' and resistance of the other. For this reason Winnicott considered this aggression to be functional and necessary (Winnicott 1965b, 1965d).

Equally, and perhaps even more important for him, was the capacity of the caretaker to 'survive' the fantasies of destruction and preserve its position as an independent being. The capacity of the caretaker to 'survive' the fantasy of destruction and act as a loving empirical self with a centre of her own makes the perspective of the other real and concrete for the child while signalling that early experiences of full connectedness can be found again in the experience of ego-relatedness and communication between two independent beings. Renouncing symbiosis and omnipotence and establishing mutual recognition are thus emotional achievements of a real and imagined dialogue between child and caretaker. This conversation continues well beyond early childhood and is recast whenever encounters between self and other take place. The transitional phenomena of the potential space, which are present in communication, in play, in art, in group work, in the symbolic function of knowledge amongst other forms of cultural expression, are exemplary of how we resolve the tension between omnipotence and the limits of reality, between being merged with the other in sameness and being able to demarcate boundaries and recognise difference. Both Mead and

Winnicott emphasised the intersubjective context of perspective-taking and recognition making clear that self can only know itself in dialogue with the concrete difference of the other, which will eventually establish the recognition of diversity and the capacity to appreciate the plurality of perspectives that constitute human experience. Their work offers not only an account of the positive role of the intersubjective but also allows us to consider why encounters between self and other are open to contradictory solutions and can promote different outcomes.

Jessica Benjamin has forcefully demonstrated this postulate in her work on the deep psychology of domination (Benjamin 1993). Drawing on Winnicott's model presented above, she shows that, depending on specific conditions of intersubjective exchange between self and other, recognition can be twisted and used as domination. When the tension between self and other is resolved by making the other an extension of self, an object of omnipotent fantasies and desires, domination sets in. Domination is the use of recognition as a means to reproduce the omnipotence of oneself over another, in fact, it is 'a twisting of the bonds of love – it does not repress the desire for recognition; rather it enlists it and transforms it' (Benjamin 1993: 219). The fantasy of omnipotence, which is equally necessary for play and creativity as it is for the sublimation of aggressive drives against the other who constrains and sets limits, becomes real in domination. Self and other are locked in a dual recognition of the omnipotence of one of the partners – disturbingly enough there is always a level of psychic participation between dominant and dominated, which shows that no project of liberation can exclude a transformation of minds. Benjamins's model takes the denial of the subjectivity of the mother, which she finds present both in sociohistorical contexts and in theoretical propositions about human development, as a paradigmatic example of processes of dominating the other and excluding her or his subjectivity. This denial has tremendous consequences in our general representations about self and its relations to others; it profoundly prevents us from seeing the world as a place of equal subjects and constitutes the deep root of domination. The infant-centric view stands as a primary representative of all situations where the response and 'survival' of the other count little or not at all. Yet, she argues, it is the difference the other can make that allows self to encounter itself and prevents the cycle of domination and separation between self and other.

The alternative to the pattern of domination is found in sustaining and coping with the tension of intersubjective spaces. If self is to recognise the other as a being whose existence goes far beyond the fantasies, desires and projections of self, then the other must provide a clear boundary and act as a being with a centre of her own: it must survive the fantasy of omnipotence by demonstrating its capacity to stand on her own and in this way to have her perspective recognised. In this case, rather than seeking pleasure in the fantasy of omnipotence and in making the other an extension of self, the sources of pleasure and gratification will be found in the reality and concrete difference of the other, in reciprocal exchanges, in sharing, in the feelings of oneness that can emerge in situations of togetherness. It is a pleasure derived from early experiences of togetherness, whose emotional basis can be appreciated in its full force in the power of the breast metaphor: the other can transform self – as when she relieves hunger; the other can complement self – as when she holds; and the other can share – as when there is mutual gaze. All of these are to be found in nursing and will persist in our psychic lives either because they have been positively experienced or because they have been missed (Stern 1974).

This intersubjective model of the child–mother interaction allows the deep psychology of self–other relations to flow directly into larger societal encounters between self and other to illuminate the social psychological dynamics underlying encounters between different knowledge systems. It provides a powerful basis for apprehending the dialogical and non-dialogical potentials embedded in the encounters between different systems of knowledge. It shows that the potential for communication between knowledges lies in the capacity of interlocutors to take the perspective of the other and establish mutual recognition while renouncing the omnipotence of a self-centred view of the world. It shows that just perceiving the other and understanding her perspective is not enough; there must be mutual recognition of perspectives and renunciation of a position where one's perspective is imposed on the other. It puts emphasis on the other and on the need for the other to stand up and make a difference; it shows that distorted recognition is concomitant with the dismissal of perspective and plurality in the formation of selves and in public spheres. It explains not only the psychology that fuels exclusionary processes and the recurring difficulties linked to perspective-taking and recognition in social life but also provides a framework for counteracting these trends and opening space to the voices that have historically been put in the position of the denied other.

The subjectivity of the excluded mother stands as a reminder of the so many others who have been denied a voice and were unable to stand up and make a difference. Because knowledge is always connected to subjective, intersubjective and objective worlds, which it seeks to represent, recognition or denial of the legitimacy of a knowledge system has consequences that go far beyond material effects and the realm of 'interests'. It impacts on the whole social psychology of the community whose knowledge is denied recognition, threatening its identity, self-esteem and way of life. In my view it is not accidental that Benjamin's psychoanalysis of domination finds echoes in the philosophy of Dussel (1995, 1996) and in the pedagogy of Freire (1970, 1973a, 2001, 2004), for both have emphasised the role of the denied other in the constitution of the dominant self. Like Benjamin, they argue that it is a true encounter between the knowledge of self and other, based on mutual recognition and dialogue, that will eventually be able not only to free the other from its dominated position but also redeem self from its domineering impetus. Common to their theoretical stances is the articulation of the redemptive potential of the intersubjective, something which in my view is missing from the otherwise superb work of Michel Foucault.

The hierarchical representation of knowledge

In the foregoing pages I have argued that communication between different knowledges is not only possible, it is also necessary in the development of human life. I have used the ontogenetic argument to show that the processes whereby an infant becomes a person are themselves processes of communication between two radically different interlocutors. I have drawn on the social psychology of Mead and on the psychoanalysis of Winnicott and Benjamin to show that while perspective-taking and mutual recognition are at the basis of self and community, the constitution of the intersubjective space on which they depend remains a contradictory process, open to both dialogue and to domination. I have suggested that these social psychological processes underlie encounters between knowledge systems and impinge on the manner in which knowledges communicate, allowing both dialogical and non-dialogical outcomes. Perspective-taking and recognition are first and foremost processes of discovering diversity and being able to live with plurality while renouncing the omnipotence of a self-centred view. Diversity and plurality give self its identity and ontological grounding by both allowing it to recognise itself as one and renounce the omnipotent fantasy of being the only one. Failure to do so distorts processes of perspective-taking, prevents mutual recognition and allows domination to set in.

As in the deep psychology of self–other relations, the basis for dialogue between knowledge systems involves decentration of perspective and mutual recognition, where interlocutors are capable and prepared to mutually recognise each other's mode of knowing as different, but legitimate. In non-dialogical encounters interlocutors meet and cannot recognise the legitimacy of a different mode of knowing because they are unable to decentre from the perspective in which they are located. Rather than recognising the legitimacy of diversity, there is a belief that the knowledge of self is the only one that deserves recognition. This is akin to processes of domination where self and other are locked in the recognition of omnipotence and the power of one over another. In both cases what is at stake is the recognition or the denial of diversity in knowledge and above all the recognition or denial that different forms of knowing are legitimate, i.e. they stand as constructs that need to be recognised for what they are and understood as legitimate in the difference they express. Thus encounters between knowledge systems depend on how different knowledges communicate and to what extent the constitution of an intersubjective space of communication allows for recognition or denial of the perspective expressed in the knowledge of the other. This recognition or denial of the other defines dialogical and non-dialogical encounters between knowledges. I shall return to this distinction later in this chapter. For now I want to focus on the problem of how representations about others and the knowledge of others permeate the processes discussed above.

Recognition or denial of diversity in perspectives are processes directly related to the second problem that concerns the social psychology of knowledge encounters: the representations that circumscribe dominant ways of recognising others and by extension, the knowledge of others. Understanding the larger social representations that permeate and shape the valuation and legitimacy of knowledge systems is central to assess how recognition takes place in the knowledge encounter. Representations about knowledge circulating in social worlds constitute a symbolic background against which, and within which, carriers of different knowledge systems meet. Recognising interlocutors as different but equal and legitimate partners is obviously a process that goes far beyond an abstract intersubjective encounter between self and other. Self and other are not abstract beings, but historically and socially situated agents, who meet in public arenas as already constituted ontologies, positioned by social and economic determinants and by a set of social and collective representations that pre-establish the overall conditions in which they meet and upon which they act.[3] In this sense it becomes necessary to establish the representations that shape, from the outset, the possibility of recognising and taking into account the perspective of the other. The extent to which partners in interaction can recognise each other as holders of legitimate knowledge is constrained by the knowledges they already carry about themselves and others and, in particular, on the representation they hold about what is knowledge. Here we must return to the problem of what constitutes knowledge and once again confront the representations that, stemming from philosophical and scientific traditions, have defined knowledge in terms of a progressive hierarchical scale with some people positioned at the bottom and others at the top.

The hierarchical representation of knowledge is widespread and can be traced back to the very heart of modern rationality. It is a representation so deeply engrained in western self-interpretation that it managed to entangle even those who attempted to construct a critique of knowledge and relate it back to emotional, social and cultural contexts. Indeed, putting different knowledges into a hierarchical scale is an offshoot of the self-interpretation of modern thought, which struggled to distinguish itself from the myths and superstitions of past by defining its own development in terms of a linear progression from the lower to the higher (see Banuri 1990; Dussel 1996; Alcoff and Mendietta 2000). This was deeply absorbed by the inaugural corpus of the social sciences, and in psychology in particular the research and debate about the development and 'education' of reason, to use Piaget's famous terminology, framed the dominant conception of what constitutes knowledge.

Indeed, the work of both Piaget and Vygotsky referred back and informed the key concern of the day: how societies evolve from the traditional to the modern, and how we can understand, with societal evolution, the evolution of the human mind. As discussed in Chapter 2, in addressing this problem it became evident that there was a fundamental relationship between the psychological and the social, between the constitution of mind, thought and knowing and the form of a society. It is in this sense that we find in Piaget and Vygotsky a comprehensive theoretical corpus to understand the plastic nature of knowledge and its fundamental relation to contexts. But they did not escape from the hierarchical view in which they were entangled and, in turn, helped to consolidate. Even in Vygotsky, there is failure to appreciate that what is called rational knowledge is no less local than any other form of knowing (see for instance, Van der Veer 1991, 1996). While for both decentration of perspective is seen as the pinnacle of psychological development, their theoretical narratives remain centred. By delocalising (universalising) one form of knowledge at the expense of all others, psychology (and its co-related disciplines) has helped to consolidate and give legitimacy to a sociopolitical project where one form of knowledge defines itself as the privileged standpoint against which all other forms of knowing and living are assessed. Not accidentally the empirical material for this debate has been the radical other: comparisons between the grown-up individual western subject on the one hand, and on the other, children, 'primitive peoples', the mad, the lay person and the crowd. The radical other has been powerfully constructed as a site of irrationality and deprived of anything that could be called knowledge. Or, to use Foucault's apposite terms, the knowledge of the other has been subjugated, derided, distorted and misrecognised (Foucault 1980).

Habermas' account of modernity and discussion of what constitutes the rationality of different worldviews is yet another example of how theoretical positions, despite being committed to the intersubjective view and a communicative model, can remain trapped in the hierarchical representation of knowledge. While in my view his work remains one of the most comprehensive and inspiring accounts of the dialogical position, it ultimately suffers from the same limitations of the Piagetian approach, from which Habermas draws extensively. Based on Piaget's concept of decentration and the concomitant abandonment of the egocentric perspective it entails, he explicitly proposes a hierarchy between worldviews: 'we placed mythical, religious-metaphysical, and modern worldviews in a hierarchy, according to the degree of decentration of the world-understanding they make possible' (Habermas 1991: 190).

This is paradoxical in itself since decentration and abandonment of egocentrism require precisely the bracketing of all hierarchies between self and other and the recognition of an equality based on the idea of perspectives. Habermas presents the formal properties needed for cultural traditions to be rational through the lenses of the Piagetian model, which do point to the need for differentiation between self and other, the con-comitant recognition of the perspective of the other, and their being intrinsically connected with the development of a reflexive attitude, i.e. the capacity to absorb the lessons coming from interaction with others. But Habermas' use of decentration is one-sided and itself oppressed by the hierarchical representation it constructs: it cannot decentre itself and recognise the knowledge of others without a hierarchical lens because it is ensnared from within by the belief that his own knowledge is at the end – and top – of the scale. Habermas, as many others who have tried to salvage modern reason, falls prey to the one-sided illusions of the modern view, something that he himself alludes to in his work.[4] The utter paradox of this illusion is that it is grounded in the very desire from which it tries to escape: the illusion of a pure rationality free from self, other and culture is ulti-mately fuelled by a reason inundated by the omnipotence of a self that sees itself at the centre and end of history.

Dussel's assessment of modernity has captured well this contradiction (Dussel 1993, 1995). European modernity, he argues, is in fact born out of a myth, which it constructs in the very moment that it tries to destroy all myths: the myth of its own supremacy, of being the centre and end of history.

> Modernity as such was 'born' when Europe was in a position to pose itself against an other, when, in other words, Europe could constitute itself as a unified ego exploring, conquering, colonizing an alterity that gave back its image of itself. The other, in other words, was not 'dis-covered' (*descubierto*) or admitted as such, but concealed, or covered-up (*encubierto*), as the same as what Europe assumed it had always been. So if 1492 is the moment of the 'birth' of modernity as a concept, the moment of origin of a very particular myth of sacrificial violence, it also marks the origin of a process of concealment or misrecognition of the non-European.
>
> (Dussel 1993: 66)

In Dussel's account what makes it possible for the European ego to see itself as the end of history is the concealment of the other and the denial of his perspective. So it is not only the experience of discovery but also of conquest that constitutes the modern subjectivity. As long as the modern ego does not recognise its own destructive tendencies, it will continue to imagine its own as the most developed and most superior civilisation, and in accordance with this sense of superiority will feel obliged to educate, to civilise and to develop lesser civilisations. For Dussel, it is only a true encounter with the reason of the Other that will eventually grant to the modern self its redemption and allow it to come to terms with its own genocidal and destructive impetus, for if to discover the other is at the same time to discover oneself, the time for discoveries has not ended. Dussel's counter-account of modernity brings back to the encounter that characterised the inception of modernity the duality which allows not only discovering but also covering up the difference of the other.

Recognition and power

Mutual recognition between knowledge systems, which is at the basis of any communicative potential between knowledges, would require dismantling the widespread assumption that there is one form of knowing that is superior to all others. This, needless to say, is no easy task. The hierarchical representation of knowledge rests on resources and power as well as on a self-interpretation that deeply believes in its own superiority. The combination of these factors affects the recognition of the validity claims which different knowledge systems put forward in the public sphere. Theoretically it is clear that all knowledges are created by the architecture of intersubjective contexts, which they seek to express. Theoretically we also know that the diversity of knowledge systems is expressive of human ecologies, human cultures and human psychologies. Epistemic claims, as we have seen, are also ontological and cultural claims; they not only propose readings of the world but declare states of being and the ways of a culture. Why thus are some knowledges granted the recognition and legitimacy of being knowledge whilst others are represented as 'non-knowledge'?

Consider for instance the knowledge held by white men in suits, sitting around a table in the headquarters of the IMF vis-à-vis the knowledge held by the Mayan women of Guatemala about their reproductive lives. As with the Mayan women, the knowledge of the men in suits is linked to a particular context, it expresses particular interests and it tries to sustain and perpetuate a specific identity and way of life. However, there are very different representations attached to each knowledge system: while the former is seen as local and not infrequently considered 'ignorance' and superstition, the latter bears full epistemological legitimacy, derived from a combination of the representation of science in the contemporary world and economic, political and cultural power. These different representations allow the knowledge of the white men in suits to cast its representational power far beyond the context of its production, penetrate other locales and propose a course of action that is more likely to take place even if not fully accepted by local peoples. The trick that allows one form of knowledge to travel beyond the context of its production and impose itself on distant locales irrespective of conditions of reception is the same trick that grants to some knowledges the aura of universality and to others the confinement of locality. It is not a trick to be found in the knowledge system itself but in the process of legitimation of different forms of knowledge. This process is related to the positioning of the knowers in the social fabric and their ability to have their knowledge recognised.

The problem of legitimation in knowledge is directly related to power differentials between knowledge systems (Jovchelovitch 1997; Campbell and Jovchelovitch 2000), a problem I am only partially addressing here. Development theorists have articulated these differentials in great detail showing that the legitimacy of different ways of knowing can only be understood in the context of social, economic and political frameworks that grant power to some knowledge systems and by the same token disqualify others (Apffell-Marglin and Marglin 1990, 1994; Escobar 1995). Asymmetries in the status and valuation of different forms of knowledge impinge directly on the ways knowledge is communicated, establishes its veracity and constructs its authority. These asymmetries are very much alive today and are well known to all who struggle to theorise common senses, lay knowledges and the knowledge of the other. The idea that these forms of knowing are a bunch of 'superstitions' and mythologies, or just 'ignorance' is pervasive and still guides many programmes of research and intervention. Thus the need to carry to the ground a reconceptualisation of knowledge, the need to give practical import to different conceptions of knowing and the need to question hard the practices deriving from mainstream conceptions. Rather than being just 'theory', these conceptions have concrete implications for all those people who are at the receiving end of the practices these representations support.

Dialogical and non-dialogical encounters

So far I have been concerned with establishing the role of recognition and perspective-taking in the social psychology of the knowledge encounter, emphasising two constitutive dimensions of these processes: (a) the nature of the intersubjective relations between self and other which allow or distort recognition and perspective-taking; and (b) the role of larger representations about the knowledge of others – in particular, the hierarchical representation of knowledge. Both are needed to understand how dialogue is facilitated or hindered in the encounter between knowledge systems. In this section I draw on the theoretical resources delineated in the pages above to systematise an analytical framework for capturing different types of encounter between knowledge systems as well as the different outcomes these encounters produce. The central criterion I use in the analysis of the knowledge encounter is recognition or denial of the diversity of knowledge, which in turn depends on the representations about, and the legitimacy granted to, different knowledge systems. I shall systematise the distinction between dialogical and non-dialogical encounters and consider some of the outcomes they make possible. I describe these as: (a) dialogical, involving coexistence and inclusion with the potential for hybridisation; and (b) non-dialogical, involving displacement and exclusion with potential for segregation and even destruction. It goes without saying that these are ideal analytical distinctions and no knowledge encounter in social life is deprived of internal contradictions that make it at times dialogical and non-dialogical. It is also important to note that in the approach I develop here the notion of dialogue can be considered at the ontological and epistemological levels. Dialogue is ontological insofar as it offers us the means to understand the constitution of being, i.e. all existing entities are formed dialogically. At the same time, dialogue is a social practice, developed under different conditions and open to empirical observation in social fields. In social psychology, Marková draws on dialogue both ontologically and epistemologically. On the one hand she uses it to understand the formation of entities in general (Marková 2003) and on the other hand she has sought to capture how dialogue is realised as social practice (Marková and Foppa 1991; Marková *et al.* 1995). This is also the case in both Habermas and Freire. Thus we can draw on dialogical approaches to understand both dialogical and non-dialogical social practices, which is precisely what I try to do here.

Before I proceed it is important to add one further qualification to this distinction. I am acutely aware that some of the outcomes I consider dialogical can be achieved in non-dialogical situations and vice versa. The transformation of knowledges is a multicausal process that can originate from a diversity of situations. Hybridisation, for instance, has been achieved throughout the colonial experience in Latin America in encounters that were far from being purely dialogical. My emphasis, however, is on the social psychological conditions that construct the *intentionality* – conscious and unconscious – with which interlocutors communicate in the knowledge encounter. The framework I present below is not exhaustive and remains open for further consideration. Let me now consider each of these processes in turn.

Dialogical encounters

The central feature of the dialogical encounter is the effort to take into account the perspective of the other and recognise it as legitimate. At the basis of these encounters is the dialogical principle where strategies of communicative action allow for the recognition of the potential clashes and potential alliances that can take place and develop in the course of the encounter. In such situations interlocutors struggle to take each other into account and reach a mutual understanding about the position, the perspective and the potential contribution each can bring to the situation at hand. Rather than idealising, romanticising or over-valuing one form of knowledge at the expense of the other, asymmetries in status and legitimacy can be recognised and worked upon by interlocutors. The aim here is to construct a critical encounter based on the dialogical principle where all stakeholders in the process can gain and develop knowledge. Dialogical encounters are, to be sure, a process. Interlocutors do not meet in conditions of a priori established communication and dialogue. There is hard work involved in processes of establishing communication and dialogical encounters *become* dialogical through the gradual development of relations in which self and other 'survive' the difficulties of the process and reach awareness of the gains involved in coexistence and inclusion of the perspective of others. In this type of knowledge encounter the transformations operated by dialogical communication produce coexistence and social inclusion of different knowledges leading to the eventual hybridisation of knowledge systems.

The coexistence of knowledge systems is expressed in many representational fields in the contemporary world, where social rather than collective representations tend to predominate. The coexistence and inclusion of different knowledge systems in the same community and even in the same individual have been amply demonstrated by social psychological research in a variety of settings and are at the basis of the process of cognitive polyphasia (Gumelli and Jacobi 1990; Gervais 1997; Gervais and Jovchelovitch 1998; Wagner *et al.* 1999; Jovchelovitch 2004). Representational fields such as these comprise heterogeneous and multiple forms of knowing which live side by side fulfilling different functions and responding to different contextual demands. They constitute patchworks of knowledge where science, belief, ideology and common sense, to cite just some, are used as *resources* and drawn upon depending on the situation and on what is at stake. Given the diversity of functions and aims of these different knowledges, coexistence via social inclusion becomes an asset for both communities and individuals.

Coexistence in time produces hybridisation in knowledge, which in the long run appears as a more integrated representational field. Hybridisation is the process that creates new representations out of the dialogues between knowledges taking place over time. Depending on how far back one goes, it becomes evident that most if not all knowledge systems are hybrids, which have incorporated and transformed elements from a variety of sources. These processes tend to occur in social life, even in those situations where there is explicit resistance to accommodate the knowledge of others. It would be wrong to suppose that they only take place when interlocutors are actively disposed towards the communicative encounter. Clearly this is not the case, as the history of all cultural borrowings shows. Yet it would be equally wrong not to theorise the space in which very different social actors genuinely struggle towards dialogue and come to recognise the legitimacy of alternative representations, patterns of action, values and relevant structures attached to any given situation. In the field of health, for instance, much of the dialogical encounters that are being advocated, and to some extent enacted, express precisely this struggle to recognise that knowledge about health and illness is a hybrid constructed through the coexistence and social inclusion of different traditions. I shall return to this problem in the last section of this chapter when addressing dialogical encounters.

Non-dialogical encounters

The central feature of non-dialogical encounters is lack of mutual recognition and the domination it makes possible – the perspective expressed in the knowledge of the other is denied and recognition remains locked in the power of one knowledge system over another. Underlying these encounters is denial of legitimacy to the knowledge of others and the belief that there is one best and superior form of knowing that can displace all others. In such encounters interlocutors are entangled in an intersubjective context where the asymmetries in the status and valuation of knowledge systems become preponderant and prevent the inclusion of perspectives. The aim is to impose on the other the perspective of self. This aim lies in the will to impose rather than in the inability to understand the other. Indeed, non-dialogical encounters do not necessarily presuppose that self cannot understand the other. The displacement and domination of the knowledge of others is usually effected in full awareness of the reality of the other because in this case what is at stake is strategic action,[5] i.e. the explicit attempt to exert an effect on the other in order to make dominant the perspective of self. In this type of knowledge encounter the transformations operated by domination produce the displacement and social exclusion of different knowledges leading to the potential segregation and even destruction of knowledge systems.

The displacement of the knowledge of others by a more powerful knowledge system has been extensively researched in a variety of fields, including education, health, development initiatives in the Third World and colonialism, amongst others. Processes of knowledge displacement have a tremendous destructive potential, as they tend to undermine and at times erase the accumulated know-hows and cultural traditions of specific groups and communities. Examples include medical knowledge vis-à-vis women's knowledge in delivering and raising children, the clashes between modern versus traditional knowledge in the colonial experience, the confrontations between experts and traditional communities in areas such as health, agriculture and the environment, and the encounter between science and common sense (Apffell-Marglin 1990; Todorov 1992; Gabe *et al.* 1994; Said 1995; Wynne 1995; Chambers 2003; Pottier *et al.* 2003). In all these encounters there is a predominant monological understanding that one form of knowing is superior to the other and the attempt to displace the views, practices and values embedded in the knowledge of the other. Deeply engrained in the practice of displacing the knowledge of others is the hierarchical representation of knowledge and the belief in its purity as a rational system that grows by becoming impersonal and detached from the context of its production. This representation and the power it carries systematically distort the potential for recognition and dialogue that are intrinsically embedded in all intersubjective contexts.

Table 5.1. summarises the framework developed above. The table contrasts dialogical and non-dialogical encounters in terms of the inclusion or

Table 5.1 Types of knowledge encounters and outcomes

Dialogical encounters	*Non-dialogical encounters*
Co-existence (Inclusion)	Displacement (exclusion)
⇩	⇩
Hybridisation (cognitive polyphasia)	Segregation/destruction (monological cognition)

exclusion of the perspective of the other. Including the perspective of others allows for the coexistence of different knowledge systems, which tend to change towards hybridisation and states of cognitive polyphasia. Non-dialogical encounters exclude the perspective of others by actively displacing different forms of knowing. This can lead to the segregation and eventual destruction of knowledges privileging states of monological cognition.

As I mentioned before, this framework is not exhaustive. My intention is not to suggest that it will capture the knowledge encounter phenomenon in its entirety. Equally, the distinction I propose between dialogical and non-dialogical should not be taken rigidly as it is clear that the hybridisation and segregation of knowledge systems are multidimensional phenomena and at times escape from neat demarcations. Having said that, I am firmly convinced that the segregation and destruction of a form of knowing rests firmly anchored in intersubjective contexts where the other is denied and violated. As far as I am aware no knowledge system has revealed a suicidal tendency without being exposed to the violence of domination from others. Surely hybridisation itself in time can destroy some elements of the sources from which it draws, but all hybrids are 'speakers' and tellers of the traditions they inherit, even if in a disguised form. In this sense, the dialogical and non-dialogical distinction remains generative to assess the conditions of realisation of processes of recognition and perspective-taking in the dynamics of the knowledge encounter. In the remainder of this chapter I seek to use the analytical framework proposed to explore two concrete examples of encounters with the knowledge of others: the case of madness and community interventions.

Classification, segregation and exclusion in madness

Perhaps no other encounter is as exemplary of processes of excluding the other and his perspective than the case of our relations to madness. From the great confinement of the Classical Age to policies of care in the community today the mad have stood as the paradigmatic other, the deposi-taries of our fears and denials, seen as sites of either unworldly or too worldly wisdoms. From the idea of possession to the more contemporary notion of losing one's mind, the mad have personified the deep angst associated with the uncontrolled and the unpredictable. That one is sovereign in relation to one's mind is the illusion that madness ultimately confronts – and for this it has paid dearly.

The encounter between so-called sanity and madness has been historically marked by a deep ambivalence, where the difficulties of the former to establish a dialogue with the latter have predominated. Madness has, for most of the time, stood as something to do away with and to erase, either by physically segregating the people considered to be mad or by trying to restore the mad back to a state of normality. This history has been well described by Michel Foucault, whose work constitutes the most comprehensive account about the history of madness and the emergence of clinical knowledge in the west. It would be impossible to do justice to the complexity of Foucault's work here; it is a vast, detailed and eloquent analysis of destructiveness towards radical others and no psychologist can possibly start to understand what constitutes her discipline without reading it and appreciating it. My intention here, however, is not to consider his work in detail but to extract from it the elements that elucidate the non-dialogical character of the encounter between sanity and madness. Equally important to the trajectory of non-dialogicity I wish to trace is the work of Goffman, Basaglia and Jodelet. I draw on the work of all to establish the discussion that follows (Basaglia 1968; Goffman 1968; Foucault 1971, 1987; Jodelet 1991).

Foucault has shown that the different representational systems and practices related to the mad in different historical periods have continuously tried to segregate and ultimately exclude mad people from so-called normal environments. Despite the differences between them, most of these representations have operated as barriers that both defined madness from the dominant perspective of self and by the same token prevented the perspective of the excluded other from being considered. The most exemplary of these representational systems was the new clinical knowledge born towards the end of the Classical Age. It consolidated the idea of madness as an illness and dealt with the ambivalence of placing the mad person between the judge and the doctor by firmly placing her in the hands of the doctor. It subjected the mad to new disciplinary practices formulated especially to domesticate and control the utter difference expressed in the reasoning and behaviour of the mad person.

A brief analysis of the practices developed by expert knowledge towards the mad reveals that it has evolved from attempts to chain and put the mad aside in large institutions where all kinds of deviants were brought together, to practices of reintegration and care in the community. The sequence of these practices is summarised in Table 5.2. Combined they show well the power of some knowledges to sustain exclusionary practices and to survive long after the material walls of the institutions they themselves construct are gone.

Table 5.2 Institutional practices towards the mad

Institutional practices
The great confinement and the birth of the asylum (17th and 18th centuries) The psychiatric hospital: total institutions (19th century) De-institutionalisation (20th century–1960s onwards) Care in the community (20th century–1970s onwards)

In the period Foucault has called the Great Confinement madness was sharply isolated from sanity and mad people were confined in special spaces with beggars, criminals and other kinds of deviants. These special spaces had no therapeutic aims; they intended to correct rather than to cure. From the late eighteenth century throughout most of the nineteenth century the psychiatric reforms initiated by William Tuke in York and Philippe Pinnel in France transformed madness into a disease and sought to cure it, through discipline, routine and therapy. It was in this context that a clear expertise was articulated, under the umbrella of medical knowledge: the science of psychiatry was born, soon followed by psychology and psychopathology. The asylum was the institution that originated from these transformations, and as the word itself reveals it was an attempt to humanise society's responses to the mad. However, from the intentions of the reformers to the realities of the total institutions that ensued we can observe the gradual consolidation of an encounter whose main drive remained the systematic segregation and exclusion of the other. As the mad person became a psychiatric patient, the emergent knowledge of psychiatry and psychopathology provided the substance and scientific justification to this drive: the history of psychiatric therapies is well documented and it cannot be recapitulated here, but from iron chains and the straitjacket, to the electroshock and chemical contention it is difficult to identify a substantial change in the underlying drive of imprisoning and colonising the mind and body of the other. As Foucault observed, it was not until the emergence of psychoanalysis that the dominant non-dialogical encounter between expert knowledge and madness was challenged, for it was Freud who suggested that it was necessary to listen and to talk in order to understand the symptom and what it expressed.

Goffman's (1968) study of total institutions as apparatuses for the mortification and liquidation of self triggered a critique of the psychiatric asylum that, combined with the non-validity of diagnostic procedures in psychiatric settings (Rosenhan 1975), helped to consolidate the movement that was to be called de-institutionalisation (Basaglia 1968). The de-institutionalisation movement was able to articulate a powerful counter-discourse that questioned the principles behind the relations between professionals and patients and the power held by the former over the latter. It moved the emphasis from cure and discipline to the creation of environments that could reframe the daily experience of patients and see them as human beings located in a context that itself needed to be changed. Clinicians working with the patients started to see the pattern that Goffman, Basaglia and others had described: the hospital and its structures were the producers of madness, not the solutions for it.

De-institutionalisation opened up the doors of the asylum and tried to reintegrate the psychiatric patient back in the community. Inspired by new theoretical readings of what is madness and what is mental health, the movement brought about new psychiatric practices such as therapeutic communities and community care. And yet, after more than two decades of continuous struggle in the field of theory, practice and policy, reformers soon came face to face with the concrete realities of practice. Conditions of care seemed to be worsening fast and patients were left vulnerable to the heavy resistance of the communities in which they were placed (Dear and Taylor 1982; Jones 1993). The idea of reintegration acquired a whole new complexity that needed to be understood and dealt with if the new practices were to be sustained.[6]

Within this context of policy crisis, Jodelet's research on social representations of madness sought to explore the nature of the representations at work when psychiatric patients live in close contact with a community (Jodelet 1991). Her ethnography powerfully shows that the contact, the closeness and the habit that characterised the intersubjective encounter between patients and community gave rise to a dynamics whose main imperative was the urgent need to demarcate difference and establish separation: knowing well who was and who was not mad was at the centre of the interaction between community and the patients. The analysis of the representations revealed that, provoked by the proximity with the radical otherness of madness, the community defended itself by constructing, in the symbolic rituals of everyday life, a knowledge that reaffirmed it as a sane community and at the same time helped to make sense of the condition of the other living in its midst. To the risk of undifferentiation and the angst and fear of fusion, the community juxtaposed practices of territorial demarcation, of separation of bodies and waters and of identity delimitation that were not too different from the material barriers and the walls of the asylum. The results made clear that everyday contact between patients and community created an intersubjective encounter where the dynamics of institutionalisation was recreated by the production of symbolic walls that maintained the rituals of separation found in the asylum.

In the practices described above we find the history of an encounter where madness and the system of thinking and knowing the world it contains was interchangeably construed as unreason, insanity and disease. Of course there have been attempts to establish a dialogue with madness and to 'liberate the word of the mad' as proclaimed the motto of the French journal *Cahiers pour La Folie*, created after 1968 to publish papers by patients and by personnel involved in their care. The stampede of publications, movements and debates that characterised the questioning of dominant psychiatric practices from the 1960s throughout the 1970s and 1980s expressed the conviction that there was something that needed to be retrieved from the experience of madness and allowed to coexist in 'normal' society. De-institutionalisation resulted precisely from this conviction, a conviction that recast theory, practice and policy and questioned deeply the foundations of psychiatry (Basaglia 1968; Mannoni 1970; Castel 1971, 1978; Aulagnier 2001). In these attempts, despite the contradictions, lacunae and ambivalence, there was a genuine desire to understand and to communicate with the experience of madness.[7] Despite this desire, attempts to understand the otherness of madness and take it into account have been systematically undermined by representations whose main drive continued to be the segregation and exclusion of the mad. It may well be, as Rose (1996) has aptly pointed out, that this results from the fact that madness resists categorisation and classification. The power of these representations continues to live in both science and everyday common sense knowledges and to this day manages to exert effects of exclusion and segregation, even if outside the hospital and through more subtle forms such as stigma (Gillman 1985; Rose 1997; Morant and Rose 1998). Decades of psychiatric reform, de-institutionalisation struggles and reflection about the nature and origins of madness have not been sufficient to dismantle the excluding apparatuses that Foucault described as foundational in the constitution of western rationality. The rationalisation of exclusion and the exclusion of a different rationality continues to a large extent, to define the encounter between sanity and insanity.

This encounter shows that dialogical and non-dialogical potentials struggle side by side when different knowledges meet in public spheres. If domination has been preponderant in relation to the mad, the attempts to recognise and listen to the experience of madness reveal that it is nevertheless possible to reframe the intersubjective contexts in which representations and practices towards the excluded other develop. Recognising the voice and the rights of all of those who struggled to 'survive' the dominant knowledge directed towards the experience of madness is increasingly seen as a necessary requisite in the task of reconstructing theory, practice and policy (Rose 2003a, 2003b). It would be naive to suppose that these efforts would alone succeed in overcoming the historical problems and contemporary difficulties that permeate the encounter sanity–madness. These problems involve issues related to the social organisation and institutionalisation of madness and certainly do not admit of easy solutions. Dialogue, however, is itself not an easy solution and as long as dominant representations about madness do not change it will be difficult substantively to change social structures. Despite the difficulties that are embedded in taking the perspective of the other who survived, establishing a dialogue with her difference and reframing the intersubjective encounter is the only path for changing these representations. To this end the anticipatory function of representations is essential for it can cast the resistance and innovative practices of the present forwards and release the hopes of producing a different future from the burdens of this heavy history.

Dialogue in the community

Is there a chance for holders of different knowledges to meet and to communicate in contemporary communities? Can people who are very different from each other in terms of cultural, ethnic and social background establish a conversation about issues of common concern and together construct a joint account about what is happening and what needs to be done? These very practical questions present themselves in a variety of settings where social psychologists work and are at the core of the social psychology of knowledge encounters. Establishing dialogues within and across communities is not an easy task and requires effort and determination for all of those who are involved in the process. In the last section of this chapter I would like to discuss the dialogical potentials embedded in knowledge encounters by considering some of the experiences developed in Latin America under the inspiration of Paulo Freire's pedagogical writings. Freire's literacy method, developed out of a theoretical and practical engagement with illiterate adults in the Brazilian Northeast, stands as an exemplary model of dialogical encounters between different knowledge systems. His work in the field of adult education generated a programme of research and intervention complemented by other Latin American theorists working in philosophy (Dussel 1993, 1995, 1996, 2004), social psychology (Bleger 1980; Pichon-Rivière 1980, 1991; Martín-Baró 1994; Hollander 1997; Guareschi 2004), action research (Fals-Borda 1985, 1988) and psychoanalysis (Langer 1987; Lira 2000). Common to all is the view that the communication between self and other is the path for the development of personal, social and material resources. The task of a critical theory is to understand what helps or hinders this possibility and develop theories and methods that can contribute to advance it.[8]

Freire's pedagogy of the oppressed, whose counterpart is a pedagogy of autonomy and a pedagogy of hope, constitutes a detailed theoretical and practical corpus about the structure of encounters between different knowledges, expressed in the encounter between educator and educatee. His point of departure is the recognition that learning can only take place if all interlocutors are prepared to learn and to recognise that everyone involved starts with knowledge of some kind. Against the passive – 'bench-sitting' – conception of education that saw the pedagogical act as a linear transfer of information from the one who knows to the one who does not know, Freire proposed that a true pedagogy must start by the recognition of the knowledge of the one who apparently 'does not know' and develop into a dialogical attitude in which both educator and educatee learn and change through communicative action.

Understanding that knowledge systems are expressive of cultural codes, identities, practices and resources lies at the heart of the dialogical encounter, for it is this understanding that brings about the ethical imperative of recognising the other and engaging in a dialogical encounter where perspectives can be understood, negotiated and eventually transformed. The combined recognition of diversity, expressiveness and limitations in all knowledge constitute the core conditions for communication between different knowledge systems. Conscientisation, that is, the gradual awakening to the full determinants of one's psychological and social circumstances comes out of the practice of communication. Underlying all genuine communication is the implicit commitment to the notion of equality, to the bracketing out of differences and to the adoption of procedures that promote and require dialogue and reciprocity. This was the central concern in Paulo Freire's work and throughout his life he tried to articulate its theoretical and practical dimensions. In this sense, Freire's pedagogy is not only conceptual but also normative and procedural, that is, it requires a set of practices that enact the normative conceptualisation it develops about knowledge, its production and transmission.

The literacy method, which informs intervention in a variety of community settings, expresses well how the conceptual and the procedural are brought together in Freire's pedagogy. The method enacts the very dialogue that is theoretically central for all literacy – for learning to read the word and the world. It consists of a number of steps in which the dyad educator–educatee uncovers the experiential universe of the community through the search for its vocabulary and the understanding of the semantic fields which link up words and concrete day-to-day experiences. Using dialogical problematisation in the manner of Socratic maieutics, interlocutors gradually construct a situation that moves from 'belonging to' to the reflexive 'entering into' the symbolic universe previously mapped. Transpositions from 'belonging' to 'entering into' and back are intended to call into question the taken-for-granted assumptions we live by and critically reflect on how they are produced and how they can be transformed. This critical reflection allows the creation of codifications that take the initial mapping of the vocabulary and semantic fields to new levels of understanding while accompanying the deconstruction and reconstruction of syllabic components of words, so that reading the words and discovering new word combinations becomes a concomitant reading of oneself, others and the political, social and cultural totality in which people are located.

Elsewhere I have suggested how Freire's method informs social psychological interventions in community and health (Campbell and Jovchelovitch 2000; Guareschi and Jovchelovitch 2004), an issue I shall return to in Chapter 6. For now I want to consider the case of rural extension, a crucial social issue in Latin America, and one that Freire has addressed directly in *Extension or Communication* (Freire 1973b). Considering the practice of rural development and the encounter between extension agents and rural communities, Freire tackled directly the problem of communication between holders of different knowledges. He was unwavering about the possibility and necessity of establishing dialogical encounters between different knowledges and projected this need into a pedagogy of hope, which accounts for the normative futures that human beings construct while living in a less than ideal present.[9] In this work Freire drew from his literacy method to offer a theoretical programme that went far beyond the rural field; he provided both a general critique of non-reciprocal relations and a dialogical model for all encounters between expert and lay knowledge. Starting from the analysis of the semantic field of the word 'extension', Freire shows that in the very meaning of the word we find the idea of transferring from one to the other, of extending one's knowledge towards other people and regions. Extension reveals in a nutshell all that is problematic and non-dialogical in the encounter between the agronomist and the peasant: it is the unilateral attempt to substitute one knowledge for another, as if knowledge could be substituted monologically without simultaneously violating personal, social and cultural worlds.

In the analysis of extension Freire produced a powerful critique of what constitutes anti-dialogue and in particular of one of its characteristics: cultural invasion. His analysis of cultural invasion resembles Benjamin's work on domination and Habermas' concept of strategic action: the other is invaded by self, who denies and silences his words by persuading, by dominating, by using propaganda and other similar instruments. The transference of knowledge, instead of communication between knowledges, ends up undermining the construction of knowledge itself, for it presupposes depositing content in a passive recipient whose task is to unreflectively introject what is given. Cultural invasion is anti-dialogical because it considers the perspective of the other empty consciousness or wrong consciousness, usually labelled 'ignorance', but never knowledge. It does not see the other as an interlocutor with a legitimate perspective of his own, but someone to be convinced and persuaded of the project self is trying to further. The non-dialogical encounter brings to the fore the ideological function of representations and exemplifies well how asymmetries in the intersubjective context lead to the domination of one form of knowing by another.

Whereas Freire was adamant that change was necessary, in particular in relation to deprived rural and urban communities whose knowledge he never idealised, he was equally adamant that genuine and ethical change can only take place with the participation of all stakeholders in the process. In this sense, Freire's theory of communication between holders of different knowledges points to the need and to the importance of constructing participatory dialogues where all interlocutors are recognised as legitimate contributors to the process. Embedded in this dialogue is the view that different knowledges are resources to be transformed and enriched through processes of communication, because no single knowledge is ever produced

Table 5.3 Dialogue and non-dialogue in Freire's method

Dialogue	Non-dialogue
A with B:	A over B:
Communication	A extends a communiqué to B
Mutual recognition between interlocutors	Belief in the superiority of one over another
Matrix: love, humbleness, hope, trust, critical	Matrix: loveless, arrogant, hopeless, mistrustful, acritical

without dialogue in the first place. The belief in the absoluteness of one's knowledge is in fact a defence that rigidifies and paralyses the very development of knowledge, scientific or otherwise. As Freire pointed out many times in his lectures and talks,[10] it is out of the critical dialogical encounters between technical knowledge and everyday knowledge that new knowledge can develop. The growth of scientific knowledge shows that it cannot preclude the world of common sense and common wisdom. Thus while Freire did not idealise common sense and everyday knowledges, he decidedly pointed to the resources they contained and the lifeworlds they expressed, a recognition that was to prove crucial in overcoming domination and constructing a critical encounter where all stake holders can gain and develop knowledge. Table 5.3 summarises the contrast between dialogue and non-dialogue in Freire's pedagogy.

In considering the reality of rural communities, whose knowledge contains strong elements of magic and participation between the natural and social worlds, he asked a question that is not different in substance to the questions social psychologists continue to pose today as they engage in the study of local social representations in fields such as health, education and community, amongst others: 'What can be done with communities which act in this way, whose thought and action – both magic, and conditioned by the structure in which they are situated, hinder their work or their lives?' For Freire it was clear that the answer did not lie in extension and replacement. This would simply amount to an act of cultural invasion, a new form of conquest as described by Dussel in his assessment of the modern subjectivity. This is the case because:

Magical thought is neither illogical nor pre-logical. It possesses its own internal logical structure and opposes as much as possible any new forms mechanically superimposed. Like any other manner of thinking, it is unquestionably bound not only to a way of acting but to a language and a structure. To superimpose on it another form of thought, implying another language, another structure, another manner of acting, stimulates a natural reaction: a defensive reaction in face of the 'invader' who threatens its internal equilibrium.

Freire 1973b: 104

Here Freire summarises a great deal of the argument I have been developing in this book. Knowledge and its corresponding structures are bound to ways of acting, to languages, to specific structures that need to be recognised as deeply linked to the identity and values of a community and as emotional and cultural assets this community has produced. While this knowledge can reveal gaps, illusions and discrepancies to the perspective of the observer, there remains the need to understand that from the perspective of the actor this is not the case. Just trying to debunk it and replace it is an act of violence, frequently resisted by local peoples and rightly so.

The possibility for changing it, which I see as a legitimate agenda that needs to be made explicit and explicated, must arise through dialogue and the mutual engagement of educator–educatee towards the development of conscientisation and the deepening of awareness about self and other (individual and collective) positions in the world. This is not a one-way road where the expert agent persuades local people to take on board the scientific knowledge on offer, but a two-way exchange where experts can also learn from the knowledge and wisdom afforded by the experience of life each day. This recognition is the truly radical requisite of the dialogical encounter for it needs, in order to be de facto realised, the rejection of a hierarchical representation of knowledge, a deep commitment to the belief that ordinary people have a contribution to make and know what they are talking about and an acceptance of the incompleteness and limitations of one's own knowledge. Freire's life work was not only a theoretical but also a political struggle towards this triple recognition, which needless to say is difficult to achieve in our personal lives and hardly a reality in our social worlds.

While non-dialogue is widespread and a permanent possibility, the central elements of Freire's work provide a working programme and a growing network of global practice that projects the normative and practical necessity of dialogue into the field. His work is a critique of cultural invasion, a powerful proposal about the nature and development of knowledge and a practical guide to how to go about it. It is a radically dialogical approach that uses dialogicity for both conceptualisation and as a method of intervention. Despite the pessimism of those who find communication between knowledges an unachievable aim, the potential embedded in dialogical encounters between knowledge systems is not only possible but it is necessary and, as lessons from the field increasingly show, constitutes a powerful resource for both individuals and communities.

6 Studying knowledge in everyday life

In this chapter I want to focus on how the theoretical issues previously discussed in this book can be translated into an applied programme of research and intervention in social psychology. Following Kurt Lewin's famous maxim that there is nothing more practical than a good theory, I want to show how the conceptual framework I proposed in this book makes a difference in research and practical interventions in social psychology. In previous chapters I have raised but not pursued questions related to the applied implications of different conceptualisations of knowledge and their consequences in social life. How do we study representations and connect empirical projects with the theoretical programme I have proposed? How can social psychological research contribute to the recognition of diversity in knowledge, to the worth of unconventional forms of expertise and to the development of dialogues between different knowledge systems? How can research be combined with intervention and lead to collaborative transformations in communities and policymaking? These are some of the questions I would like to address in this final chapter.

In order to do so I want to recall two aspects of the approach to knowledge I have developed in this book that have concrete implications to the direction of research and practice. The first is the idea that all knowledge is *expressive* insofar as it seeks to represent subjective, intersubjective and objective worlds. Far from being a monological cognitive construct, knowledge systems are produced by intersubjective triads that connect knowledge to persons and the public contexts in which it is produced. To all knowledge there corresponds a relationship between people and between people and their environment that is both natural and social. In this sense, the study of social knowledge is neither the listing of themes about an object in the social world nor the description of the cognitive processes underlying it. Rather, it involves the study of the relationships that are at the basis of knowledge formation and sensitivity to the logic that underlies these relations by connecting the content of knowledge to its cognitive processes and these to the personal and social logics that permeate acts of knowing. Whereas some of these may seem illogical to the observer, they possess reasons of their own and respond to needs that are specific to the people who enact them.

Knowledge systems project identities, values and ways of life into social fields and these need to be considered, at least initially, without reference to an ideal and 'right' set of representations. It is from the idea that all knowledge is expressive that the practical requirement to map out and diagnose local representations drawing on the melancholic attitude as defined by Bauer and Gaskell (1999) arises: the capacity to suspend convictions, interests and prejudices and ultimately to put into parenthesis the researcher's agenda in order to listen to the other. Allowing communities and persons to speak and display a voice in the research process is central to the dialogical process of uncovering representations usually undermined, displaced or made invisible by the power structures of public spheres. There is an emancipatory potential embedded in the task of recognising the validity of a community's knowledge and engaging in a critical dialogue with it.

The second and related point refers to the idea that different forms of knowing can live side by side fulfilling different functions and responding to different needs in the life of communities. Rather than conceiving of knowledge as the end product at the top of a linear developmental scale, displacing and erasing lower forms, knowledge is seen as a plural and heterogeneous phenomenon capable of comprising different rationalities and forms. Recognising the diversity of knowledge and the coexistence of different knowledge systems in the same community (and even same individual) raises questions about how different knowledges compare and what happens when they meet in public spheres. Encounters and comparison between knowledge systems brings about problems related to the evaluation of knowledges, the legitimacy that is granted to knowledges and the obstacles and possibilities comprised in the communication between knowledges. In this sense, studying knowledge means to study the array of practices, relationships and concrete contexts in which knowing, as social action, occurs. It means to be sensitive to what knowledge expresses and to the interrelations between one form of knowing and others, since they are not only connected to the identities, values and the ways of life of a community but also to how the knowledge of communities fares in unequal public arenas. It also means to consider how encountering the knowledge of others can contribute to the process of critically evaluating one's own knowledge, the development of conscientisation and ultimately the empowerment of communities for productive transformations.

These issues have been present, albeit in insipient form, throughout the trajectory of the social psychology of knowledge, and in particular within the tradition of social representations research. They can be found at the core of classical studies that established the field, such as Moscovici's study on psychoanalysis and Jodelet's study of madness. Underlying these investigations was the attempt to uncover representational fields that expressed the reality of a society, a community, an historical period, as known and understood by ordinary people in contexts of everyday life. They belong to what I called in Chapter 2 the phenomenology of everyday life, the study of the understandings, mentalities and practices that shape the constitution of worldviews and ways of life. The commitment with the expressiveness of everyday knowledges and the concomitant need to listen carefully to what they reveal has always been central to this tradition of research. Against the idea that everyday knowledge is 'ideological', in the old sense of distortion or 'false consciousness', the aim has been to retrieve the epistemological dignity of the knowledges linked to the everyday and understand the understandings they express. In many respects this is akin to what Freud did when he decided to talk and listen to his patients in turn of the century Vienna, what Piaget did when he talked to children about their conceptions of the world, what Lévy-Strauss did in the Brazilian Xingu, his *Tristes Tropiques*, what Weber did in relation to the 'spirit of capitalism', what Goffman did in relation to the asylum. Common to all is the attempt to understand the universes of signification that underlie the full texture of lived experience, be it inside a hospital or in the experience of mental unrest, be it amidst massive social transformations or simply in the experience of life each day.

While subsequent research on social representations is far from being a unified field and reveals much of the contradictions of social psychology as a whole (Allansdottir *et al.* 1993; for a recent and comprehensive assessment see Wagner and Hayes 2005), a great deal of the work that is being carried out today is concerned with understanding the interface knowledges/community/culture (see Jovchelovitch and Campbell 2000; Jodelet 2002; Montero 2002; Campbell 2003; Campbell and Murray 2004; Cornish 2004; De-Graft Aikins 2004; Howarth 2004; Howarth and Foster 2004). This is the stream that I have emphasised throughout this book and seek to develop further in this chapter. I shall start with a brief review of Moscovici's and Jodelet's classical studies on social representations, emphasising how the original empirical programme they put forward relates back to the issues I have discussed and informs more recent developments in the field. Against the background of current research, I discuss what is involved in the mapping of local representational systems and suggest some key entry points for conducting investigations in this area. In the second section of the chapter I explore issues of participation, conscientisation and empowerment that derive from the reflexive understanding of local knowledges and their interrelations in public spheres. In the third section I shall consider the standpoint from where interventions are carried out and develop the argument that research is itself a dialogical act. Bringing together these threads of argumentation, I conclude the chapter with a discussion of the main issues I have addressed in the book and the ethical dimensions linked to the study of diversity in an unequal and globalised world.

Studying social representations

In previous chapters I have argued that knowledge systems are enabled by representational processes that express at once subjective, intersubjective and objective worlds. Contrary to the idea that knowledge is a cognitive mental construction, which we achieve by progressively detaching ourselves from emotional, social and cultural links, knowledge is a variable system related to the intersubjective architecture of the representations that produce it. The relational genesis of knowledge makes it a variable and plastic phenomenon that changes depending on the 'who', 'how', 'what', 'why' and 'what for' of representation. These different dimensions of the representational process constitute contexts of knowing and it is to these contexts that we need to turn if we are to understand the expressiveness of a knowledge system.

This conceptualisation has consequences for research and for the assessment of programmes of social intervention. If we assume that there is only one way of knowing, which in our contemporary world is equated to science and technical knowledge, investigating representations becomes a process of describing the content and logic of knowledge and comparing these with a pattern that is considered to be right. This assumption, while widespread, ignores the very complexity of knowledge as well as the rich potentials that are embedded in the arrangements ordinary people construct while dealing with their social and natural environments. Its consequences reach far beyond the poverty of research results; they also impact on the manner in which the knowledge of local communities is treated and on the practices that are deployed to deal with it. In most cases, the practical aim of this type of non-dialogical research is to debunk, displace and destroy the knowledge that is there by considering it ignorance and distortion of a state of affairs. Projects of this kind abound in fields such as health, education and development initiatives in Third World countries (for an overview see Apffell-Marglin and Marglin 1990, 1994). Not accidentally, international agencies, technocrats and experts are starting to realise the inefficacies of such programmes. They provoke resistance, are blind to its causes and tend to fail because they ignore the lives and realities of local people.

Research on social representations has clearly demonstrated just how problematic it is to ignore the expressiveness and epistemological status of local knowledges. Moscovici's original study of psychoanalysis developed within the context of an intellectual battle between science and common sense and concern about what happens to scientific knowledge once it enters the semantic universes of ordinary people. What in France and other Latin countries was called the process of 'vulgarisation' or 'popularisation' of science roughly corresponds today to the field of public understanding of science in the Anglo-Saxon world. The use of the word vulgarisation in the 1960s was not accidental; vulgarisation refers to a process of disqualification and loss of credentials. The drive behind studies of vulgarisation was to assess the extent to which science could be 'extended' – in Freire's sense – to the lay public and yet retain its integrity (Barbichon and Moscovici 1965; Dulong and Ackermann 1972; Schiele and Jacobi 1988; Jacques and

Raichvarg 1991). The view of transportation, of extension, of transference was recurrent then and it has not completely lost its appeal today.

Yet, studies on the public understanding of science show that people invest it with ideas, values and meanings that are linked to their social and psychological contexts (Wynne 1989; Hilgartner 1990; Farr 1993a). In this process, science is, of course, transformed. *La Psychanalyse: son Image et son Public* (Moscovici 1961) tried to capture precisely this transformation by showing how representations of psychoanalysis in the public sphere went far beyond the idea and practice of psychoanalysis described in books and held by its professional practitioners. But rather than seeing it as distortion and vulgarisation, Moscovici saw the process as an expression of what happens to knowledge systems when they move from one context to another through communication and social exchanges. The appropriations and social transformation of psychoanalytic knowledge expressed the symbolic and social dimensions of all knowledge and debunked the idea of transfer and extension. Moscovici juxtaposed to the idea of vulgarisation the view that contexts of reception actively appropriate the symbolic materials they receive. As in Freire, communication rather than extension was the key to understand the transformation of knowledges.

In addition to this, Moscovici's original study provided a powerful analysis of how different forms of knowledge live side by side in the same community and in the same individual. The concept of cognitive polyphasia, as discussed in Chapter 2, was first proposed in the study on psychoanalysis, and developed through an extended dialogue with debates about the epistemological status of common sense and the nature of development in knowledge. Moscovici's study presented, in very clear form, the issue of expressiveness in knowledge and the issue of communication between knowledges.

Jodelet's (1991) classical study of madness equally showed that without a clear appreciation of everyday knowledges any attempt to reintegrate mental patients in the community would remain partial and unlikely to succeed. Her detailed ethnography of community life as it meets in close-up the reality of madness linked the production of social knowledge to the complex architecture of the encounter between sane–insane. Whereas her study emphasised the logic of identity and identity protection in the construction of knowledge, its main lesson was that ignoring local knowledge is something experts and policymakers do at their own peril. Jodelet's study revealed how the need to demarcate identity and differentiate the mad from the sane in a context where demarcation and differentiation were difficult to realise, led to strong strategies of separation that revived, in the register of symbolic experiences, the material walls of the asylum. The question of who was and who was not mad became the primary and urgent guiding force in the daily knowledge of a community whose experience of madness evoked fears of fusion and contagion. In addition to the logic of identity demarcation, Jodelet also found the ancestral symbols which, in western culture, link madness to the foreigner, to errant and nomadic groups, to those who live at the margins. Thus the rituals of separation enacted by the community: separation of bodies, separation of territories, separation of cooking and eating utensils and separation of waters – from body fluids to washing up and laundry, all responding to the need of keeping the other at bay.

What is clear in this set of representations and practices? That the ideals of reformers who wished to bring the mental patient back to the community were clashing head on with the representations of the community about reintegration. Symbolically, the community rebuilt the asylum and, as discussed in Chapter 5, it will take many more years of dialogue to overcome the barriers that in our societies still seek to segregate and displace the reality of madness. This study shows that a central mistake of those who discard local knowledge as ignorance, distortion or superstition is to assume that local communities are a vessel waiting to be filled by the superior knowledge and practices of experts and outside aid professionals. Failure to understand and appreciate what is there provokes resistance and dissimulation. Indeed local communities are more and more aware of what they need to do to satisfy the aid industry, and as soon as experts leave town they turn around and carry on with life as they know it (see in this regard, Novellino 2003).

What accounts for the continuous interest in Moscovici's and Jodelet's classical studies is the very contemporary nature of the issues they have addressed. These issues have not aged. How to understand local knowledges and the dynamics they express, how to conceive the relationship between knowledges and in particular the relationship between science and common sense; what happens with knowledge – any form of social knowledge – as it moves context and penetrates the lives of different social groups and is reworked by a variety of modes of communication and interaction; these remain pertinent and challenging questions opened not only to social psychology but to the social sciences as a whole. The programme initiated by Mosocovici and Jodelet has served as a platform from where researchers have continued to pursue the connection between knowledges and lifeworlds and the investigation of local realities at the interface knowledge/community/culture. The questions that guide this research effort are the questions Jodelet proposed in her assessment of the field of study of social representations: 'Who knows and from where does one know? How and what does one know? About whom and with which effects does one know?' (Jodelet 1989: 43, my translation). Responding to these questions makes the study of social representations a field of inquiry into how a community of people constructs knowledge, how this knowledge is linked to its identity, and how it expresses the cultural codes and practices which define, in different historical moments, the way of life of a community. Throughout the disciplinary spectrum there is evidence of the importance granted to such issues; the very notion of local knowledge has come to symbolise precisely the importance of paying attention to the lived dimensions of knowledge, to the strategies ordinary people develop to cope with the everyday and the traditions in which they are grounded.

Mapping representational systems: environment, health and public spheres

Local representational systems are sources of insight into the conditions of living, cultural codes, practices and resources – material and symbolic – of a community of people. They constitute a plural and multifaceted system of different knowledges, practices and cultural traditions, involving mythologies, folk beliefs, scientific expertise, practices and rituals. They are expressive, because as human activity they have the power to *represent*: they re-present history, context and identity, revealing the histories and social memory of the community as well as the societal and institutional arrangements that define the context in which people both find themselves and actively construct. In this sense, mapping local representations involves studying the subjective, intersubjective and objective worlds they comprise.

Gervais' (1997) study of representations of the environment in the wake of an environmental disaster in a remote Scottish community has articulated the concerns discussed above exemplarily. In the early 1990s the *Braer* tanker spilled some 85,000 tons of oil into the sea off the coast of the Shetland archipelago, destroying much of the natural habitat around the islands and threatening the livelihood of its inhabitants. This event put into motion a process that shook the lifeworld of islanders to the core and made it necessary to reconstruct the representations they held about the social and natural world they once knew and now knew no more. Faced with the strangeness coming from the disaster and the outsiders that came into the Shetlands in its wake, the local community reorganised the representations it historically held about nature to accommodate the unfamiliar and defend identity, locale and livelihood. The Shetlanders were not only coping with the actual disaster, which was difficult enough, but with the politicians, environmentalists and journalists who brought their clashing views, knowledges and practices into the community. Gervais' ethnography of community life as it is shaken by the disaster powerfully mapped the polyphasic structure of the representational fields about nature which the community held and suddenly needed to transform. These representational fields expressed not only the self-interpretation of the community, its cultural identity and history but also the interrelations it established with others, and the appropriations and symbolic exchanges that changed the knowledge of both Shetlanders and outsiders. Through the study of symbolic representations she was able to capture both the reality of the local community and the exchanges that transformed its knowledge. More, the study has convincingly shown how local communities are open to this transformation by resourcefully appropriating external knowledge and combining it with their own to accommodate new realities and needs.

Nuilla's (2001) study of representations of reproductive health in Mayan communities in the western highlands of Guatemala displayed similar concerns. Conducted in a context where extremely high fertility rates live side by side with external programmes of mass sterilisation, Nuilla sought to uncover the patterns of thinking and the practices attached to reproduction that were prevalent in the community. The clashes between governmental programmes in reproductive health and local Mayan people persistently showed the failure of external interventions to recognise local knowledge and understand the perspective from where it is produced. For most of the time interventions use a monological strategy that focuses on extension: agents seek to promote contraceptive use by transferring knowledge to local people while neglecting their psychological, social and cultural reality. To counteract this trend, Nuilla's research strategy consisted of retrieving her connection with the community and establishing a sustained relationship over time. In paying attention to the lifeworld of Mayan people, she found an extremely rich cosmology linking the reproduction of oneself, the reproduction of Mayan people and the production of crops to the core idea of 'mother Earth' and the nine months Mayan calendar. To think about reproduction for this community is to think about cultural, historical and personal continuity in time through the productive link they hold with the land, which is both a source of living and the place they call home. Only when we understand this system of knowledge can we start to understand why local people are so suspicious of reproductive health programmes and anything to do with birth control, and why they reject widely contraceptive methods and the information that comes from outsiders. Nuilla's study does not idealise local knowledge and makes no claims that it should not be changed. It is a call, however, for the construction of collaborative partnerships between local people and external agents based on a dialogical approach that recognises the legitimacy of local perspectives.

The recognition of local perspectives is the guiding thread in the research conducted by Guareschi and colleagues in the south of Brazil (Guareschi and Jovchelovitch 2004). Mapping out how local people living in very poor areas define notions such as community, participation, and citizenship has been central to interventions that aim to understand the relationship between deprived populations and participation in the public sphere. In situations of extreme poverty and deprivation, it is important for communities to develop reflexive awareness of the difference social solidarity and social capital can make. In our research, notions of togetherness, union, solidarity and mutual help were identified as emotional and practical resources for the feelings of empowerment the community considers as a requisite for effective social action. Without experiencing and feeling their power as a community of people, there is little or no disposition to participate and to engage in the hard battles associated with obtaining resources.

For these communities, sanitation and electricity can make a tremendous difference as can a weekly baby clinic held in the community centre. To produce pressure from below, the community must feel empowered about the legitimacy of its know-how, its capacity to act, express its needs and have them recognised by both local government and policymakers (Briceno-Leon 1998). Indeed, very few researchers, if any, know with the same depth what the community itself knows about its ways of life and living conditions. The aim of the project is not only to recognise the potentials and resources of local people to deal with an extremely harsh everyday life but also to sensitise carriers of scientific expertise to the fact that local people are not 'ignorant'. They hold knowledge: it is of a different kind, but most of the time it is resourceful and can lead to productive alliances with health professionals, planners and policymakers.

In these projects social representations are seen as local systems of knowledge that express social and cultural realities and integrate a diversity of psychosocial phenomena. Rather than defining these systems of knowledge as ignorance, distortion and error, they are understood as the practical means of a community to express itself, its identity and way of life (Campbell and Jovchelovitch 2000). Contrary to the idea that local representational systems need to be changed or improved as a matter of course, the first task of researchers is to 'understand the understandings' of local people and listen to the other in the disinterested manner proposed by Bauer and Gaskell (1999). If we are to establish strategies of communication rather than extension, the primary task is to listen and understand the community under study from the perspective of its actors. This underlying assumption allows us to suggest that mapping out local representational systems involves some key entry points.

Narratives of community life

Narratives contain a plot linking actors, context and social objects. They offer a series of stories, myths and memories of the social group and introduce the different angles that make communities a plural and heterogeneous reality. Narratives carry history, they carry memories and they carry personal perspectives. They provide reasons and explanations about what goes on and allow communities to elaborate and work through their past and present realities. Stories can also project futures and help to realise the hopes and expectations of the not-yet-become dimension of representations. Equally, they are a privileged method for carrying out dialogical research for the very act of telling and listening to stories is entangled in a dialogical intersubjective structure. Narratives are powerful instruments for generating and analysing data about local representational systems as well as for interventions that seek to produce critical reflexivity about local knowledge. They are particularly apt in situations where knowledge about specific events is being investigated and the focus is on the different perspectives that combine to produce the overall account about the situation in questions. Narratives are a flexible tool for intervention insofar as they can be adjusted to accommodate situations in which dialogue and verbal narration cannot be assumed, i.e. in severe trauma or impaired language capacity. In these situations narration can be enacted through drawings (especially if working with children, see Sharabi 2005), through drama and visual images, and of course through writing if literacy skills are in place.

Rituals of community life

Rituals are rich containers of symbolic meaning, which indicate how representations are enacted and guide action and behaviour. By observing the manner in which an organisation, group or a community does things, organises its everyday practices and structures its mode of going about we can learn a great deal about representational systems, and in particular about representational systems that remain unspoken in verbal language. Language, of course, is central but so are rituals, action and cultural artefacts. In the same way that oral narratives, conversation and written texts produce social knowledge, so do ritualised practices, gestures, relations of production, tools, images and art. They are all means of sustaining, producing and transforming patterns of signification in social life. Sometimes, as with rural communities in the south of Brazil, social knowledge is sustained through certain gestures and practices associated with labour in the fields (Oliveira 1981). Throughout Latin America deprived communities display a law of silence that keeps them verbally closed to the outside. In these places, language or dialogue cannot be taken for granted, and the ways in which people communicate lie in a certain way of looking after children, of preparing food, of cleaning tools, of going to church, of dressing in a specific way. Indeed, a great deal of community and group life is expressed in rituals that enact that which communities cannot speak of.

In Jodelet's study it was the understanding of rituals of separation that revealed the barriers between sane and insane, barriers that were absent from the verbal discourse of the community. In Nuilla's study two ritualised practices provided much insight into representations that remained unspoken: the burial of the placenta and the use of the temescal, a thermal bath with hydrotherapeutic properties. Ritualised behaviour captures well the meanings that remain absent from texts and verbal discourse, and reveal in the routines and repetitions they establish the symbolic and affective value of what is being hidden. Rituals are very efficient tools for controlling anxiety in representational processes and keeping at bay the forbidden and unconscious dimensions of representations. Understanding that which is absent is as important as understanding that which is present (Gervais *et al.* 1999) in mapping the 'why' of representational processes and the type of logic that guides the specific outlook on an event or social object.

The diagnostic of different knowledge systems and how they communicate

Local representations are often hybrids comprising a melange of knowledge systems (e.g. Jovchelovitch and Gervais 1999; Wagner *et al.* 2000); no locale is able to sustain full 'purity' in knowledge since no community context is closed in itself. The framework I suggested in Chapters 4 and 5 can help to identify the key elements that constitute the local knowledge of communities and to map which are the dominant knowledges defining the way in which a group of people represents a given social object. In the same manner that communities and social groups meet, clash and establish alliances in contemporary public spheres, so does knowledge. This is the case at the level of small groups and communities as it is when one is considering large public spheres. The large international research programme on representations of biotechnology developed by Bauer and Gaskell (Gaskell and Bauer 2001; Bauer 2002; Bauer and Gaskell 2002) sought to map precisely the confluence of different knowledge systems in various public spheres coming to terms with this new technology. The overall framework of the research took into account science, everyday knowledges, media coverage and policy to trace how large public spheres elaborate and bring about a new object as it fights to establishes its 'reality' in the social world. In this research it was not a case of science constructing biotechnology and *ex post factum* being received and represented by the public; rather the research sought to examine the controversies, dialogues and disputes between different representational systems and national public spheres struggling to project into the future what biotechnology should or should not be. In this case, the mapping of local systems of knowledge – large national public spheres were systematically studied and compared – involved the diagnosis of the different representations that framed biotechnology and the unparallel dynamics they displayed in the different cultural contexts.

Institutional arrangements, social and material resources

Whereas institutional arrangements and social and material resources may be located in political and sociological dimensions, these should not be ignored by social psychological analysis. The concrete social conditions within which knowledge develops are intrinsic to the process of knowledge formation and shape the internal structure of knowledge. They frame the everyday experience of communities and indicate the constraints and everyday obligations organising the practices of the group. These dimensions have been well explored by studies of situated cognition (Scribner and Cole 1973; Rogoff and Lowe 1984; Lave 1988). Nunes and colleagues (1993) showed well how the institutional arrangements of formal schooling impaired the learning of mathematics for children unaccustomed to such settings. Scribner's extensive research on work conditions also demonstrated how the organisation of work shapes modes of knowing and engaging with the world (Scribner 1984, 1986). Organisational settings imply complex administrative arrangements, hierarchies, division of labour, demarcation of spaces and access to power and resources that define to a large extent the production of representations inside and.outside its boundaries. This connection between the social, economic, institutional and political structures of a context and the production of psychological phenomenon is one of the avatars of the sociocultural approach to knowledge. We know that forced repetitive tasks jeopardise creative thinking and we also know that in communities where levels of deprivation are severe there is a narrowing of cognitive resources and communicative strategies. Severe deprivation expresses itself not only at the economic level but also at the cognitive and discursive levels, thus shaping the process of production of knowledge.

The dimensions above are not exhaustive and there is plenty of scope for developing further strategies for mapping out local representational systems. They do offer, however, a path for the investigation of how communities produce knowledge and what are the aspects that need to be taken into account in this process. Equally they allow us to connect the study of local representational systems with interventions that aim at capacity building at the individual, community and political levels.

Knowledge, conscientisation and empowerment

So far I have been concerned with showing how the multiple expressiveness of knowledge translates into empirical investigations. Recognising that knowledge represents subjective, intersubjective and objective worlds is central to the study of how ordinary people, in a variety of settings, come to construct a way of knowing both themselves and the social world in which they are located. There is, however, another dimension that needs to be considered when studying local representational systems. This refers to how local representations are worked through in the process of being uncovered and how researchers tune their intervention to allow critical reflexivity about what is going on in the field. One possibility is to map out and describe representations through unilateral methodologies that provide a picture of the field in a given moment of the community being studied. There are certainly merits to this type of research, not least its capacity to register and systematise semantic universes across wide populations. Large surveys and questionnaires can do just that. They provide breadth rather than depth and their usefulness lies in the capacity they have to capture common trends across large populations.[1] Another possibility is to construct the process of mapping out representations as a dialogue with the community with the specific aim of producing transformations in its realities. In these cases, the uncovering of local representations becomes a qualitative procedure of critically assessing local knowledges and engaging in a process of change that may redefine the outlook of the community. This second modality of research is a clear intervention and I want to discuss some of its potentials for developing community participation and capacity building. I shall use as a background reference research on community participation and health in Brazil (Guareschi and Jovchelovitch 2004).

Community participation has become an important process in the struggle against social inequalities and in the consolidation of citizenship rights for all. In deprived and marginalised communities in particular, participation can be a powerful tool in enhancing community awareness and conscientisation (Cooke and Kothari 2001; Howell and Pearce 2001). This in turn is dialectically linked to the capacity of communities to act and to compete for resources in unequal public arenas (Conway 2004). The construction of participatory action to reduce inequalities is a highly complex phenomenon that cannot be understood without social psychological categories. As noted before (Campbell and Jovchelovitch 2000) identities, local knowledges and power are key dimensions for understanding the social psychology of participation. They are deeply interrelated and clearly show that disposition to act and intervene in public spheres involves social psychological constructs in a dynamic relationship to larger social, economic and political contexts. Thus in considering what moves individual and communities to participate it is necessary to take the following into account:

- *identities*, as an arena of understanding and struggle about 'who I am or who we are', what shapes and circumscribes the life I/we live and what I/we can, should and would do to provoke change or let things be as they are;
- *social representations*, as an arena of knowledge constructed by communities about their identities, cultural traditions, ways of life and strategies for survival and living; about a variety of objects in the social field and about the relations communities establish with other communities;
- *power*, as an unequal arena of resources for action and realisation of interests that enables or disables communities to have their identities, knowledge, projects and needs recognised and worked upon.

Consideration of these three dimensions is a reflexive process that involves communication within the community, between researcher and community and between community and wider interlocutors in the public sphere. It is in communicative process, usually developed in the context of group work and participation in the rituals of community life, that researchers encourage critical reflexivity on the three arenas of struggle identified above and work towards the development of critical consciousness.

Conscientisation, or the development of critical consciousness, is the unifying thread in Freire's work and cannot be understood without reference to his dialogical method. As discussed in Chapter 5, Freire's literacy method is based on the idea that to read the word is, at the same time, to read the world. Learning how to do these readings depends upon dialogical encounters between self and other, where interlocutors through their differences and similarities expand each other's understanding. By progressively increasing the scope of decodings of the local reality and people's insertion in it, educator and educatee enlarge their reading capacities, so that participants can achieve depth in understanding problems, are able to provide causal explanations, learn to assess their own implication in what happens and are open for revision through practices of argumentation and dialogue. These aims offer to the investigative process a pedagogical edge so that reading the representations held by the community also becomes a larger reading about what they mean, why they came about and whether they need to be changed.

Whereas the development of critical awareness offers a number of gains at the cognitive, personal and social levels, the procedures upon which it depends are also constitutive of other capacities that can be located in the interface between local level/state institutions. Critical awareness not only contributes to processes of self-understanding and the empowerment of individuals and communities, but it puts their voices back in the centre of institutionalised public spheres while affording new levels of understanding to those populations systematically excluded from them. Underlying the participation of deprived communities there is both a politics and a psychology of recognition, where socially excluded subjects come into the public arena to state who they are, what they know and what they want. To speak and to be present in participatory fora is a way of saying 'look at us, listen to what we have to say and pay attention to how we want to develop our projects'. This redefines the very nature of the public sphere as it introduces a new dialogue with communities that have been historically damaged by chronic poverty and social exclusion. It also shows that demands for and the construction of redistributive policies are entangled with recognition policies. Whereas the pitfalls of participation are much discussed today as international agencies and governments appropriate the concept to legitimise unilateral action (Rahman 1995; White 1996; Morgan 2001), the gains it offers should not be easily dismissed (Van Vlaenderen 2001). As with so many other concepts, we must be careful not to discard it because it is misused. Figure 6.1 shows the main elements of a psychosocial intervention for community development based on the principles presented above.

The levels of diagnosis, intervention and reflexivity are interlinked and in turn relate to the development of participation and empowerment. In this conception social psychological interventions can be conceived as dialogical encounters between researchers and communities involving the recognition of the meeting points, potential clashes and potential alliances that can take place between the different knowledges at stake, between the agenda of researchers and the reality of the community. It involves dealing with the

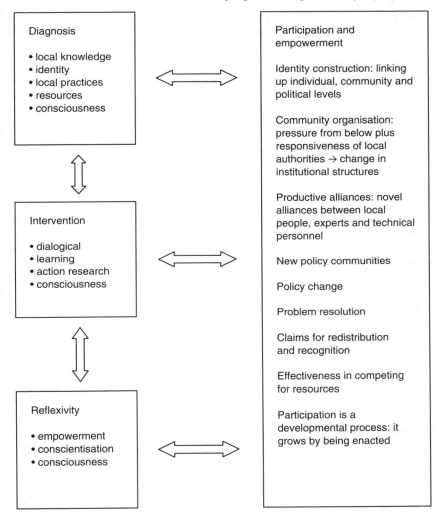

Figure 6.1 Community-based intervention for participation and empowerment

obstacles and separations between stakeholders and making an effort to work through and resolve problems with a view to construct productive alliances between researchers, practitioners, policymakers and community members that can improve and change the lives of dispossessed populations. It also poses to the institutional structures of the state the need to incorporate and take into account the insights and demands coming from informal public spheres. This type of work has an agenda that must be made explicit and explicated: it pays attention to the local level but does not idealise it. Rather than idealising the knowledge of communities, the aim is to construct a critical encounter based on the dialogical principle, where all stakeholders in the project can gain and develop knowledge. Processes such as this, of course, are time consuming and not easy; they are developmental in nature and cannot be evaluated within a short cycle of expected outcomes. They need a strategic long-term orientation to grow and to consolidate. Positions that deny their potential because of the obstacles they present are ultimately self-fulfilling and self-defeating prophecies. If we are to sustain the idea of inclusive public spheres we must engage strategically with the challenges they present and recognise the need for long-term thinking for the consolidation of the emancipatory potentials they carry.

Research as a dialogical act

All research is a social act conducted by actors who carry knowledges and agendas of their own. Whereas this statement applies to all research, it acquires a more acute character when applied to the practice of the social sciences (Habermas 1990). The symbolically structured domain of inquiry that concerns social scientists puts in evidence issues of time, space and identity between subject and object of knowledge that cannot be simply posited under the procedures of the natural sciences. In psychology, as we know, this has not been a simple issue. Indeed, the very beginnings of psychology as an independent discipline reveal that in order to establish its epistemological credentials as a science, psychology sought to place itself within the framework of the natural sciences, rearranged its foundations and turned away from social and cultural concerns (Danzinger 1974; Farr 1996). In social psychology this process produced some deep scars. The overwhelming emphasis on methodological operations has served well to disguise the absence of theoretical elaboration (Elejabarrieta 1989). Theoretical presuppositions frequently remained understated or unexamined under the formulation of hypotheses that, through sophisticated statistics, acquire the value of scientific findings. However, methodological questions do not relate simply to technical procedures and are not a matter of either applying a questionnaire or conducting in-depth interviews. Although the debate has often centred on a presumed opposition between qualitative and quantitative methodologies, such an opposition is entirely false and does not touch upon the fundamental questions. Methodology relates and actually depends upon theoretical issues, which in their turn are bound to epistemological conceptions. It is the close connection and penetration between the three that guides and opens the research options.

If we wish to grasp the social and historical character of social psychological phenomena and understand the contexts of meaning in which they are produced, we need to adopt a hermeneutic stance that goes beyond the deep-seated constraints imposed by the behaviourist tradition. Behaviourism, as we know, has restricted psychology to the study of observable behaviour while at the same time detaching from the structures of action the domain of symbolically constructed experiences. This was handy to the behaviourist intention of producing a public psychological science (in the sense of being observable and open to scrutiny and replication) free from introspection, but remains partial if we seek to understand the social and psychological processes that underlie what is immediately observable. Behavioural facts are also facts of meaning which originate in interactive contexts. The unit of analysis is not monological subject–object but dialogical self–other–object: it centres on the intersubjective triads that produce representation as well as all social psychological phenomena.

This theoretical position encapsulates not only the internal dynamics of what is studied and observed but also the very act of observing (Von Cranach 1982). As in the Borges short story, the dilemma of the researcher is the dilemma of the map-maker whose attempts to draw an exhaustive map of the world stumble on the need to include himself drawing himself drawing the map. Recognising that any full picture of the world must include the person taking the picture shatters the dream of a knowledge capable of providing full correspondence between itself and the reality it tries to capture. The predicament of the cartographer in Borges' short story reminds us that no person has access to reality in its 'naked truth' and that although it is possible to reflect about the problems involved in the making of the map there is no such a thing as a 'view from nowhere'. In this sense all research is participant research because the people who are involved in the act of observation are themselves interacting with the object being observed. This is as clear in face-to-face clinical interviews as it is in large-scale surveys where considerations about the wording of questionnaires and who is to conduct fieldwork where are paramount (O'Muircheartaigh 1997).

When conducting research as psychosocial intervention at the community level – which applies to any social context conceptualised as community, i.e. institutions, organisations, geographical communities, etc. – the above issues become prominent. Intervention, as the name suggests, implies interfering with a state of affairs and trying to change its course in order to produce an effect. It comprises a proposal of change as well as a set of procedures about how to set change into motion. Researchers who combine investigation and intervention carry languages, cultures, agendas, working hypotheses and projects related to both policy communities and to the views of contractors who bring them into a field. There is an *implication* of the researcher in the research process that needs to be recognised and dealt with instead of denied. This needs to be done at two interrelated levels. First, there is the level of recognising belonging: whoever has conducted research knows that phenomenologists were right. We all start from a position of belonging to a *Mitwelt*, a world we share with others: we belong to a culture, to a place, to a nation, to a historical period, to a scientific tradition, and these belongings frame from the outset the position from where we speak and from which we act. To bracket out such belongings and to free the gaze of the researcher from the lenses of her own traditions, customs and outlook is one of the many aspirations of the research attitude.

Recognising that we belong to and that we can never completely escape from the constraints that belonging imposes, is central to the investigative effort and takes us to the second level of the researcher's implication with the field of research. This level is procedural and involves consideration of what is the nature of our relationship to the field. As with any other type of knowledge encounter, interventions can be dialogical or non-dialogical. The dialogical attitude involves exchanges based on mutual recognition between different and separate interlocutors, where partners struggle to establish communication and to deal with the many obstacles that are often linked to this process. The dialogical attitude in research is based both on the act of listening to the other and allowing the field to express itself as much as possible and on the constant assessment of how the reality of the field shakes and reshapes the researcher's working hypothesis, theory and previous presuppositions. Through the dialogical act both the previous knowledge and assumptions of researchers and the reality of the field impact on each other, producing readjustment, change and hopefully enlarging the boundaries of all knowledges involved.

The position of disinterest that constitutes a central requisite for listening and engaging in a dialogue with the field is not a datum, but a conscious and deliberate effort of researchers, never fully realised. It is not easily done and requires training, practice, discipline and the pains of self-critique. How to produce distance in a field that is all too close is one of the main concerns of the dialogical method. This is the case because communicating with the reality of the field should not be confused with a quest for sameness between researcher and participants: the task of the researcher is to retain a level of separatedness so that the difference of others we want to understand, i.e. the otherness of the field of research, can be recognised for what it is and speak back with its own voice. This effort is paradoxical because at first sight separation and disinterest may suggest that researchers are cold to the field and unengaged with its reality. In fact, it is rather the opposite: it is because there is a communicative space between researchers and the field of research, which produces its own dynamics and has a range of consequences in the research process, that the need for stepping back and engaging in critical reflection arises. Distanciation is sought precisely because of the realisation that understanding our own biases, prejudices and agendas can contribute to a better approximation. Without being able to step back and distance oneself from the situation, the very activity of listening is compromised. If researchers are too entangled in the field or with their own agendas, they may find it difficult to sustain listening without acting out their own concerns. Dealing with the tension between distanciation and participation in a field is central to effective research interventions, to the aim of producing critical reflexivity and enlarging the parameters of all knowledges involved in the process.

The tension between participation and distanciation has been widely theorised in the field of psychology and is at the heart of the clinical method, both in clinical settings proper and in social research. The analysis of this tension has provided the basic tenets to articulate how dialogical encounters between independent interlocutors lie at the centre of knowledge production, be it knowledge of self, others or world. These tenets go back to Socrates' maieutics and his disavowal of knowledge. The Socratic method is a method of knowledge production that draws on metaphors of midwifery, labour pains, delivery and birth. Socrates believed his pupils to be 'pregnant' while he himself was barren of wisdom. He claimed to be a midwife, just like his mother, and saw his task as that of a facilitator, just like midwives are. His method of delivery was dialogue, which he compared to labour pains: a chain of questions and answers, each carefully examined and critically assessed, that would eventually deliver true knowledge. Genuine dialogue can be painful, and indeed for most of the time it is, because it involves gaining awareness of one's own illusions and mistakes, coping with one's limitations and learning how to revise one's errors. The maieutics of Socrates combines the disavowal of his own knowledge with his active participation in the dialogical encounter. His disavowal, to be sure, can be seen as an artefact and to some extent ironically, as he knew all too well what to ask and how to blast open the inconsistencies of the responses he got. But there remains in his act a principle that persists in all dialogical encounters: a measure of self-denial and a measure of self-participation.

Freud expanded on the issue when he brought to the heart of the psychoanalytic method the understanding and examination of transference and countertransference processes, Freire extensively discussed the problem in his pedagogy and so did Piaget in his studies of the child. When Freud described the processes of transference and countertransference he was aware that the communicative setting proposed by the therapy was a two-way road with effects on both therapist and client. Using free speech and the intersubjective setting as therapeutic tools, psychoanalysis presupposes that the client does the talking and the therapist the listening, but the therapist, of course, speaks back seeking to interpret what is said in order to produce new and enlarged levels of awareness. In this process both therapist and client are greatly helped by the analysis of transference and countertransference, which brings to the centre of the therapeutic situation the vast range of emotional and procedural phenomena that emerge when therapist and client communicate. So rather than seeing the process as a one-way effect moving from self towards the other, there is a mutual process of interference that must be acknowledged by both partners and worked through in the therapeutic context. The Freudian model can be easily translated into the dynamics of social research (see Devereux 1967; Habermas 1987; Giami 2001), for the act of allowing the other to speak feeds back into the listener, sometimes with very unsettling results. These must not be regarded as errors but need to be understood and interpreted as integral to the process. When Freire discussed his dialogical pedagogy he was also keenly aware that learning is a dual process and that a true pedagogy must consider that which the teacher learns from others he is trying to teach. His literacy method, as we have seen, takes on Socratic midwifery to construct a series of dialogical steps aiming at the development of a new consciousness for the participants involved. In Piaget's description of the clinical method the same principles are at stake. He emphasised that the researcher must combine what appears as two contradictory qualities: to be detached in order to observe and to participate at the critical moment when intervention is required. The common thread uniting the work of these theorists is the notion that intersubjective structures based on dialogue, however difficult and painful, are the inroad for processes of discovery: to know is to dis-cover in communication with others. This insight can be applied not only to conceptualise knowledge in contexts of everyday life but also to guide the very processes whereby we, as researchers, seek to constitute this knowledge.

The questions we try to answer when we study knowledge apply well to the research process and can help us to visualise the nature of our interventions in the social world. What does science want? Which are the strategies it deploys to pursue its aims? How do we go about producing representations about the events and realities we study? Many years ago, Luria referred to these issues when he contrasted the idea of romantic versus classical science and described the different aspirations and strategies of each. The crux of the matter is always how to preserve the richness of a living reality and what is the price we pay if we want to do so. The loss of firm formulations, the entanglement with the 'human, all too human' dimensions of our studies should not deter us, or so Luria thought. The tensions between belonging and detachment, discovering and covering up are of a very practical nature and present themselves quite concretely when we conduct research. The idea of research as dialogue can help us to navigate these tensions and recuperate the connection between investigation and life, which is always there anyway, whether we acknowledge it or not.

Re-thinking knowledge and its rationality

The approach to knowledge that I have presented in this book relies heavily on the concept of representation understood as a social psychological construct expressive of subjective, intersubjective and objective worlds. Representation, I have argued, is the stuff of which all knowledges are made and to understand a knowledge system we need to understand who, how, what, why and what for it tries to represent. Knowledge without representation is a dream, and a legitimate and understandable one for that matter. It corresponds to the old human search for certainty and security, to the rather elusive possibility of stating that the world *is* the knowledge we have of it. This dream, expressed in all collective representations, has been exemplarily rearticulated by modernity as it coped with the anxieties triggered by the questioning of myth, tradition and religious experience. It reappeared in the form of a theory of knowledge as full correspondence with the reality of the world, something that could be achieved once the act of knowing is cleansed from the impurities of person, society and culture. The dream of knowledge without representation became the dream of representation without its representational function. Deprived of its expressiveness, representation was to emerge as the individual mental act of describing the world as it is, i.e. a set of empirical regularities that pre-exists the labours of human cognition. The world is there, waiting to be known and the task of knowledge is to capture it as it is.

This twist in representation, which deprived it from its connection with person and context, explains why the theory of knowledge as correspondence with reality has been criticised as the representational view of knowledge. Trapped by the Cartesian project of representation as a detached copy of the world, theorists have tried to discard the notion opting instead for a linguistic turn. Language, goes the argument, can circumvent the monological character of representation because language is inherently social. That language is itself a representational system remains peculiarly unexamined. The fact is that this conceptual framework deals more with the dream of representation without the impurities of person, society and culture and less with the phenomenon of representation. It is a framework haunted by the dream of a pure rationality and its corresponding anxiety, which, as with all anxieties, prevents it from engaging with the more complex and messy reality it is trying to avoid.

The theory of representation as mental copy, while widespread and powerful, does not withstand closer inspection. It treats representation as a given while remaining blind to issues of genesis and development. It does not ask questions about how representation comes about and how it develops, which is precisely what allows the ahistorical and asocial character of its formulations. It detaches psychological phenomena from its sources and conditions of realisation, transforming representation into arid cognitive maps without emotional and social components. Even a brief observation of the human mind at work in natural settings will show that representation goes far beyond the processing of information and the mind is not a modular entity with separate compartments. Observe a child in a primary school: intermingled with the acquisition of content and the development of logical structures, there are social and emotional logics that do not walk away when the child struggles with the formal content of schooling. Little children construct public spheres both in the classroom and in the playground, which shape the way in which they learn and construct knowledge about the world. In children's play there is society's play, as Furth so aptly demonstrated. Observe children playing on twosome or threesome basis and very fast one will see the emergence of politics: the negotiation of differences, the identification of similarities, striking a joint procedure, the formation of alliances, exclusions, minute coups d'état, the changing of agendas and so on. How can we possibly separate processes such as these from the structures of knowledge? If we do it, we do it at the cost of our own understanding.

Once detached from the ground in which they emerge, psychological phenomena became abstractions that can be artificially attached back to a subject considered in his own self-centred totality, without history and culture. A subject with a history and a mind without a subject are the two related outcomes of this separation between the psychological and the contextual. Vygotsky argued that if we cannot demonstrate the mode of constitution of phenomena in time and space we cannot apprehend the fundamental historicity of all that is human – this applies as much to psychological as to any other level of phenomena. The genetic approach is an essentially historical approach because it searches the developmental trajectory of mind and sees it as an evolving and dynamic process rather than as a finished product.

The approach to representation that I have developed throughout this book sought to offer an account of representation that is developmental and social, communicative and intersubjective. The trajectory of the human child, as shown well in the psychologies of Piaget, Vygotsky, Mead and Winnicott, is above all a journey of constructing connections with others and the object-world, connections that ultimately allow the child to become a person and establish a connection with its own existence as an independent being. The construction of these relations – with others, with oneself, with the object-world – is a communicative process that simultaneously constructs representation and impregnates it with expressiveness, which constitutes the source of its symbolic character. Because representation is fundamentally intertwined with interrelations involving many and not one, it is not a one-way copy but a symbolic effort that produces meaning and allows for signification and sense-making. Neither theorists of cognitive processes as mental individual cognition nor critics of representation as a monological mirror of nature have engaged with the psychological genesis of representation and the sociocultural theories that show its connection to meaning and the symbolic order. As soon as we take into account the development of the human child, it becomes clear that representational processes are an achievement of intersubjectivity, constructed by the infant as she co-constructs with others her relations to object, word and world.

The sociogenetic view of representation reconnects it to micro and macro categories such as body, person, history and culture and opens the structure of knowledge to the inherent variability of contexts of knowing. It allows us to understand why children and women have produced forms of knowing that are distinct enough to be recognised, and it gives us tools to understand why different cultures and communities produce knowledge in different ways. Once we understand the constituents of the representational form and how representation relates to knowledge, we can (a) escape from the view of knowledge as a pure individual rationality obtained through detachment from self, society and culture; (b) do away with the task of dividing epistemic forms simply in terms of how well they represent reality; (c) move knowledge away from a monological theory of consciousness and insert it in a communicative theory of mind. The variability of representational processes precludes the closure of human knowledge and calls for frameworks that can engage with the difference of its forms without resorting to a centric perspective which, blind to its own historicity and positioning, declares itself as the standard against which everything else is assessed.

Within the disciplinary context of social psychology the last decades have witnessed a systematic shift from concern with knowledge as an individual property to its grounding in the intersubjective world of a community (see, for instance, Billig 1987; Billig *et al.* 1988; Potter 1996; Potter and Wetherell 1987; Semin and Gergen 1990, amongst many others). Despite the power of the Cartesian project of the solitary knower, there has been a considerable effort both to retrieve and renew the approaches that seek to study how human communities come to know and make sense of the world in which they both find themselves and construct. In much of the work being conducted today within the social psychology of knowledge there is a clear attempt to retrieve the relative wisdom of all knowledge systems and to rehabilitate the worth of those knowledges traditionally seen as error and distortion. This concern not only with the knowledges of everyday life, but also with how they transform and create in encounters with other knowledges such as science, expresses the impetus to construct a wiser theory of knowledge that is not blind to the link between knowledge and life, between reason and passion, between knowing and belonging. The basic tenets of such a social psychology of knowledge can be summarised as follows.

The primacy of inter-subjectivity

Shifting the way we conceive knowledge involves recognising the primacy of intersubjective structures in its genesis and social realisation. To every form of knowing there corresponds a set of fundamental relationships between people and between people and the environment in which they live, which is both social and natural. These relationships frame the representational aims of knowledge and need to be understood if we are to explain the rationality of knowledge and what, at times, seems irrational for the observer who does not understand the context in which that form of knowing is grounded. It is the social psychological nature of these relationships, their quality and location in space, place and time that needs to be considered if we are going to be serious about treating social context as more than an added variable to understand knowledge. This involves exploring the social psychology of contexts of knowing by considering 'who', 'how', 'what', 'why' and 'what for' of representational processes.

Diversity in styles of knowing

The study of knowledges in context demonstrates that there is diversity in styles of reasoning, which in turn do not correspond perfectly to different forms of knowing. Indeed, states of cognitive polyphasia refer precisely to the fact that communities hold knowledges which comprise different logics and rationalities. This applies equally to scientific communities. Social studies of science show that scientific knowledge, despite its efforts, is permeated by rationalities and logics that are other than the alleged pure rationality of the sciences. Rather than seeing knowledge as a monological and singular construct, it should be seen as a heterogeneous and plastic form comprising multiple rationalities, whose logic is not defined by some transcendental norm but is dependent on the social psychological logic of contexts. Accepting diversity in knowledge involves engagement with two problems: the first is how different knowledges are treated; the second is whether different knowledges can communicate. These two problems are related to the social psychology of self–other relations and in particular to issues of recognition and perspective-taking. Recognising difference involves renouncing the fantasy of being the only one and using one's own assumptions to frame the experience of others. The recognition of diversity in systems of knowing is usually hindered by the power of the hierarchical representation of knowledge. Dialogical relations between knowledges presuppose the recognition of diversity and active rejection of the hierarchical view of knowledge. There are, of course, many obstacles in the way of dialogical relations between knowledges but these should not prevent us from theoretical and empirical efforts towards the dialogical. All knowledges contain dimensions related to the future and to the not-yet-become; awareness of limitations and constraints involves not only compromise but also a vision of what the world could and should be. The study of diversity and communication between knowledges requires a social psychology of hope, committed to the construction of futures.

The evolution and transformation of knowledge

Understanding the heterogeneity of knowledge involves dismantling the classic, often implicit, presupposition that there is one best and better developed way of knowing. The idea of linear evolution from lower to higher forms has produced the rather self-aggrandising view that there is an optimal state to be achieved at the end of a hierarchical scale, occupied so it happens by a specific group of people. The construction of developmental frameworks based on a continuous path with different stages of development has been central to the self-interpretation of the west, as it legitimatised its way of life, its modes of knowing and its patterns of behaviour and its intervention in 'non-developed' contexts which needed to progress towards the optimal state. Needless to say this view has had devastating consequences in all places affected, not least in the west itself, which has been prevented from achieving a better grasp of the limitations embedded in its own way of life and its position as one amongst many others. Whereas the self-interpretation of the west is exemplary of the issues we have discussed, it can serve as a model to question all situations in which individuals and communities put themselves in a position unable seriously to consider the perspective and knowledge of others. Debunking the idea of linear evolution allows us to perceive that the hierarchical view of knowledge is a cultural construction that expresses inability to recognise difference without undermining it. At the same time, it opens up new spaces of awareness about human diversity and its potentials. Contrary to the idea that 'higher' forms of knowing will eradicate 'lower' ones, we suggest that different forms of knowing coexist fulfilling different functions and identity needs. These can be used by social actors as a resource from where to draw answers to the different kinds of demands of the everyday. Rather than treating difference in knowledges through a progressive and hierarchical scale, there is a need to elaborate the possibilities and dangers embedded in processes of communication between different forms of knowing.

The social psychology of knowledge that I presented in this book is inspired by these assumptions and its impetus lies in a deep commitment with the potentials inherent in human communication. It is an impetus present in Moscovici's social psychology as it is in all those theoretical perspectives that put emphasis on the redeeming power of the intersubjective. I identify this impetus in the work of Dussel, Freire and Martin-Baró in Latin America, in the work of Habermas, in the psychoanalytical tradition inaugurated by Freud and continued in the work of Winnicott, in the social psychology of Mead and Rommetveit, in the sociocultural school of developmental psychology. Despite their differences and the criticisms that can be levelled at different aspects of their work, they have provided us with elements to understand and to pursue the intersubjective.

The conditions we experience today, characterised by the interconnectedness between different worlds and ways of life, give to this view an unavoidable ethical dimension for the plight of others is seen, known and difficult to deny. Yet, paying attention to the many sites of suffering produced by injustice and inequality and to the nature of the experience that comes out of dispossession and exclusion does not mean that we need to renounce the commitment with the potential realisation of human communication and understanding. No matter how heavy the oppressions, barbarities and injustices of the world weigh on us, there remains in human life the absolute requirement for the intersubjective, and with it the possibility of communication, of encountering the other and in this encounter encountering oneself.

I would like to conclude with a final word on relativism, a danger that, I know well, lurks in my book. Recognising the legitimacy of different forms of knowledge can easily take us into relativism. If all knowledges have their worth then there is no way we can establish what one would call reality or truth. I want to distance myself from an easy relativism or the denial of the possibility of sustaining the idea of truth by reaffirming once again the struggle for communication. And I use the word struggle because if there is one thing we psychologists should know well it is that to communicate is an immense effort, a continuous struggle. Fundamentally speaking, every human community constitutes a unique cultural reality and ontologically speaking every human being is a world of her own. But transposing these existential distances is the essence of human culture and the essence of the development of the self. Moving towards the other and constructing a shared understanding is the process that allows the precarious, but nevertheless necessary, establishment of criteria for what a human community considers right and wrong, good and bad, truth and falsity. To recognise that truth is social does not make it less necessary and does not imply that we must disregard it as an ideal that needs to be preserved. The recognition of diversity and legitimacy in different types of knowledge does not lead to the unconditional acceptance of all knowledges. Error and illusion are part and parcel of human reality and they are a possibility inherent in all forms of human knowledge. It is the human capacity for critique, for revising errors, for learning from previous mistakes and from the experience of others, through communication, reflection and self-critique, which provides both the antidote for the isolation and loneliness proposed by relativism and at the same time the elements for the growth and development of all knowledge.

Notes

1 Knowledge, affect and interaction

1 As Taylor observes (1989), Descartes and Locke democratised the separation between subject and world, something that was only possible in the pre-modern period to some special individuals such as monks and philosophers. The *vita comtemplativa*, where reflexivity and contemplation become widespread and accessible to many is a direct product of the separation between subject and world and becomes 'universalised' with the advent of modernity.

2 That the development of psychological functions is a qualitative process rather than a mere quantitative one is central to the approach I am developing in this book. A clear account of the terms of the debate between developmental and cultural psychologists and cognitivists can be found right at the birth of the journal *Cognition*, when Fodor (1972) heavily criticised Vygotsky's *Mind in Society*, which had just appeared in the USA. In his virulent attack on Vygotsky (and Piagetian developmental psychology) Fodor states that the differences between adults and children are quantitative rather than qualitative and it would be wrong to imagine development as a process of qualitative changes. Leontiev and Luria (1972) quickly responded to this attack, restating the project of a historical and developmental approach to mind.

3 It would be foolish for social psychology to ignore our biological make-up. Any human psychology must reckon with the embodiment of psychic structures, not least because the genesis of thought and knowledge is to be found in the action of the body and not the reverse. If biological make-up would not be important any organism should serve to produce a person. We know, however, that attempts to engage communicatively with some of our closest genetic relatives, the bonobos, failed to produce a distinctive human form of communication (Savage-Rumbaugh and Fields 2000; Strayer 2000). Biology, of course, matters and it is a central key to understanding what makes humans psychological and social beings. But psychology must proceed and tackle that which biology alone cannot account for. When the biological foundations are taken further by the development of a subject that is both psychological and social the scope of scientific explanation must also be taken further. Representation, as a psychological and social phenomenon, is a key concept in this task.

4 Consider the following extracts. Freud remarked that 'the contrast between individual psychology and social or group psychology, which at a first glance may seem to be full of significance, loses a great deal of its sharpness when it is examined more closely (. . .) In the individual's mental life someone else is invariably involved, as a model, as an object, as a helper, as an opponent; and so

from the very first individual psychology, in this extended but entirely justified sense of the words, is at the same time social psychology as well' (1921: 95).

Winnicott (1964) observed: 'There is no such thing as a baby – meaning that if you set out to describe a baby, you will find your are describing a baby and someone. A baby cannot exist alone, but is essentially part of a relationship.' Piaget and Inhelder (1969: 95) also made clear that: 'The decentring of cognitive constructions necessary for the development of. the operations is inseparable from the decentering of affective and social constructions. But the term "social" must not be thought of in the narrow sense of educational, cultural or moral transmission alone; rather, it covers an interpersonal process of socialization which is at once cognitive, affective, and moral.' In the same vein, Vygotsky and Luria (1994: 116) stated: 'The road from object to child and from child to object lies through another person.'

5 While Vygotsky criticised psychoanalysis he did not easily dismiss it. Throughout his writings there are references to Freud's work. (For a detailed analysis of continental European thought on Vygotsky's thinking, see Valsiner 1988.) Piaget is also widely criticised for his lack of concern with the emotional dimension in the development of cognitive structures. Commentators fail to take Piaget at his word. At various points throughout his writtings he has articulated an explicit statement about the role of unconscious and affective life in the formation of cognitive structures and in particular when he discusses the formation of the symbol in the child. This also can be applied to the dimension of the social, consistently criticised in Piaget's work for being allegedly absent. (For a superb rebuttal of both criticisms see Furth 1987.)

2 Social representations and the diversity of knowledge

1 In what follows I draw on Moscovici's writings on social representations and social theory. The best source in English to assess Moscovici's original voice on the issues I address is *Social Representations: Explorations in Social Psychology* (Moscovici 2000c). A translation of *La Psychanalyse, son Image et son Public* is forthcoming with Polity Press.

2 Different approaches include Abric's structural approach (1989, 2001), Jodelet's socio-cultural approach (1989, 1991, 2002), the genetic approach of Doise and his colleagues in Geneva (1990) and Marková's dialogical approach (2003). These approaches are not radically distinct; indeed they interpenetrate and have been cross-fertilised by the practices of researchers who use them. Other important contributions to the conceptual corpus of the theory are to be found in Farr (1993a, 1993b, 1998; Farr and Moscovici 1984), Doise and Palmonari (1986) and Von Cranach *et al.* (1992). For more recent developments see Arruda (2003), Duveen (1998, 2001b), Bauer and Gaskell (1999), Castro (2003), Joffe (1999, 2002) and Wagner and Hayes (2005) as well as my own work (Jovchelovitch 1996, 2000, 2002, 2004).

3 This view, however, has not gone unchallenged. The crowd has also been seen as a site of daydreaming, creativity and feelings of union and identity formation, from the poetry of Baudeleire, to the writings of Elias Canetti (1973). In contemporary social psychology, Steve Reicher (1987) has produced the most articulated and systematic attempt to reconceptualise the social psychology of the crowd.

4 Marx and Engels (1970) address these issues in *The German Ideology*, a text that, in my view, remains essential reading for social psychologists. It is there that Marx discusses the relations between the ideal and the material, between life and consciousness. It is there that we find the influential statement 'Life is not

determined by consciousness, but consciousness by life', a statement that still haunts us today as we struggle with unresolved issues related to the origins of psychological processes and mind, the nature versus nurture debate and the impact of social and economic processes on the psychology of individuals.

5 However, both Durkheim and Moscovici have used the terms indistinctively. Durkheimian sociologists, such as Alexander (2003, 2006), continue to use both social and collective representations to refer to Durkheim's original description of the concept. Here I make the distinction for the sake of theoretical clarification and to substantiate the point I shall advance in Chapter 3 related to the changes in representational systems from traditional to de-traditionalised societies.

6 This, of course, does not preclude the possibility of establishing comparative frameworks to enlarge our understanding of different modalities of thinking. On the contrary, such frameworks are needed if we are to understand how knowledges change as they undergo processes of communication and social interaction. But comparison does not need to rest in criteria ruled by hierarchical overtones. I shall examine these issues in Chapter 4.

7 It is important to note that we cannot transpose literately the meaning of the word 'primitive' from Vygotsky's to our context. During the first decades of the twentieth century there were a great deal of positive connotations associated with the idea of the primitive, which was seen as 'natural' and 'genuine' as opposed to the deformations of cultivation. As Jane Cox points out in her introduction to the book, this view was specially fuelled by Mayakovsky's Futurist Manifesto, which exalted the purity of the primitive.

3 Knowledge, community and public spheres

1 Most of these processes, to be sure, are also found in the construction of groups and here one could easily ask how is community different from any other type of group. Indeed there is a vast area of social psychology that deals with groups and intergroup relations, which I do not address here. There are two reasons for this. First, and perhaps less importantly, there is an issue of scale. Community is an intermediate structure that superposes the group, it is larger than the group and its purpose and aims in social life cannot be immediately compared to those of groups. Second, I wish to escape from the limitations that have constituted the psychology of small groups, most notably the tendency to work with artificial groups in the laboratory and exclude from the analysis the social, psychological and historical genesis of group formation. Equally, social psychology has been prodigal in reducing communities to small groups, not infrequently small artificial groups. This practice needs to be overcome since communities are not reducible to small groups, something Habermas (1989a) has convincingly demonstrated while criticising the social psychological liquidation of the concept of public opinion.

4 The forms and functions of knowledge

1 From the Greek *maieutiké*, the art of the midwives, the art of helping to procreate. Midwifery, the Socratic method for teaching and seeking knowledge, based on the dialogue between teacher and pupil, is exposed clearly in Theaetetus, where we find Socrates' famous disavowal of knowledge:

Well, my midwifery has all the standard features, except that I practise it on men instead of women, and supervise the labour of their minds, not their bodies. And the most important aspect of *my* skill is the ability to apply every conceivable test to see whether the young man's mental offspring is illusory and false or viable and true. But I have *this* feature in common with midwives – I myself am barren of wisdom.

Socrates's midwifery is at the basis of the psychoanalytical relationship and the dialogical pedagogy of Paulo Freire, to which I return in Chapter 6.

2 Surely social representations are not exclusively symmetric phenomena; they are permeated by asymmetries that shape its form and define its content. The same can be said of science. Social representations, however, have the potential to be shaped by symmetrical relations, a potential that seems to be less present in collective modalities of representation. As I argue later, both modalities of representations are ideal types and cannot be conceived without the inter-penetrations that give shape to representational fields.

3 My use of the word 'invest' corresponds to the Freudian concept of investment (*Besetzung*), which as Furth (1987) points out is the clearest connection in Freud between knowledge and the drives. It simply refers to the process whereby the psychological energy of drives is invested in objects through the symbolic labour of representation.

4 My approach to the ideological function of representations follows Thompson's (1990) reappraisal of the concept. It refers to the interrelations between symbolic forms and power and to the use of symbolic forms to exert domination. To dominate and to oppress constitute key functions of representations in an unequal world and I refer to this as the ideological function.

5 In my view there is nothing to apologise for in the scientific attitude that seeks the bracketing of subjective and intersubjective dimensions. This is an attitude required whenever there is a serious intention of understanding otherness; it is present in the listening act and it is at the basis of any true pedagogy. Recog-nising the inevitable presence of the subjective in knowledge does not mean that it rules alone nor that knowing is necessarily equated with full emotional disclosure. The subjectivity of researchers is best if well controlled in the research process, something that can be achieved through training.

5 Encountering the knowledge of others

1 As discussed earlier in Chapter 1, this is not unique to the social psychology of Mead. Most psychological systems have described the barred nature of self, conceiving it as a territory of many rather than just one.

2 This task is facilitated by the maturation of the cognitive abilities of the infant and by the help received by the caretaker from a third party – in psychoanalytic terms, the father and the law of culture he represents, which confirm that dyads are in fact *triads* in the foundation of the subject (Winnicott 1965d).

3 Any social psychological analysis must be aware of its own limitations to tackle such a complex issue. Without a consideration of larger socioeconomic factors we cannot fully understand what is involved when interlocutors, for most of the time very unequal, meet in public arenas to propose representations of the world. Yet, socioeconomic relations also depend on social psychological subjects, who invest these relations with meaning and subjective value, linking them to identities and ways of life. This is the dimension that I am interested in unpacking here.

4 In the first volume of *The Theory of Communicative Action* Habermas admits: 'it could very well be the case that even with a decentred understanding of the

world there arises a special illusion – namely, the idea that the difference of an objective world means totally excluding the social and subjective worlds from the domains of rationally motivated agreement' (1989b: 73). In Habermas' (2005) new book, yet to be translated into English, he addresses again the relations between different worldviews and knowledges, revising some of his hierarchical conceptions.

5 See Habermas (1991) contrast between communicative and strategic action. In strategic action it is power that bends interaction out of its dialogical potentials by distorting communication.

6 Commentators have pointed to issues such as the lack of a proper understanding of the nature of chronic mental illness, the failure to understand that the asylum was a home for chronic patients and what are the social, psychological and economic resources needed for a community to be therapeutic (see Murphy 1991, 1996 and Barnes and Bowl 2000).

7 I remember well the force of this conviction. From the mid to the late 1980s I participated directly in the de-institutionalisation movement in Brazil and the inspiration we drew from the theories and practices developed in France, Italy and England were guiding attempts to redefine the psychiatric hospital, to listen to the reality of patients and construct policies that could give them back citizenship rights. For all of us involved in clinical practice at the time there was no stronger imperative than the activity of 'listening'; it was towards listening that most of our training and efforts were directed.

8 This view connects to, and actually precedes, many dimensions of Habermas' theory of communicative action and his attempt to characterise what are the universal conditions for reaching mutual understanding. Notwithstanding the hierarchical representation of knowledge that permeates his work, this does not incapacitate the tremendous effort of Habermas to elaborate the foundations of a theory for reaching mutual understanding. See Ramella and De La Cruz (2000) for a theoretical and practical articulation of the works of Freire and Habermas.

9 It is important to note that this text was elaborated during Freire's exile in Chile where he actively participated in the educational initiatives of Salvador Allende's government. As with the writings of the other theorists I refer to here, there is a direct connection between intellectual production and political struggle, as well as involvement with the poor and dispossessed of Latin America. None of these writers makes apologies for this and none of them sits exclusively within the protected walls of academia. This was made particularly evident in the assassination of Martin-Baró by the El Salvadorian government. I am convinced that this connection explains the unequivocal hope that paradoxically permeates their work.

10 As many other psychologists of my generation in Brazil I was privileged enough to have Paulo Freire's teachings and vivid voice inspiring and guiding the practices we were developing. When he returned to Brazil after exile he was tireless in making himself available to all, and in particular to the generation that grew up during the dictatorship era.

6 Studying knowledge in everyday life

1 Questionnaires and surveys are valuable tools for community-based research and both can be productively used for conscientisation and empowerment. Indeed the lack or unreliability of large data banks in developing countries is yet another tool for domination. Large-scale surveys consolidate knowledge over time and offer excellent resources for reflecting about inequalities and other social conditions (see Bauer *et al.* 2000).

Bibliography

Abric, J.-C. (1989) 'L'étude experimental des representations socials', in D. Jodelet (ed.) *Les Représentations Socials*, Paris: Presses Universitaires de France.

Abric, J.-C. (2001) 'A structural approach to social representations', in K. Deaux and G. Philogéne (eds) *Representations of the Social*, Oxford: Blackwell.

Alcoff, L. M. and Mendietta, E. (eds) (2000) *Thinking from the Underside of History: Enrique Dussel's Philosophy of Liberation*, Lanchan, MD: Rowan and Littlefield.

Alexander, J. C. (2003) *The Meanings of Social Life: A Cultural Sociology*, New York: Oxford University Press.

Alexander, J. C. (2006) *The Civil Sphere*, New York: Oxford University Press.

Allansdottir, A., Jovchelovitch, S. and Stathopoulou, A. (1993) 'Social representations: the versatility of a concept', *Social Representations* 2, 1: 3–10. Online. Available HTTP: <http://www.psr.jku.at/psrindex.htm> (accessed 14 February 2006).

American Psychiatric Association (APA, 1994) *Diagnostic and Statistic Manual of Mental Disorders*, 4th edn, Arlington: American Psychiatric Association.

Anderson, B. (1991) *Imagined Communities: Reflections on the Origin and Spread of Nationalism*, London: Verso.

Apffell-Marglin, F. (1990) 'Smallpox in two systems of knowledge', in F. Apffell-Marglin and S. A. Marglin (eds) *Dominating Knowledge: Development, Culture and Resistance*, Oxford: Oxford University Press.

Apffell-Marglin, F. and Marglin, S. A. (eds) (1990) *Dominating Knowledge: Development, Culture and Resistance*, Oxford: Oxford University Press.

Apffell-Marglin, F. and Marglin, S. A. (eds) (1994) *Decolonizing Knowledge: From Development to Dialogue*, Oxford: Clarendon Press.

Arce, A. and Fisher, E. (2003) 'Knowledge interfaces and practices of negotiation: cases from a women's group in Bolivia and an oil refinery', in J. Pottier, A. Bicker and P. Silitoe (eds) *Negotiating Local Knowledge: Power and Identity in Development*, Sterling, VA: Pluto Press.

Arendt, H. (1958) *The Human Condition*, Chicago: University of Chicago Press.

Arruda, A. (2003) 'Living is dangerous: research challenges in social representations', *Culture and Psychology* 9, 3: 339–359.

Ashenden, S. and Owen, D. (eds) (1999) *Foucault contra Habermas*, Thousand Oaks, CA: Sage.

Aulagnier, P. (2001) *Violence of Interpretation: From Pictogram to Statement*, London: Brunner-Routledge.

Bachelard, G. (1938) *La Formation de l'Esprit Scientifique: Contribuition à une Psychanalyse de la Connaissance*, Paris: Librairie Philosophique J. Vrin.

Bachelard, G. (1971) 'The cogito of the dreamer', in G. Bachelard *The Poetics of Reverie: Childhood, Language and the Cosmos*, Boston: Beacon Press.

Bachelard, G. (1987) *The Psychoanalysis of Fire*, London: Quartet.

Banuri, T. (1990) 'Modernization and its discontents: cultural perspectives on theories of development', in F. Apffell-Marglin and S. A. Marglin (eds) *Dominating Knowledge: Development, Culture and Resistance*, Oxford: Clarendon Press.

Barbichon, G. and Moscovici, S. (1965) 'Diffusion des connaissance scientifique', *Social Science Information* 4, 1: 7–22.

Barnes, M. and Bowl, R. (2000) *Taking over the Asylum: Empowerment and Mental Health*, Basingstoke: Palgrave.

Barthes, R. (1973) *Mythologies*, London: Paladin.

Bartlett, F. C. (1923) *Psychology and Primitive Culture*, Cambridge: Cambridge University Press.

Bartlett, F. C. (1932) *Remembering: A Study in Experimental and Social Psychology*, Cambridge: Cambridge University Press.

Basaglia, F. (1968) *L'Institution en Negation*, Paris: Editions du Seuil.

Bauer, M. W. (2002) 'Arenas, platforms and the biotechnology movement', *Science Communication* 24, 2: 144–161.

Bauer, M. W. and Gaskell, G. (1999) 'Towards a paradigm for research on social representations', *Journal for the Theory of Social Behaviour* 29, 2: 163–186.

Bauer, M. W. and Gaskell, G. (eds) (2002) *Biotechnology: The Making of a Global Controversy*, Cambridge: Cambridge University Press.

Bauer, M., Gaskell, G. and Allum, N. C. (2000) 'Quality, quantity and knowledge interests: avoiding confusions', in M. W. Bauer and G. Gaskell (eds) *Qualitative Researching with Text, Image and Sound: A Practical Handbook*, London: Sage.

Bauman, Z. (2001) *Community: Seeking Safety in an Insecure World*, Cambridge: Polity Press.

Beck, U., Giddens, A. and Lash, S. (1994) *Reflexive Modernization: Politics, Tradition and Aesthetics in the Modern Social Order*, Cambridge: Polity Press.

Benhabib, S. (1992) *Situating the Self: Gender, Community and Postmodernism in Contemporary Ethics*, Cambridge: Polity Press.

Benhabib, S. (1999) 'Civil society and the politics of identity and difference in a global context', in N. J. Smelser and J. C. Alexander (eds) *Diversity and its Discontents: Cultural Conflict and Common Ground in Contemporary American Society*, Princeton: Princeton University Press.

Benhabib, S. (2002) *The Claims of Culture: Equality and Diversity in the Global Era*, Princeton: Princeton University Press.

Benhabib, S. (2004) *The Rights of Others: Aliens, Residents and Citizens*, Cambridge: Polity Press.

Benjamin, J. (1993) *The Bonds of Love: Psychoanalysis, Feminism and the Problem of Domination*, London: Virago.

Berger, P. and Luckman, T. (1966) *The Social Construction of Reality*, Harmondsworth: Penguin.

Billig, M. (1987) *Arguing and Thinking: A Rhetorical Approach to Social Psychology*, Cambridge: Cambridge University Press.

Billig, M., Condon, S., Edwards, D., Gane, M., Middleton, D. and Radley, A. (1988) *Ideological Dilemmas*, London: Sage.

Bleger, J. (1980) *Temas de Psicologia: Entrevista e Grupos*, São Paulo: Martins Fontes Editora.

Bloch, E. (1986) *The Principle of Hope*, Oxford: Blackwell.

Bloch, E. (1988) 'The conscious and known activity within the not-yet-conscious: the utopian function', in E. Bloch *The Utopian Function of Art and Literature*, Cambridge, MA: MIT Press.

Blumenberg, H. (1985) *Work on Myth*, Cambridge, MA: MIT Press.

Boog, B. W. M., Keune, L. and Tromp, C. (2003) 'Action research and emancipation', *Journal of Community and Applied Social Psychology* 13, 6: 419–503.

Bourdieu, P. (1994) *Language and Symbolic Power*, Cambridge: Polity Press.

Brandão, C. R. (1982) *Pesquisa Participante*, São Paulo: Brasiliense.

Briceno-Leon, R. (1998) 'El contexto político de la participación comunitária em América Latina', *Cadernos de Saúde Publica* 14, 2: 141–147.

Bruner, J. (1990) *Acts of Meaning*, Cambridge, MA: Harvard University Press.

Brunswik, E. (1952) *The Conceptual Framework of Psychology*, Chicago: University of Chicago Press.

Calhoun, C. (ed.) (1992) *Habermas and the Public Sphere*, Cambridge, MA: MIT Press.

Campbell, C. (2003) *'Letting them Die': How HIV/AIDS Programmes often Fail*, Bloomington: Indiana University Press.

Campbell, C. and Jovchelovitch, S. (2000) 'Health, community and development: towards a social psychology of participation', *Journal of Applied and Community Social Psychology* 10, 4: 255–270.

Campbell, C. and Murray, M. (2004) 'Community health psychology: promoting analysis and action for social change', *Journal of Health Psychology* 9, 2: 187–195.

Canetti, E. (1973) *Crowds and Power*, Harmondsworth: Penguin.

Castel, R. (1971) 'L'institution psychiatrique en question', *Revue Française de Sociologie* 12, 1: 57–92.

Castel, R. (1978) *O Psicanalismo*, Rio de Janeiro: Graal.

Castro, P. (2003) 'Dialogues in social psychology – or how new are new ideas?', in J. László and W. Wagner (eds) *Theories and Controversies in Social Psychology*, Budapest: New Mandate.

Chambers, R. (2003) *Whose Reality Counts? Putting the First Last*, London: ITDG.

Chryssochoou, X. (2000a) 'Changes in globalised societies and the redefinition of identities', *Journal of Community and Applied Social Psychology* 10, 5 (special issue).

Chryssochoou, X. (2000b) 'Muticultural societies: making sense of new environments and identities', *Journal of Community and Applied Social Psychology* 10, 5: 343–354.

Cohen, A. P. (1995) *The Symbolic Construction of Community*, London: Routledge.

Cole, M. (1985) 'The zone of proximal development: where culture and cognition create each other', in J. Wertsch (ed.) *Culture, Communication and Cognition*, New York: Cambridge University Press.

Cole, M. (1996) *Cultural Psychology: A Once and Future Discipline*, Cambridge, MA: Belknap Press.

Conway, J. M. (2004) *Identity, Place, Knowledge: Social Movements Contesting Globalisation*, Halifax, Nova Scotia: Fernwood.

Cooke, B. and Kothari, U. (eds) (2001) *Participation: The New Tyranny?* London: Zed Books.

Cornish, F. (2004) 'Making context concrete: a dialogical approach to the society–health relation', *Journal of Health Psychology* 9, 2: 281–294.

Danziger, K. (1990) *Constructing the Subject: Historical Origins of Psychoanalytical Research*, Cambridge: Cambridge University Press.

Davis, M. and Wallbridge, D. (eds) (1981) *Boundary and Space: An Introduction to the Work of D. W. Winnicott*, London: Karnac.

Dear, M. J. and Taylor, S. M. (eds) (1982) *Not in Our Street: Community Attitudes to Mental Health Care*, London: Pion.

De-Graft Aikins, A. (2004) 'Strengthening quality and continuity of diabetes care in rural Ghana: a critical social psychological approach', *Journal of Health Psychology* 9, 2: 295–309.

Descartes, R. (1641/1989) *A Discourse on Method: Meditations and Principles*, London: Everyman's Library.

Devereux, G. (1967) *From Anxiety to Method in the Behavioural Sciences*, The Hague: Mouton.

Doise, W. (1990) 'Les représentacions sociales', in R. Ghiglione, C. Bonnet and J. F. Richard (eds) *Traité de Psychologie Cognitive*, vol. 3, Paris: Dunod.

Doise, W. (1986) *Levels of Explanation in Social Psychology*, Cambridge: Cambridge University Press.

Doise, W. (2001) 'Un projet européen pour la psychologie sociale', in F. Buschini and N. Kalampalikis (eds) *Penser la Vie, le Social, la Nature: Mélanges en l'honneur de Serge Moscovici*, Paris: Éditions de la Maison de Sciences de l'Homme.

Doise, W. and Mugny, G. (1984) *The Social Development of the Intellect*, Oxford: Pergamon.

Doise, W. and Palmonori, A. (eds) (1986) *L'Étude des Représentacions Socials*, Neuchâtel: Delachaux and Nestlé.

Doise, W., Mugny, G. and Perrot-Clermont, A. N. (1975) 'Social interaction and the development of cognitive operations', *European Journal of Social Psychology* 5, 3: 367–383.

Dulong, R. and Ackermann, W. (1972) 'Popularisation of science for adults', *Social Science Information* 11, 1: 113–148.

Durkheim, E. (1898/1996) 'Représentations individuelles et représentations collectives', in E. Durkheim *Sociologie et Philosophie*, Paris: Presses Universitaires de France.

Durkheim, E. and Mauss, M. (1905/1963) *Primitive Classification*, Chicago: Chicago University Press.

Durkheim, E. (1955/1983) *Pragmatism and Sociology*, Cambridge: Cambridge University Press.

Durkheim, E. (1973) *On Institutional Analysis*, Chicago: University of Chicago Press.

Dussel, E. (1993) 'Eurocentrism and modernity', *boundary 2* 20, 3: 65–76.

Dussel, E. (1995) *The Invention of the Americas: Eclipse of the 'Other' and the Myth of Modernity*, New York: Continuum.

Dussel, E. (1996) *The Underside of Modernity: Apel, Ricouer, Rorty, Taylor and the Philosophy of Liberation*, Atlantic Highlands, NJ: Humanities Press.

Dussel, E. (2004) 'Deconstruction of the concept of "intolerance": from tolerance to solidarity', *Constellations* 11, 3: 326–333.

Duveen, G. (1997) 'Psychological development as social process', in L. Smith and J. P. Tomlinson (eds) *Piaget, Vygotsky and Beyond*, London: Routledge.

Duveen, G. (1998) 'The psychosocial production of ideas', *Culture and Psychology* 4: 455–472.

Duveen, G. (2000) 'Introduction: the power of ideas', in S. Moscovici *Social Representations: Introductions and Explorations*, Cambridge: Polity Press.

Duveen, G. (2001a) 'Genesis and structure: Piaget and Moscovici', in F. Buschini and N. Kalampalikis (eds) *Penser la Vie, le Social, la Nature: Mélanges en l'honneur de Serge Moscovici*, Paris: Éditions de la Maison de sciences de l'homme.

Duveen, G. (2001b) 'Representations, identity and resistance', in K. Deaux and G. Philogène (eds) *Representations of the Social: Bridging Theoretical Traditions*, Oxford: Blackwell.

Duveen, G. (2002a) 'Construction and constraint in psychological development', paper presented at the workshop 'Exploring Psychological Development as a Social and Cultural Process', Cambridge, September.

Duveen, G. (2002b) 'Construction, belief, doubt', *Psychologie et Societé* 3: 139–155.

Eco, U. (1966) 'Narrative structure in Flemming', in O. del Buono and U. Eco (eds) *The Bond Affair*, London: MacDonald.

Elejabarrieta, F. (1989) 'Las paradojas de los rigores metodológicos en psicología social', *Revista Vasca de Psicología* 2, 1: 81–90.

Eley, G. (1992) 'Nations, publics and political cultures: placing Habermas in the nineteenth century', in C. Calhoun (ed.) *Habermas and the Public Sphere*, Cambridge: MIT Press.

Elliot, A. (1992) *Social Theory and Psychoanalysis in Transition: Self and Society from Freud to Kristeva*, Oxford: Blackwell.

Erikson, E. (1964) 'Psychological reality and historical actuality', in E. Erikson *Insight and Responsibility*, New York: Norton.

Escobar, A. (1995) *Encountering Development: The Making and the Unmaking of the Third World*, Princeton: Princeton University Press.

Fals-Borda, O. (1985) *Conocimiento y Poder Popular: Leciones con Campesinos de Nicarágua, México y Colombia*, Bogotá: Siglo XXI.

Fals-Borda, O. (1988) *Knowledge and People's Power: Lessons with Peasants in Nicaragua, Mexico and Colombia*, New York: New Horizons Press.

Fals-Borda, O. and M. A. Rahman (1991) *Action and Knowledge: Breaking the Monopoly with Participatory-Action Research*, London: Intermediate Technology Books.

Fanon, F. (1967) *Black Skin, White Masks*, New York: Grove Press.

Farr, R. M. (1991) 'The long past and the short history of social psychology', *European Journal of Social Psychology* 21, 5: 371–380.

Farr, R. M. (1993a) 'Common sense, science and social representations', *Public Understanding of Science* 2: 111–122.

Farr, R. M. (1993b) 'Theory and method in the study of social representations', in D. Canter and G. Breakwell (eds) *Empirical Approaches to Social Representations*, Oxford: Clarendon Press.

Farr, R. M. (1996) *The Roots of Modern Social Psychology*, Oxford: Blackwell.

Farr, R. M. (1998) 'From collective to social representations: aller et retour', *Culture and Psychology* 4: 275–296.

Farr, R. M. and Moscovici, S. (eds) (1984) *Social Representations*, Cambridge: Cambridge University Press.

Farr, R. M. and Rommetveit, R. (1995) 'The communicative act: an epilogue to mutualities in dialogue', in I. Marková, C. Graumann and K. Foppa (eds) *Mutualities in Dialogue*, Cambridge, Cambridge University Press.

Fodor, J. (1972) 'Some reflections on L. S. Vygotsky's thought and language', *Cognition* 1, 1: 83–95.

Foucault, M. (1971) *Madness and Civilization: A History of Insanity in the Age of Reason*, London: Routledge.

Foucault, M. (1974) *Les Mots et les Choses. The Order of Things: Archaeology of the Human Sciences*, London: Tavistock.

Foucault, M. (1980) *Power/Knowledge: Selected Interviews and Other Writings, 1972–1977*, Brighton: Harvester.

Foucault, M. (1987) *Mental Illness and Psychology*, Berkeley: University of California Press.

Foucault, M. (1991) 'Introduction', in G. Canguilhem *The Normal and the Pathological*, New York: Zone Books.

Fraser, N. (1990) 'Rethinking the public sphere: a contribution to the critique of actually existing democracy', *Social Text* 25: 56–80.

Freire, P. (1970) *Pedagogy of the Oppressed*, Herder and Herder: New York.

Freire, P. (1973a) 'Education as the practice of freedom', *Education for Critical Consciousness*, New York: Seabury Press.

Freire, P. (1973b) 'Extension or communication', in P. Freire *Education for Critical Consciousness*, New York: Seabury Press.

Freire, P. (1996) *Pedagogia da Autonomia: Saberes Necessários à Pratica Educativa*, 19th edn, Rio de Janeiro: Editora Paz e Terra.

Freire, P. (2001) *Pedagogy of Freedom, Democracy and Civic Courage*, Oxford: Rowman & Littlefield.

Freire, P. (2004) *The Pedagogy of Hope*, London: Sage.

Freud, S. (1900) 'The interpretation of dreams', *Standard Edition*, vol. 5, London: Hogarth Press and Institute of Psychoanalysis.

Freud, S. (1908) 'On the sexual theories of children', *Collected Papers*, vol. 2, London: Hogarth Press and Institute of Psychoanalysis.

Freud, S. (1911) 'Formulations on the two principles of mental functioning', in *On Metapsychology: The Theory of Psychoanalysis*, Pelican Freud Library, vol. 2, Harmondsworth: Penguin.

Freud, S. (1912) 'The dynamics of transference', *Collected Papers*, vol. 2, London: Hogarth Press and Institute of Psychoanalysis.

Freud, S. (1919/2003) *The Uncanny*, Harmondsworth: Penguin.

Freud, S. (1920) 'Beyond the pleasure principle', *Standard Edition*, vol. 18, London: Hogarth Press and Institute of Psychoanalysis.

Freud, S. (1921) 'Group psychology and the analysis of the ego' in *Civilization, Society and Religion*, Pelican Freud Library, vol. 12, Harmondsworth: Penguin.

Freud, S. (1930/2002) 'Civilization and its discontents', *The New Penguin Freud*, Harmondsworth: Penguin.

Furth, H. (1987) *Knowledge as Desire: An Essay on Freud and Piaget*, New York: Columbia University Press.

Furth, H. (1996) *Desire for Society: Children's Knowledge as Social Imagination*, New York: Plenum Press.

Gabe, J., Kelleher, D. and Williams, G. (eds) (1994) *Challenging Medicine*, London: Routledge.

Gadamer, H.-G. (1975) *Truth and Method*, London: Sheed and Ward.

Gaskell, G. and Bauer, M. W. (eds) (2001) *Biotechnology, 1996–2000*, London: Science Museum.

Gaskell, G., Bauer, M. W. and Durant, J. (1998) 'The representation of biotechnology: policy, media and public perception', in J. Durant, M. W. Bauer and G. Gaskell (eds) *Biotechnology in the Public Sphere: A European Sourcebook*, London: The Science Museum.

Gellner, E. (1992) *Reason and Culture: The Historic Role of Rationality and Rationalism*, Oxford: Blackwell.

Gergen, K. (1985) 'The social constructionist movement in modern psychology', *American Psychologist*, 40, 3: 266–275.

Gervais, M.-C. (1997) 'Social representations of nature: the case of the Braer oil spill in Shetland', unpublished PhD thesis, University of London.

Gervais, M. C. and Jovchelovitch, S. (1998) 'Health and identity: the case of the Chinese community in England', *Social Science Information* 37, 4: 709–729.

Gervais, M.-C., Morant, N. and Penn, G. (1999) 'Making sense of "absence": towards a typology of absence in social representations theory and research', *Journal for the Theory of Social Behaviour* 29, 4: 419–444.

Giami, A. (2001) 'Counter-transference in social research: George Devereux and beyond', *Papers in Research Methodology Qualitative Series no. 7*, London: Methodology Institute, LSE.

Giddens, A. (1971) *Capitalism and Modern Social Theory: An Analysis of the Writings of Marx, Durkheim and Max Weber*, Cambridge: Cambridge University Press.

Giddens, A. (1978) *Durkheim*, London: Fontana.

Giddens, A. (1991) *Modernity and Self-Identity: Self and Society in the Late Modern Age*, Cambridge: Polity Press.

Gillman, S. (1985) *Difference and Pathology: Stereotypes of Sexuality, Race and Madness*, Cornell: Cornell University Press.

Goffman, E. (1968) *Asylums: Essays on the Social Situations of Mental Patients and other Inmates*, London: Pelican.

Guareschi, P. (2004) *Psicologia Social Crítica: Como Prática de Libertação*, Porto Alegre: EDIPUCRS.

Guareschi, P. A. and Jovchelovitch, S. (2004) 'Health and the development of community resources in southern Brazil', *Journal of Health Psychology* 9, 2: 311–322.

Guimelli, C. and Jacobi, D. (1990) 'Pratiques nouvelles et transformation des representations sociales', *Revue Internationale de Psychologie Sociale* 3: 307–334.

Gutmann, A. (ed.) (1994) *Multiculturalism: Examining the Politics of Recognition*, Princeton: Princeton University Press.

Habermas, J. (1987) *Knowledge and Human Interest*, Cambridge: Polity Press.

Habermas, J. (1989a) *The Structural Transformation of the Public Sphere: An Inquiry into a Category of Bourgeois Society*, Cambridge: Polity Press.

Habermas, J. (1989b) *The Theory of Communicative Action: Life World and System, a Critique of Functionalist Reason*, Cambridge: Polity Press.

Habermas, J. (1990) *On the Logic of the Social Sciences*, Cambridge: Polity Press.
Habermas, J. (1991) *The Theory of Communicative Action: Reason and the Rationalization of Society*, Cambridge: Polity Press.
Habermas, J. (1992) 'Further reflections on the public sphere', in C. Calhoun (ed.) *Habermas and the Public Sphere*, Cambridge, MA: MIT Press.
Habermas, J. (2005) *Naturalismus und Religion: Philosophische Essays*, Frankfurt: Suhrkamp.
Halbwachs, M. (1997) *La Mémoire Collective*, Paris: Édition Albin Michel.
Halbwachs, M. (1992) *On Collective Memory*, Chicago: University of Chicago Press.
Hall, S., Held, D. and McGrew, T. (eds) (1992) *Modernity and its Futures*, Oxford: Oxford University Press and Open University.
Halldén, O. (1999) 'Conceptual change and contextualization', in W. Schnotz, S. Vosniadou and M. Carretero (eds) *New Perspectives in Conceptual Change*, Amsterdam: Pergamon.
Halldén, O., Petersson, M. S., Ehrlén, K., Haglund, L., Österlind, K. and Stenlund, A. (2002) 'Situating the question of conceptual change', in M. Limón and L. Mason (eds) *Reconsidering Conceptual Change: Issues in Theory and Practice*, London: Kluwer.
Heelas, P., Lash, S. and Morris, P. (eds) (1996) *Detraditionalization: Critical Reflections on Authority and Identity*, Oxford: Blackwell.
Heider, F. (1958) *The Psychology of Interpersonal Relations*, New York: Wiley.
Herzlich, C. (1973) *Health and Illness: A Social Psychological Analysis*, London: Academic Press.
Hilgartner, S. (1990) 'The dominant view of popularisation: conceptual problems, political uses', *Social Studies of Science* 20, 3: 519–539.
Himmelweit, H. T. and Gaskell, G. (eds) (1990) *Societal Psychology*, London: Sage.
Hollander, N. C. (1997) *Love in a Time of Hate: Liberation Psychology in Latin America*, New Brunswick, NJ: Rutgers University Press.
Honneth, A. (1995) *The Struggle for Recognition. The Moral Grammar of Social Conflicts*, Cambridge: Polity Press.
Honig, B. (2001) *Democracy and the Foreigner*, Princeton: Princeton University Press.
Howarth, C. (2004) 'Re-presentation and resistance in the context of school exclusion: reasons to be critical,' *Journal of Community and Applied Social Psychology* 14, 5: 356, 377.
Howarth, C. and Foster, J. (2004) 'Exploring the potential of the theory of social representations in community-based health research and vice-versa', *Journal of Health Psychology* 9, 2: 229–243.
Howell, J. and Pearce, J. (2001) *Civil Society and Development: A Critical Exploration*, Boulder: Lynne Rienner.
Hsu, E. (1999) *The Transmission of Chinese Medicine*, Cambridge: Cambridge University Press.
Ibañez, T. (1991) 'Social psychology and the rhetoric of truth', *Theory and Psychology* 1, 2: 187–201.
Israel, J. and Tajfel, H. (1972) *The Context of Social Psychology: A Critical Assessment*, London: Academic Press.
Ivinson, G. and Duveen, G. (2005) 'Classroom structuration and the development of representations of the curriculum', *British Journal of Sociology of Education* 26, 5: 627–642.

Jacques, J. and Raichvarg, D. (1991) *Savants et Ignorants: Une Histoire de la Vulgarisation des Sciences*, Paris: Editions du Seuil.

Jodelet, D. (1985) 'Civils et bredins: representations sociales de la maladie mentale et rapport à la folie en milieu rural', unpublished thesis of Doctorat d'Etat, Paris, École de Hautes Études en Sciences Sociales.

Jodelet, D. (1989) 'Représentations sociales: un domaine en expansion', in D. Jodelet (ed.) *Représentations Socials*, Paris: Presses Universitaires de France.

Jodelet, D. (1991) *Madness and Social Representations*, London: Harvester/ Wheatsheaf.

Jodelet, D. (2002) 'Les representations socials dans le champ de la culture', *Social Sciences Information* 41, 1: 111–133.

Joffe, H. (1999) *Risk and the Other*, Cambridge: Cambridge University Press.

Joffe, H. (2002) 'Risk: from perception to social representation', *British Journal of Social Psychology* 42, 1: 55–73.

Jones, K. (1993) *Asylums and After*, London: Athlone Press.

Jovchelovitch, S. (1995) 'Social representations in and of the public sphere: towards a theoretical articulation', *Journal for the Theory of Social Behaviour* 25, 1: 81–102.

Jovchelovitch, S. (1996) 'In defense of representations', *Journal for the Theory of Social Behaviour* 26, 2: 121–135.

Jovchelovitch, S. (1997) 'Peripheral communities and the transformation of social representations: queries on power and recognition', *Social Psychological Review* 1, 1: 16–26.

Jovchelovitch, S. (2000) Representações Sociais e Esfera Pública: *Um Estudo Sobre a Construção Simbólica dos Espaços Públicos no Brasil*, Rio de Janeiro: Petrópolis.

Jovchelovitch, S. (2001) 'Social representations, public life and social construction', in K. Deaux and G. Philogene (eds) *Representations of the Social: Bridging Theoretical Traditions*, Oxford: Blackwell.

Jovchelovitch, S. (2002) 'Re-thinking the diversity of knowledge: cognitive polyphasia, belief and representation', *Psychologie & Societé* 5, 1: 121–138.

Jovchelovitch, S. (2004) 'Psicologia social: saber, comunidade e cultura', *Psicologia e Sociedade* 16, 2: 20–31.

Jovchelovitch, S. and Campbell, C. (eds) (2000) 'Health, community and development', *Journal of Community and Applied Social Psychology* 10, 4 (special issue).

Jovchelovitch, S. and Gervais, M. C. (1999) 'Social representations of health and illness: the case of the Chinese community in England', *Journal of Community and Applied Social Psychology* 9, 4: 247–260.

Kaës, R. (1984) 'Le travail de la représentations et les fonctions de l'intermédiare: étude psychanalytique', in C. Belisle and B. Schele (eds) *Les Savoirs dans les Pratiques Quotidiennes: Recherches sur les Representations*, Paris: Editions du Centre National de La Recherche Scientifique.

Knorr-Cetina, K. and Mulkay, M. (1983) *Science Observed: Perspectives on the Social Study of Science*, London: Sage.

Kruger, A. C. and Tomasello, M. (1986) 'Transactive discussions with peers and adults', *Developmental Psychology* 22, 5: 681–685.

Landes, J. (1988) *Women and the Public Sphere in the Age of the French Revolution*, Ithaca: Cornell University Press.

Langer, M. (1987) *Cuestionamos*, Buenos Aires: Ediciones Busqueda.

Latour, B. (1987) *Science in Action: How to Follow Scientists and Engineers through Society*, Cambridge: Harvard University Press.

Latour, B. (1993) *We Have Never Been Modern*, London: Prentice Hall.

Latour, B. and Woolgar, S. (1986) *Laboratory Life: The Construction of Scientific Facts*, 2nd edn, Princeton: Princeton University Press.

Lave, J. (1988) *Cognition in Practice: Mind, Mathematics and Culture in Everyday Life*, New York: Cambridge University Press.

Leenhardt, M. (1975) 'Preface', in L. Lévy-Bruhl, *The Notebooks on Primitive Mentality*, Oxford: Blackwell.

Leman, P. J. (1998) 'Social relations, social influence and the development of knowledge', *Papers on Social Representations* 7: 41–56. Online. Available HTTP: <http://www.psr.jku.at/psrindex.htm> (accessed 14 February 2006).

Leman, P. J. (2002) 'Argument structure, argument content and cognitive change in children's peer interaction', *Journal of Genetic Psychology* 163, 1: 40–45.

Leman, P. J. and Duveen, G. (1999) 'Representations of authority and children's moral reasoning', *European Journal of Social Psychology* 29, 5–6: 557–575.

Leontiev, A. N. and Luria, A. R. (1972) 'Some notes concerning Dr Fodor's "Reflections on L. S. Vygotsky's Thought and Language"', *Cognition* 1, 2–3: 311–316.

Lévy-Bruhl, L. (1975) *The Notebookss on Primitive Mentality*, Oxford: Blackwell.

Lévy-Bruhl, L. (1910/1985) *How Natives Think*, Princeton: Princeton University Press.

Liebes, T. and Katz, E. (1993) *The Export of Meaning: Cross Cultural Readings of Dallas*, 2nd edn, Cambridge: Polity Press.

Lira, E. (2000) 'Verdad, justicia y impunidad: memoria, perdón y olvido', in J. J. Vazques (ed.) *Psicología Social y Liberación en América Latina*, Mexico City: Universidad Autónoma Metropolitana, Iztapalapa.

Livingstone, S. (1989) *Making Sense of Television: The Psychology of Audience Interpretation*, Oxford: Pergamon.

Luria, A. R. (1931) 'Psychological expedition to Central Asia', *Science* 74: 383–384.

Luria, A. R. (1976) *Cognitive Development: Its Cultural and Social Foundations*, Cambridge, MA: Harvard University Press.

Luria, A. R. (1979) 'Romantic science', in A. R. Luria *The Making of Mind: A Personal Account of Soviet Psychology*, Cambridge, MA: Harvard University Press.

Lynch, M. and Woolgar, S. (1990) *Representation in Scientific Practice*, Cambridge, MA: MIT Press.

Mannoni, O. (1970) *Le Psychiatrie, son 'Fou' et la Psychanalyse*, Paris: Editions du Seuil.

Marková, I. (1983) *Paradigms, Thought and Language*, Chichester: Wiley.

Marková, I. (2003) *Dialogicality and Social Representations: The Dynamics of Mind*, Cambridge: Cambridge University Press.

Marková, I. and Foppa, K. (eds) (1991) *Asymmetries in Dialogue*, Hemel Hempstead: Harvester Wheatsheaf.

Marková, I., Graumann, C. and Foppa, K. (eds) (1995) *Mutualities in Dialogue*, Cambridge: Cambridge University Press.

Marx, K. and Engels, F. (1970) *The German Ideology*, London: Lawrence & Wishart.

Martín-Baró, I. (1994) *Writings for a Liberation Psychology*, Cambridge, MA: Harvard University Press.

Mead, G. H. (1932) *The Objective Reality of Perspectives: The Philosophy of the Present*, Illinois: Open Court.

Mead, G. H. (1934) *Mind, Self and Society from the Standpoint of a Social Behaviourist*, Chicago: University of Chicago Press.

Merlau-Ponty, M. (1986) *Phenomenology of Perception*, London: Routledge and Kegan Paul.

Micale, M. S. and Dietle, R. L. (eds) (2000) *Enlightement, Passion, Modernity: Historical Essays in European Thought and Culture*, Stanford: Stanford University Press.

Montero, M. (2002) 'On the construction of reality and truth: towards an epistemology of community social psychology', *American Journal of Community Psychology* 30, 4: 571–584.

Morant, N. and Rose, D. (1998) 'Loucura, multiplicidade e alteridade', in A. Arruda (ed.) *Representando a Alteridade*, Petrópolis: Vozes.

Morgan, L. M. (2001) 'Community participation in health: perpetual allure, persistent challenge', *Health Policy and Planning* 16, 3: 221–230.

Moscovici, S. (1961) *La Psychanalyse, son Image et son Public*, Paris: Presses Universitaires de France.

Moscovici, S. (1976a) *La Psychanalyse, son Image et son Public*, 2nd edn, Paris: Presses Universitaires de France.

Moscovici, S. (1976b) *Social Influence and Social Change*, London: Academic Press.

Moscovici, S. (1984) 'Introduction: la domaine de la psychologie sociale', in S. Moscovici *Psychologie Sociale*, Paris: Presses Universitaires de France.

Moscovici, S. (1985) *The Age of the Crowd: A Historical Treatise in Mass Psychology*, Cambridge: Cambridge University Press.

Moscovici, S. (1988) 'Notes towards a description of social representations', *European Journal of Social Psychology* 18, 211–250.

Moscovici, S. (1989) 'Des représentations collectives aux représentations sociales: éléments pour une histoire', in D. Jodelet (ed.) *Les Représentations Sociales*, Paris: Presses Universitaires de France.

Moscovici, S. (1993) *The Invention of Society: Psychological Explanations for Social Phenomena*, Cambridge: Polity Press.

Moscovici, S. (1998) 'Social consciousness and its history', *Culture and Psychology* 4, 3: 411–429.

Moscovici, S. (2000a) 'Ideas and their development: a dialogue between Serge Moscovici and Ivana Marková', in S. Moscovici *Social Representations: Explorations in Social Psychology*, Cambridge: Polity Press.

Moscovici, S. (2000b) 'The history and actuality of social representations', in S. Moscovici *Social Representations: Explorations in Social Psychology*, Cambridge: Polity Press.

Moscovici, S. (2000c) *Social Representations: Explorations in Social Psychology*, Cambridge: Polity Press.

Murphy, E. (1991) *After the Asylums: Community Care for People with Mental Illness*, London: Faber and Faber.

Murphy, E. (1996) *Asylum in the Community*, London: Routledge.

Nagel, T. (1986) *The View from Nowhere*, New York: Oxford University Press.

Nature (2005) 'Don't keep your distance, 437, 7058: 451.

Needham, R. (1972) *Belief, Language, and Experience*, Oxford: Blackwell.

Novellino, D. (2003) 'From seduction to miscommunication: the confession and presentation of local knowledge in "participatory development"', in J. Pottier, A. Bicker and P. Silitoe (eds) *Negotiating Local Knowledge: Power and Identity in Development*, Sterling, VA: Pluto Press.

Nuilla, A. (2001) 'Representations of reproductive health: a study about a Mayan community in the western highlands of Guatemala', unpublished PhD thesis, University of London.

Nunes, T., Schliemann, A. D. and Carraher, D. (1993) *Street Mathematics and School Mathematics*, Cambridge: Cambridge University Press.

Oliveira, C. (1981) 'Olhai os homens do campo', unpublished paper, Papers of the Psychiatric Hospital São Pedro, Porto Alegre, Brazil.

O'Muircheartaigh, C. (1997) 'Measurement error in surveys: a historical perspective', in L. Lynberg, P. P. Biemer, M. Collins, E. DeLeeuw, C. Dippo, N. Schrtz and D. Trewin (eds) *Survey Measurement and Process Quality*, New York: Wiley.

Perret-Clermont, A.-N. (1980) *Social Interaction and Cognitive Development in Children*, London: Academic Press.

Piaget, J. (1929) *The Child's Conception of the World*, London: Routledge and Kegan Paul.

Piaget, J. (1962) *Child, Dreams and Imitation in Childhood*, London: Routledge and Kegan Paul.

Piaget, J. (1964) *Six Psychological Studies*, London: London University Press.

Piaget, J. (1971) *Structuralism*, London: Routledge and Kegan Paul.

Piaget, J. (1995a) 'Genetic logic and sociology', in *Sociological Studies*, London: Routledge.

Piaget, J. (1995b) 'Individuality in history: the individual and the education of reason', in J. Piaget *Sociological Studies*, London: Routledge.

Piaget, J. (1995c) 'Logical operations and social life', in J. Piaget *Sociological Studies*, London: Routledge.

Piaget, J. (1995d) *Sociological Studies*, London: Routledge.

Piaget, J. and Inhelder, B. (1969) *The Psychology of the Child*, London: Routledge and Kegan Paul.

Pichon-Rivière, E. (1980) *O Processo Grupal*, São Paulo: Martins Fontes Editora.

Pichon-Rivière, E. (1991) *Teoria do Vínculo*, São Paulo: Martins Fontes Editora.

Plato (1987) *Theaetetus*, Harmondsworth: Penguin.

Potter, J. (1996) *Representing Reality: Discourse, Rhetoric and Social Construction*, London: Sage.

Potter, J. and Wetherell, M. (1987) *Discourse and Social Psychology: Beyond Attitudes and Behaviour*, London: Sage.

Pottier, J., Bicker, A. and Sillitoe, P. (eds) (2003) *Negotiating Local Knowledge: Power and Identity in Development*, London: Pluto.

Psaltis, C. and Duveen, G. (forthcoming) 'Social relations and cognitive development: the influence of conversation type and representations of gender', *European Journal of Social Psychology*.

Putnam, R. (2000) *Bowling Alone: The Collapse and Revival of American Community*, New York: Simon and Schuster.

Rahman, M. A. (1995) 'Participatory development: toward liberation or co-optation?', in G. Craig and M. Mayo (eds) (1995) *Community Empowerment: A Reader in Participation and Development*, London: Zed Books.

Ramella, M. and De La Cruz, R. B. (2000) 'Taking part in adolescent sexual health promotion in Peru: community participation from a social psychological perspective', *Journal of Community and Applied Social Psychology* 10, 4: 271–284.

Reicher, S. (1987) 'Crowd behaviour as social action', in J. Turner (ed.) *Rediscovering the Social Group: A Self-Categorisation Theory*, Oxford: Blackwell.

Rogoff, B. and Lowe, J. (1984) *Everyday Cognition: Its Development in Social Context*, Cambridge: Cambridge University Press.

Rommetveit, R. (1974) 'On the architecture of intersubjectivity', in R. Rommetveit *On Message Structure: A Framework for the Study of Language and Communication*, Chichester: Wiley.

Rommetveit, R. (1984) 'The role of language in the creation and transmission of social representations', in R. M. Farr and S. Moscovici (eds) *Social Representations*, Cambridge: Cambridge University Press.

Rorty, R. (1980) *Philosophy and the Mirror of Nature*, Princeton: Princeton University Press.

Rose, D. (1996) 'Representations of madness on British television: a social psychological analysis', unpublished PhD thesis, University of London.

Rose, D. (1997) 'Television, madness and community care', *Journal of Community and Applied Social Psychology* 8, 3: 213–228.

Rose, D. (2003a) 'Collaborative research between users and professionals: peaks and pitfalls', *Psychiatric Bulletin*, 27: 404–406.

Rose, D. (2003b) 'Partnership, co-ordination of care and the place of user involvement', *Journal of Mental Health* 12, 1: 59–70.

Rosenhan, D. L. (1975) 'On being sane in insane places', in D. Brisset and C. Edgley (eds) *Life as Theatre: A Dramaturgical Sourcebook*, Chicago: Aldine.

Said, E. (1995) *Orientalism: Western Conceptions of the Orient*, Harmondsworth, Penguin.

Savage-Rumbaugh, E. S. and Fields, W. M. (2000) 'Linguistic, cultural and cognitive capacities of Bonobos (Pan paniscus)', *Culture and Psychology* 6, 2: 131–153.

Schiele, B. and Jacobi, D. (1988) 'La vulgarisation scientifique: themes de recherche', in B. Schiele and D. Jacobi (eds) *Vulgariser la Science: Le Proces de l'ignorance*, Champ-Vallon: Seyssel.

Schutz, A. (1944) 'The stranger: an essay on social psychology', *American Journal of Sociology* 49: 500–507.

Schutz, A. (1967a) 'The dimensions of the social world', in A. Schutz *Collected Papers II: Studies in Social Theory*, The Hague: Martinus Nijhoff.

Schutz, A. (1967b) *Collected Papers I: The Problem of Social Reality*, The Hague: Martinus Nijhoff.

Scribner, S. (1975) 'Models of thinking and ways of speaking: culture and logic reconsidered', in P. N. Johnson Laird and P.-C. Wason (eds) *Thinking*, New York: Cambridge University Press.

Scribner, S. (1984) 'Cognitive studies of work', *Quarterly Newsletter of the Laboratory of Comparative Human Cognition* 6: 1–48.

Scribner, S. (1985) 'Vygotsky's uses of history', in J. Wertsch (ed.) *Culture, Communication and Cognition*, New York: Cambridge University Press.

Scribner, S. (1986) 'Thinking in action: some characteristics of practical thought', in R. J. Sternberg and R. K. Wagner (eds) *Practical Intelligence: Nature and Origins of Competence in the Everyday World*, Cambridge, MA: Harvard University Press.

Scribner, S. and Cole, M. (1973) 'Cognitive consequences of formal and informal education', *Science* 182: 553–559.

Semin, G. R. and Gergen, K. J. (eds) (1990) *Everyday Understanding*, London: Sage.

Sharabi, Asi (2005) 'Behind the narrative bars: taking the perspective of the other in the Israeli-Palestinean conflict. A case study with Israeli children', unpublished PhD thesis, University of London.

Shotter, J. (1993) 'Harré, Vygotsky, Bakhtin, Vico, Wittgenstein: academic discourses and conversational realities', *Journal for the Theory of Social Behaviour* 23, 460–482.

Smith, L. T. (1999) *Decolonizing Methodologies: Research and Indigenous People*, London: Zed Books.

Spitz, R. A. (1945) 'Hospitalism: an inquiry into the genesis of psychiatric conditions in early childhood', *Psychoanalytic Study of the Child* 1: 68.

Spitz, R. A. (1959) *A Genetic Field Theory of Ego Formation: Its Implications for Pathology*, New York: International Universities Press.

Stern, D. (1974) 'Mother and infant at play: the dyadic interaction involving facial, vocal and gaze behaviour', in M. Lewis and L. Rosenblum (eds) *The Effect of the Infant on Its Caregiver*, New York: Wiley.

Stern, D. (1985) *The Interpersonal World of the Infant: A View from Psychoanalysis and Developmental Psychology*, New York: Basic Books.

Strayer, F. F. (2000) 'Decentration, communication and collective survival: reflections on the evolution of human culture', *Culture & Psychology* 6, 2: 161–168.

Tajfel, H. (ed.) (1984) *The Social Dimension: European Developments in Social Psychology*, vols I and II, Cambridge: Cambridge University Press.

Taylor, C. (1989) *Sources of the Self: The Making of the Modern Identity*, Cambridge: Harvard University Press.

Taylor, C. (1994) 'The politics of recognition', in A. Gutmann (ed.) *Multiculturalism: Examining the Politics of Recognition*, Princeton: Princeton University Press.

Thompson, J. (1990) *Ideology and Modern Culture*, Cambridge: Polity Press.

Thompson, J. (1995) *The Media and Modernity: A Social Theory of the Media*, Cambridge: Polity Press.

Thompson, J. B. and Held, D. (1982) *Habermas: Critical Debates*, London: Macmillan.

Todorov, T. (1992) *The Conquest of America: The Question of the Other*, London: Harper Perennial.

Trevarthen, C. (1980) 'Communication and cooperation in early infancy: a description of primary intersubjectivity', in M. Bullowa (ed.) *Before Speech: The Beginning of Interpersonal Communication*, New York: Cambridge University Press.

Tul'viste, P. (1987) 'L. Lévy-Bruhl and the problems of the historical development of thought', *Soviet Psychology* 25, 3: 3–21.

Valsiner, J. (1988) *Developmental Psychology in the Soviet Union*, Brighton: Harvester.

Valsiner, J. (1991) 'Construction of the mental: from the "cognitive revolution" to the study of development', *Theory & Psychology* 1: 477–494.

Valsiner, J. (2000) *Culture and Human Development*, London: Sage.

Valsiner, J. (2003) 'Beyond social representations: a theory of enablement', *Papers on Social Representations* 12: 7.1–7.16. Online. Available HTTP: <http://www.psr.jku.at/psrindex.htm> (accessed 14 February 2006).

Van der Veer, R. (1991) 'The anthropological underpinning of Vygotsky's thinking', *Studies in Soviet Thought* 42: 73–91.

Van der Veer, R. (1996) 'The concept of culture in Vygotsky's thinking', *Culture and Psychology* 2: 247–263.

Van der Veer, R. and Valsiner, J. (1991) *Understanding Vygotsky*, Oxford: Blackwell.

Van der Veer, R. and Valsiner, J. (1994) 'Reading Vygotsky: from fascination to construction', *Introduction to The Vygotsky Reader*, Oxford: Blackwell.

Van Vlaenderen, H. (2001) 'Psychology in developing countries: people-centred development and local knowledge', *Psychology in Society* 27: 88–108.

Von Cranach, M. (1982) 'The psychological study of goal-directed action: basic issues', in M. V. Cranach and R. Harré (eds) *The Analysis of Action: Recent Theoretical and Empirical Advances*, Cambridge: Cambridge University Press.

Von Cranach, M., Doise, W. and Mugny, G. (eds) (1992) *Social Representations and the Social Basis of Knowledge*, Lewiston, NY: Hogrefe & Huber.

Vygotsky, L. S. (1978) *Mind in Society: The Development of the Higher Psychological Processes*, Cambridge, MA: Harvard University Press.

Vygotsky, L. S. (1997) 'The history of the development of higher mental functions', *The Collected Works of L. S. Vygotsky*, vol. 4, New York and London: Plenum Press.

Vygotsky, L. S. and Luria. A. R. (1993) *Studies in the History of Behaviour: Ape, Primitive and Child*, Hillsdale, NJ: Lawrence Erlbaum Associates, Inc.

Vygotsky, L. S. and Luria, A. (1994) 'Tool and symbol in child development', in R. Van der Veer and J. Valsiner (eds) *The Vygotsky Reader*, Oxford: Blackwell.

Wagner, W. and Hayes, N. (2005) *Everyday Discourse and Common Sense: The Theory of Social Representations*, Basingstoke: Palgrave.

Wagner, W., Duveen, G., Themel, M. and Verma, J. (1999) 'The modernization of tradition: thinking about madness in Patna, India', *Culture and Psychology* 5, 4: 413–445.

Wagner, W., Duveen, G., Verma, J. and Temel, M. (2000) '"I have faith and at the same time I don't believe": cognitive polyphasia and cultural change in India', *Journal of Community and Applied Social Psychology* 10, 4: 301–314.

Weber, M. (1976) *The Protestant Ethic and the Spirit of Capitalism*, Hemel Hampstead: Unwin.

Wertsch, J. V. (1985a) *Vygotsky and the Social Formation of Mind*, Cambridge, MA: Harvard University Press.

Wertsch, J. V. (ed.) (1985b) *Culture, Communication and Cognition*, New York: Cambridge University Press.

Wertsch, J. V. (1993) 'Preface', in L. S. Vygotsky and A. R. Luria, *Studies in the History of Behaviour: Ape, Primitive and Child*, Hillsdale, NJ: Lawrence Erlbaum Associates, Inc.

White, S. C. (1996) 'Depoliticising development: the uses and abuses of participation', *Development in Practice* 6, 1: 6–15.

Winnicott, D. W. (1964) 'Further thoughts on babies as persons', in D. W. Winnicott *The Child, the Family and the Outside World*, Harmondsworth: Penguin.

Winnicott, D. W. (1965a) 'From dependence towards independence in the development of the individual', in D. W. Winnicott *The Maturational Process and the Facilitating Environment*, London: Hogarth Press.

Winnicott, D. W. (1965b) 'The capacity to be alone', in D. W. Winnicott *The Maturational Process and the Facilitating Environment*, London: Hogarth Press.

Winnicott, D. W. (1965c) *The Maturational Process and the Facilitating Environment*, London: Hogarth Press.

Winnicott, D. W. (1965d) 'The theory of parent–infant relationship', in D. W. Winnicott *The Maturational Process and the Facilitating Environment*, London: Hogarth Press.

Winnicott, D. W. (1967) 'The location of cultural experience', in D. W. Winnicott (1974) *Playing and Reality*, Harmondsworth: Penguin.

Winnicott, D. W. (1971) *Playing and Reality*, London: Tavistock Publications.

Winnicott, D. W. (1984) 'Varieties of psychotherapy', in D. W. Winnicott *Deprivation and Delinquency*, London and New York: Tavistock Publications.

Winnicott, D. W. (1985) 'Transitional objects and transitional phenomena', in D. W. Winnicott *Collected Papers: Through Paediatrics to Psycho-Analysis*, London: Hogarth Press.

Winnicott, D. W. (1988) *Human Nature*, London: Free Association Books.

Wolman, B. B. (1960) *Contemporary Systems and Theories in Psychology*, New York: Harper.

Wynne, B. (1989) 'Sheep farming after Chernobyl: a case-study in communicating scientific information', *Environment* 31: 33–40.

Wynne, B. (1995) 'Public understanding of science', in S. Jasanoff, G. E. Markle, J. C. Peterson and T. Pinch (eds) *Handbook of Science and Technology Studies*, Beverly Hills: Sage.

Index